THE
COLORADO
TRAIL

EIGHTH EDITION

THE OFFICIAL GUIDEBOOK OF
The Colorado Trail Foundation

The Colorado Trail
Foundation

Rocky Mountain columbine, the Colorado state flower.
PHOTO BY PETE KARTSOUNES

THE
COLORADO
TRAIL

EIGHTH EDITION

The Colorado Trail
Foundation

THE OFFICIAL GUIDEBOOK OF
The Colorado Trail Foundation

THE COLORADO MOUNTAIN CLUB PRESS
GOLDEN, COLORADO

The Colorado Trail: The Official Guidebook of the Colorado Trail Foundation
Eighth edition

© 2011 The Colorado Trail Foundation
710 10th Street, Room 210, Golden, CO 80401
(303) 384-3729 • ctf@ColoradoTrail.org • ColoradoTrail.org
Please alert the CTF to any errors or outdated information at the address above.

PUBLISHED BY:
The Colorado Mountain Club Press
710 10th Street, Suite #200, Golden, CO 80401
(303) 996-2743; (800) 633-4417; email cmcpress@cmc.org

Founded in 1912, The Colorado Mountain Club is the largest outdoor recreation, education, and conservation organization in the Rocky Mountains. Look for our books at your local bookstore or outdoor retailer or online at www.cmc.org

Jerry Brown, Bear Creek Survey Service, Inc.	GPS trail data
Tim Burroughs	developmental editor
Ann W. Douden	design, composition, production
Joyce Dunne	proofreader
Bill Manning, CTF Managing Director	project manager
Susan Hill Newton	copyeditor
Alan Stark	publisher

Front cover photo: The Colorado Trail three miles to the North of Kennebec Pass.
Photo by Kennan Harvey, kennanharvey.com
Title page photo by Lori Brummer

DISTRIBUTED TO THE TRADE BY
Mountaineers Books
1001 SW Klickitat Way, Suite 201, Seattle, WA 98134
800-533-4453 | www.mountaineersbooks.org

We gratefully acknowledge the financial support of the people of Colorado through the Scientific and Cultural Facilities District of greater metropolitan Denver for our publishing activities.

Warning: Although there has been an effort to make this book as accurate as possible, some discrepancies may exist between this guide and the trail. Before beginning an excursion on The Colorado Trail, users should be capable of independent backcountry travel and be experienced in relevant mountaineering and orienteering techniques. Failure to have the necessary knowledge, equipment, and conditioning may subject users of The Colorado Trail to physical danger, injury, or death. Some routes described in this book have changed and others will change; hazards described may have expanded and new hazards may have formed since the book's publication. Users of The Colorado Trail may be held liable for all costs incurred if a rescue is necessary. For updates on trail changes and reroutes, go to ColoradoTrail.org.

ISBN 978-0-9842213-3-2
Printed in Korea

CONTRIBUTORS

This book is a collaborative effort by The Colorado Trail Foundation (CTF) and its volunteers, the builders and stewards of the 486-mile Colorado Trail. To find out more about the CTF, or to join in preserving and maintaining The Colorado Trail, visit ColoradoTrail.org.

Many people helped the CTF develop the eighth edition of The Colorado Trail guidebook and we thank each one. Jerry Brown surveyed the trail, completing it five times (plus), gathering accurate trail data with professional-grade GPS equipment. George Neserke compiled trail features data for the guidebook as well as *The Colorado Trail Databook* and *Map Book* for improved consistency. Morgan and Robyn Wilkinson refined the guidebook's trail descriptions. Roger Forman helped sort through all the great photographs taken and donated by many Colorado Trail users. Paul Magnanti used his "triple-crowner" experience to write about lightweight backpacking. Jack Reed drew on his many years with the United States Geological Survey to rewrite the chapter on geology. Tim Burroughs donated his professional expertise and edited this entire guide. Carrie Dittmer assisted with maps. Coordinating the entire effort was CTF Managing Director Bill Manning.

Many other volunteers assisted, including George Miller, Jon Greeneisen, Gudy and David Gaskill, Carl Brown, Ken Swierenga, Chuck Lawson, Jim Gigone, Pat Rush, Liz Truitt, Cindy Johnson, and Bryan Martin, as well as CTF Office Manager Laura Becker. This edition relies, in part, on earlier editions developed by Terry Root, Merle McDonald, Marilyn Eisele, Suzanne Reed, and others. Also contributing were many Colorado Trail users who report to the CTF office about necessary refinements to the book. The CTF needs, and is grateful for, all of our good Friends of The Colorado Trail, the CTF volunteers and donors. Your involvement helps preserve The Colorado Trail.

Support from the U.S. Forest Service, Department of Agriculture, Rocky Mountain Region acknowledged and appreciated.

A volunteer works to clear the trail. Hundreds of fallen trees are removed every year by CTF volunteers who maintain The Colorado Trail.

PHOTO BY MARK RITCHEY

CONTENTS

For ease of navigation, sections of this guidebook are organized by color.

Waterton Canyon Trailhead to Kenosha Pass (Segments 1–5)

Kenosha Pass to Mount Massive Trailhead (Segments 6–10)

Mount Massive Trailhead to Marshall Pass (Segments 11–15)

Marshall Pass to San Luis Pass (Segments 16–20)

San Luis Pass to Junction Creek Trailhead (Segments 21–28)

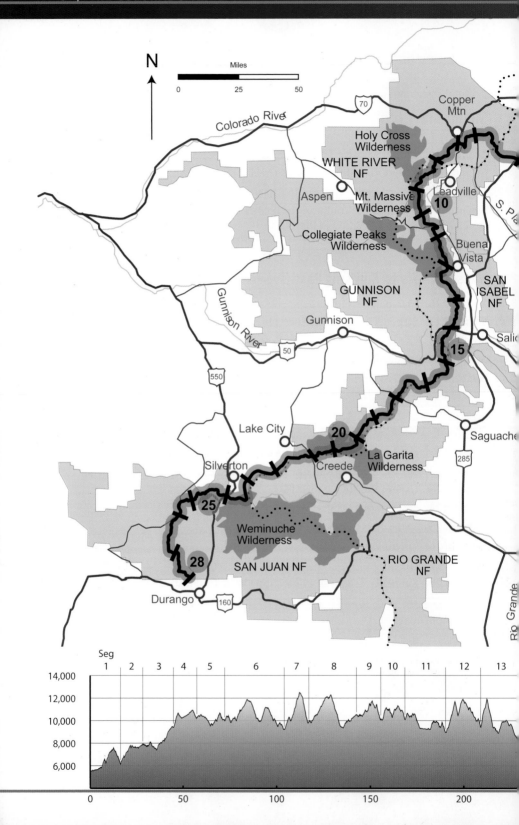

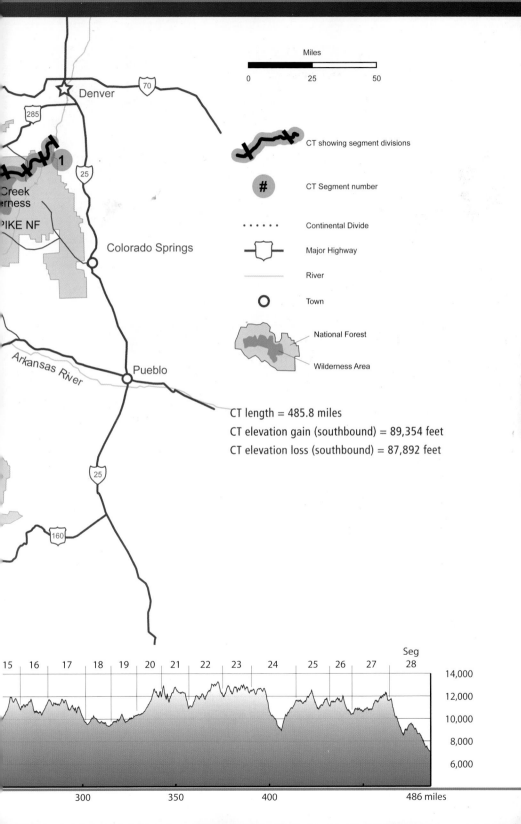

Miles

0   25   50

CT showing segment divisions

CT Segment number

· · · · · ·   Continental Divide

Major Highway

River

○   Town

National Forest

Wilderness Area

Denver

Colorado Springs

Pueblo

Arkansas River

Creek
·rness

·IKE NF

CT length = 485.8 miles
CT elevation gain (southbound) = 89,354 feet
CT elevation loss (southbound) = 87,892 feet

Seg
15 16 17 18 19 20 21 22 23 24 25 26 27 28

14,000
12,000
10,000
8,000
6,000

300   350   400   486 miles

FOREWORD by GUDY GASKILL

COLORADO. The name rolls off the tongue and brings to mind images of red rock walls, cascading waterfalls, lofty peaks, alpine meadows bedecked with wildflowers, and a unique outdoor lifestyle. This lifestyle has created a state of vigorous, healthy, and robust men and women who flock to the mountains to practice their climbing, hiking, mountain biking skills in the summer and a multitude of snow sports in the winter. It is truly a magnificent state.

I have traveled all over the world, climbed and hiked in many different climates and environments, but each time the plane brings me safely down to terra firma my mind always comes back to the same question: Why did I ever leave Colorado? Colorado is home; a big friendly state with such a variety of scenery. Who could ever forget the azure blue sky, the color deepening as the day draws to an end, the spectacular cumulus clouds that billow up before the afternoon showers, and the show of golds, oranges, and crimsons in the sky on a late summer evening? Who could forget a tunnel of golden aspens, with a treasure of gold coins covering the fragrant earth on a crisp autumn day? Or the brilliance of ice crystals shimmering a million colors in the early morning sun? This is heaven underfoot.

The Colorado Trail, a wilderness path traversing some of the most scenic areas of the Rockies and Continental Divide, is a unique experience for both body and soul. This revised guidebook to the trail describes the wonders and beauty that you will see along the way. It points out the flora and fauna native to the region. It will stir your imagination with its geological observations, creating a desire to know more of the area's ancient history and the powers of nature that formed this landscape. The Colorado Trail also provides a living history lesson as it crosses the paths of the area's earlier inhabitants, from American Indians to nineteenth-century miners and railroad barons.

As early as 1970, the late Merrill Hastings, publisher, ski industry pioneer, and co-conceptualizer of The Colorado Trail, wrote of the increasing need for the conservation of our public lands as the nation looks more and more to the American West in its search for peace and contentment away from the pace of metropolitan life. An idea was born, and in 1987 The Colorado Trail became a reality.

Gudy Gaskill.
PHOTO BY ERIC WUNROW

THE COLORADO TRAIL FOUNDATION

The Colorado Trail

THE "TRAIL TO NOWHERE": That is how the *Empire* magazine section of *The Denver Post* characterized The Colorado Trail in 1984. Bill Lucas of the U.S. Forest Service and Merrill Hastings of *Colorado Magazine* had conceived the idea of a long-distance trail between Denver and Durango in 1973. In 1974, several focus groups were held to develop a plan for building the trail.

Gudy Gaskill, an active member of The Colorado Mountain Club since 1952 and later the first women president of the CMC, attended the first focus group. Subsequently, in those early years, she never missed a planning meeting. The Colorado Mountain Trails Foundation, predecessor to The Colorado Trail Foundation, was formed to plan, develop, and manage The Colorado Trail, and Gudy Gaskill was asked to chair the committee.

The task ahead was immense: A route had to be scouted through eleven Forest Service districts, linking early trails with existing mining and logging roads. Inquiries had to be sent to each district to get permission to build. Gudy made

Roundup Riders of the Rockies were early CT advocates and remain involved today.

numerous trips to persuade reluctant district rangers to buy into the idea of The Colorado Trail. After a year of intense work, most districts agreed to the plan. At the same time, Gudy was recruiting and training volunteers, leading trail crews, and purchasing supplies.

Despite the massive effort of Gudy and her "dirt-digging volunteers," The Colorado Trail seemed to languish. Hence the "Trail to Nowhere" designation by *Denver Post* writer Ed Quillen. (This article and others are posted at ColoradoTrail.org under Who We Are, Trail History.) That article was just what The Colorado Trail needed. It caught the attention of then Governor Dick Lamm and his wife, Dottie. They joined a trail crew, hosted a fundraiser, and rekindled support and cooperation between the state and Forest Service.

In 1986, Gudy founded The Colorado Trail Foundation, whose nonprofit mission was to complete and maintain the trail. CTF volunteers subsequently built the trail for about $500 per mile, compared with an estimated Forest Service cost of $25,000 per mile.

Gudy was a true visionary in realizing that volunteers were the heart, soul, and future of outdoor stewardship. With the Forest Service providing technical assistance, Gudy's volunteers provided the labor. The then 468-mile-long trail between Denver and Durango was completed in 1987.

Today, Gudy is still active in The Colorado Trail Foundation and the organization remains volunteer-driven. Its board of directors, adopters, crew leaders, and participants, and hundreds of others from all over the world, volunteer their time each year, and on Sept. 25, 2004, The Colorado Trail celebrated its thirtieth anniversary.

It is Gudy's inspiration and can-do attitude that permeates this effort. For that, the "Mother of The Colorado Trail" has been honored by two U.S. presidents and in 2002 was inducted into the Colorado Women's Hall of Fame.

Volunteers Build and Maintain the Trail

Volunteers "keep" The Colorado Trail, all 486 miles of it. In 1974 volunteers began building the trail and they connected it end-to-end in 1987. Volunteers continue to maintain and improve it today. The entire effort is organized and led by The Colorado Trail Foundation , a nonprofit, in coordination with the United States Forest Service.

A volunteer trail crew, one of many that build and maintain The Colorado Trail.

PHOTO BY DALE ZOETEWEY

Keeping the trail in good shape is a monumental task. Mother Nature has the greatest impact on the trail, toppling trees that block the path and sending runoff that erodes the tread. The toll is continuous, and without annual maintenance the trail would degrade quickly and become impassable in just a few years. Clearing downed trees and diverting runoff to prevent erosion are just some of the tasks volunteers perform. Where plant growth is prolific, volunteers rework the edges and trim overgrowth. They build bridges and walkways. They clear new tread when needed. It has been a decades-long labor of love by the friends of Colorado's best-known trail.

CTF volunteers find joy in giving back to the trail.

PHOTO BY CAROLYN BURTARD

CT trekkers hike toward Searle Pass in Segment 8.

PHOTO BY KEITH EVANS

There are many ways volunteers contribute:

Adopters—Colorado Trail Adopters carry out routine trail maintenance. Working through the CTF, they take responsibility for an average of 8 miles of the trail. Each season, just after the snow melts, adopters and their helpers embark on a trail maintenance excursion. Their goal is to clear the trail of fallen trees and debris and dig away the silt and rocks from water diversions. Typical adopters spend several days each year on their section, working and camping until each is clear and in good shape. They also report to the CTF on trail conditions and any additional work needed.

Trail Crews—Volunteer trail crews take on larger trail improvements. For example, when a bridge needs rebuilding, some twenty or so volunteers team up to build a new structure. Crews also build reroutes where needed, construct retaining walls, install signs, build cairns, and establish new water diversions. About fifteen weeklong and weekend crews are scheduled each summer, usually from mid-June to mid-August. Crew schedules are usually announced in February, giving volunteers time to integrate one or more outings into their summer plans. Schedules are sent to those on the CTF mailing list and are posted on the CTF website (ColoradoTrail.org) as well. The typical volunteer enjoys traveling The Colorado Trail and finds working on a crew not only fun and a good way to meet new friends, but also a great way to give back. Despite the hard work, many return year after year.

Trekking on The Colorado Trail—For two decades, the CTF has offered weeklong supported treks, and many trail volunteers and supporters have first experienced The Colorado Trail on one of these trips. Camping gear is transported ahead of the hikers and guides lead the way. After a day's hike, trekkers arrive at camp to appetizers, cold drinks, comfortable camp chairs, and a backcountry shower. They also enjoy back-country gourmet meals prepared by the staff. Space is limited to about twelve participants each week, and spots fill quickly. For more information and to register, visit ColoradoTrailHiking.com.

Funding—CTF funding comes almost entirely from private donations, which are essential to sustaining The Colorado Trail. Funding goes to trail maintenance, including volunteer food and equipment; publications to spread the word about the trail; signs and bridges; insurance for trail volunteers; office expenses; and even thank-you cards for the many volunteers. The foundation is able to accomplish great work with modest resources and is proud of its volunteer tradition and its ability to leverage donations into top-notch trail preservation. The organization is a 501(c)(3) nonprofit and donations are tax deductible.

Help Keep the Trail Clear: The CTF Pocket Chainsaw

People frequently ask the CTF, "How can I get involved?" Here's a great way to contribute, one that you can begin on your next Colorado Trail excursion.

The trail continuously needs to be cleared of fallen trees; they topple with surprising frequency. While CT Adopters do their best and remove most of the fallen trees, they cannot monitor all 486 miles all the time. It is common for trail users to encounter fallen trees and, if carrying a pocket chainsaw, they can eliminate the blockage on the spot.

The pocket chainsaw is a motorless wonder tool. Weighing less than 8 ounces and stored in its own carrying case, the pocket chainsaw is easy to take on every trail outing. Two people team up to make a cut and users find that cutting a log is unexpectedly easy, even one as big as 15 inches in diameter.

The more users who contribute to trail clearing, the clearer The Colorado Trail stays. Pocket chainsaws are available for sale at the CTF website, ColoradoTrail.org (click on CT Store).

A pocket chainsaw is ultra-light, useful, and worth carrying.

HOW TO USE THIS GUIDE

THE COLORADO TRAIL is divided into 28 segments, each of which is covered by a chapter in this guide. Segments were established based on convenient access points to the trail. Most can be hiked in a day, although admittedly some require a very long day, even with a light pack. The map of The Colorado Trail on pages 8–9 shows the entire length of the trail, plus major highways, towns, national forests, and wilderness areas along the route. The information presented is from Denver to Durango, in a southbound direction.

Segment Color Coding

This guide is separated into color-coded sections, representing five multi-segment stretches of the trail. Look for the colored tabs to find the section you are interested in.

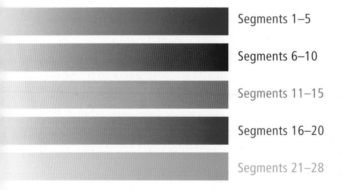

Segments 1–5

Segments 6–10

Segments 11–15

Segments 16–20

Segments 21–28

The Segments

Each segment chapter begins with a short summary of pertinent information for the segment, including the starting and ending points, one-way distance, and approximate elevation gain and loss. The elevation gain (southbound) is the sum of the major ascending portions and, in addition to mileage, is a general indicator of how much effort is required to complete the segment. Elevation loss (southbound) is included as well.

Following that is a list of maps relating to the segment. The first, included in the guidebook, is a vicinity map, which is useful for general orientation purposes. Based on U.S. Forest Service visitor maps, these also provide road information and show trail access points. Listed next are the topographic maps in *The Colorado Trail Map Book*, which is available at ColoradoTrail.org. These full-color maps show The Colorado Trail in detail. Next are the National Geographic Trails Illustrated maps that pertain to that segment. These waterproof, tear-resistant maps cover surrounding areas and trails as well. Pertinent Latitude 40° maps are also listed.

A trekker hops a stream in the San Juan Mountains.

COURTESY OF COLORADO MOUNTAIN EXPEDITIONS

Beneath the map listings is the jurisdiction (the U.S. Forest Service ranger district) for that segment. Contact addresses for the districts are listed on page 282. Because most of The Colorado Trail passes through federally managed public lands, contact the appropriate office if you have questions about regulations.

The symbols for access from Denver (right-facing car) and access from Durango (left-facing car) indicate the normal condition of access roads to the trail from the Denver and the Durango ends of that section. (For thru-hikers going from Denver to Durango, the first is the start of that segment and the latter is the end of that segment.) Please note that a dirt or gravel road listed as easily negotiable by a normal passenger car can become impassible in wet weather. Also, many of these secondary roads are not kept open during winter.

Next are symbols that indicate the likely availability of water in the segment during late summer. More detailed information about the location of water sources is provided in the trail description for each section.

Finally, there is symbol that pertains to bicycling in that segment. If a mandatory bicycle wilderness detour applies, a page number for the detour is listed.

Key to Symbols

 Paved or graded-dirt access road

 Rough, dirt access road

 Four-wheel-drive access road

 Plentiful water sources

 Scattered water sources

 Water is difficult to obtain

 Bicycles allowed

 Bicycles prohibited in wilderness

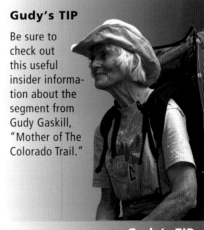

Gudy's TIP

Be sure to check out this useful insider information about the segment from Gudy Gaskill, "Mother of The Colorado Trail."

Gudy's TIP

One of the many styles of CT markers.
PHOTO BY JAMIE COMPOS

ABOUT THIS SEGMENT

This section provides general information, interesting facts, and local history about each segment.

TRAILHEAD/ACCESS POINTS

Instructions for reaching the trailheads and trail access points, along with symbols that indicate normal road conditions, are given in this section. All of the beginning and ending points are accessible by vehicle. Many segments have additional trail access points, some of which are accessible by road, some that are not. Generally, a *trailhead* refers to an official access point with a parking area, though these are sometimes primitive and skimpy. *Trail access* refers to a point where the trail crosses or approaches a road, but where no official parking is provided.

SERVICES, SUPPLIES, AND ACCOMMODATIONS

This section describes nearby supply points and services. For major supply points, a town or city map is included, as well as a list of services such as grocery stores, showers, post offices, and laundries. Larger towns offer multiple lodging and dining options. Check with the local chamber of commerce for more information. It should be noted that on some remote segments of The Colorado Trail, no convenient points of resupply are available.

TRAIL DESCRIPTION

Detailed trail descriptions progress from Denver to Durango. They indicate the distance between recognizable features (indicated in bold) from the beginning of the trail segment. Generally, accompanying the mileage is the altitude of that feature in parentheses. The mileages were obtained using professional-grade GPS equipment.

> ⚠ **Warning**
> Be alert for this symbol ⚠ and box. It highlights a particular caution or warning for that segment.

MAPS, ELEVATION PROFILES, AND GPS

Each segment chapter ends with a vicinity map, based on U.S. Forest Service visitor maps. They were chosen for this book, in part, because they show all types of roads and road access reasonably well. The trail in that segment is indicated by a solid line with red highlighting. A dashed line shows adjacent segments. Key features (usually trail intersections, stream crossings, or trail access points) also are shown.

At the bottom corner of each vicinity map page, a trail elevation profile shows the ups and downs encountered along that segment. Note that the hill steepness is not consistent in each segment due to the variations in the scale of miles. A chart in the other bottom corner lists key features. The distance of these features from both the start of the segment as well as the Denver and Durango ends of The Colorado Trail are indicated, along with GPS coordinates designating the UTM (NAD83) and zone. For more information about using the GPS waypoints, see pages 31–33.

For those who like to have detailed topographical maps, The Colorado Trail Foundation recommends *The Colorado Trail Map Book*, which includes GPS-generated data as well. Information on the *Map Book* and how to purchase one is available on the CTF website, ColoradoTrail.org/store.

Another valuable publication is *The Colorado Trail Databook*, available at many retailers. Though it contains only the ultra-simple mini maps, many users find that the *Databook* is all they need for their CT excursion.

Map Key

———————— CT (current segment)

- - - - - CT (adjacent segment)

▬▬▬▬▬ CT Bicycle Wilderness Detour

1.8► CT Feature Mileage & Location

And There's More!

Additional information boxes provide interesting facts or useful information to help you get the most out of your Colorado Trail experience.

🚶 Indicates helpful tips for hikers, and highlights other hikes or climbs in the segment

📷 Indicates a special viewing opportunity in this segment

🚲 Indicates information for mountain bikers, including other rides in the area that might be of interest

PLANNING FOR THE COLORADO TRAIL

In mid-June, the snow-covered Tenmile Range looms ahead in Segment 7.

PHOTO BY BERNARD WOLF

WINDING 486 MILES through the magnificent heart of the southern Rockies from Denver to Durango, The Colorado Trail is one of the nation's most beautiful and varied long-distance trails. For recreationalists—hikers, backpackers, mountain bikers, and horse packers—the CT offers an unparalleled path into the scenic wonders of Colorado's mountains, crossing eight mountain ranges, six national forests, and countless streams and rivers. The topography ranges from the high plains of eastern Colorado to the alpine peaks along the Continental Divide.

The enjoyment of the CT experience is dependent in large part on users' ability to respond to the demands, challenges, and even dangers imposed by this remarkable path through the backcountry. Relatively few people consider thru-hiking the entire trail—it's not an endeavor for the unprepared or out of shape. Most users opt instead for day trips or outings of a few days at a time. However long your excursion is, planning is crucial.

Consider the Season

The Colorado Trail traverses a landscape ranging in altitude from 5,522 feet at its eastern end to over 13,000 feet in the lofty San Juan Mountains in the southwestern corner of the state. Much of the trail is above 9,000 feet, where winters are long and extreme. Snow covers the trail for much of the year, usually persisting through June along high ridges or in shady ravines. For that reason, it is important to carefully consider the time of year for your trek or ride.

Furthermore, while it is possible to travel some segments of the CT in the winter (Segment 9 at Tennessee Pass, for instance, is the start of several classic ski tours), most of the secondary access roads mentioned in this guide are closed to traffic during the winter and well into the spring.

Unlike thru-hikers, day or short-term users can pick and choose among individual segments based on snow cover. Segments 1 through 3 can have scant snow cover (or none at all) between winter storms. By early May, these lower-elevation sections are often snow-free and showing their early wildflowers. Likewise, the first half of Segment 28 at the western end of the trail is low enough in altitude to be hiked in late spring.

An early-season hiker "post-holes" through snow near Georgia Pass in Segment 6.

PHOTO COURTESY COLORADO MOUNTAIN EXPEDITIONS

By early June, significant portions of the trail up to 9,000 feet are mostly free of snow, including Segments 4 and 5, as well as that part of the CT traversing the lower flanks of the Sawatch Range in Segments 13 and 14.

The eastern half of the trail holds late-melting snow on Georgia Pass, the Tenmile Range, Searle and Kokomo passes, as well as the north-facing forested slopes nearby. Last to be free of the icy grip of winter are the high reaches of the western half of the trail, especially Segments 20 through 28, where snow can linger well into July.

Crossing significant snowpack can turn even a short trip into a monumental, even unsafe, outing. For one thing, The Colorado Trail is not signed for snow travel. Until the snows melt, many CT signs and trail markers are buried in the snow. Also, the signs are too infrequent to guide users traveling atop snow, with trail markers appearing at approximately half-mile intervals. Users can easily get off track.

Another hazard is "post-holing" (sinking deeply into the snowpack while hiking), which quickly becomes exhausting and presents the risk of sprained ankles (and worse) from stepping on branches and rocks hidden beneath the snow. Even if the snow is firm enough to walk atop, hikers can encounter slick, icy surfaces that are hard to negotiate.

Together, heavy snowpack, icy slopes, and cornices make travel difficult and dangerous, suitable only for those trained and equipped for winter mountaineering.

Thru-Hiking

So, when should thru-hikers start? The Colorado Trail near the Denver area is generally accessible by the end of the first week of June, sometimes earlier. Based on the average snowpack west of Kenosha Pass, however, thru-hikers hoping to avoid lengthy stretches of deep snowpack should not set out earlier than mid- to late June. Eastbound hikers shouldn't take off from Durango until July because of the lingering snow at the higher elevations of the trail in southwest Colorado. Winter can return to the high country by late September, so hikers should plan to finish their trek before then.

The Colorado Trail Foundation recommends that thru-hikers begin their trek from the eastern end, starting at Segment 1 and ending at Segment 28, as described in the pages of this guide. Not only does the trail tend to clear of snow earlier on the eastern end, but by starting at the lower-elevation Denver end of the trail, hikers do not encounter tree line until Georgia Pass in Segment 6, some 80 miles into the trek. Hikers starting from Durango, on the other hand, reach tree line much more quickly, barely 20 miles into Segment 28, which doesn't allow much time to acclimatize to higher elevations.

In addition, the average elevation overall for the eastern half of the CT is much lower than the western half, which is dominated by long alpine sections through the San Juan Range, some of the loftiest mountains in the state. The conditioning gained while hiking east to west can help hikers better handle the strenuous, higher-elevation western half.

Foot Care

Experienced hikers report that attention to your feet is most important, both in planning a hike and while on the trail, and that it is particularly important for those on multiday hikes. Why? Because sore feet limit enjoyment, and blisters are common and painful. But, careful attention to your feet can help. Keep in mind that blisters result from a combination of friction, heat, and moisture; plan to minimize these.

Begin focusing on your feet when planning your trip and doing your training hikes. Carefully choose your footwear and socks. Consider lightweight and lower-height shoes that have proven adequate even for a thru-hike and offer advantages including less heat buildup. Cooler feet can mean drier feet and can help avoid blisters. Choose good-quality socks that help wick moisture and dry fast; avoid cotton. Try lighter-weight socks, as some find that they reduce heat buildup. Train in the shoe/sock combination you plan to take on your trip and refine your footwear until you're using what works best for you. Attempt to strengthen and toughen your feet; it will pay off on your CT hike. Some hikers have found that applying a preventative anti-friction/anti-chafing product (stick or cream) during training and even on the trail helps fend off blisters. Study foot care. A highly rated resource is *Fixing Your Feet: Prevention and Treatments for Athletes* by John Vonhof. Secure supplies such as tape, Moleskin, scissors, ointment, and skin-cleaning wipes and know how to use them. Consider carrying extra pairs of socks.

On the trail, from your first steps, employ your knowledge gained in training and planning. Tape your feet in advance if that's what works best. Keep your shoes and socks as dry as you can. If you feel a hot spot, stop right away and care for it to keep from forming blisters or allowing them to grow larger.

Getting to and from the Trail

Both Denver and Durango are served by several national and regional airlines. Express bus and van service is available between Denver International Airport and several resort communities close to The Colorado Trail, including Breckenridge, Frisco, and Copper Mountain. The Regional Transportation District (rtd-denver.com), a bus and light-rail system serving the Denver metropolitan area, provides service trail users have found helpful, including weekday, express bus service to the Lockheed Martin facility (about a 20 minute walk from the Waterton Canyon trailhead) on line 63X.

Commercial bus lines run between some of the towns and cities listed as resupply points in this guide. Schedules and routes change frequently, however, so inquire about service before setting off on your trip. A few towns have shuttles that CT users can take between the trail and town; notably, the Summit County Stage in Segments 6 and 7. Phone the chambers of commerce mentioned in the Services, Supplies, and Accommodations section of each chapter for information about local shuttle services or taxis.

A unique way to access Segment 24 from either Durango or Silverton is aboard the historic Durango & Silverton Narrow Gauge Railroad. You can book trips and check fares and schedules at durangotrain.com, or call 888-TRAIN07 (888-872-4607).

Resupplying

For those planning an extended or thru-trip on The Colorado Trail, you'll probably want to resupply. While the entire trail has been traversed without resupply, not many will want to carry all the provisions (and weight) for such a trip. Resupply towns are noted in the Services, Supplies, and Accommodations section of each chapter. Many CT thru- and long-distance hikers have reported being able to resupply with relative ease by taking side trips to the nearby towns. However, planning is warranted, as some of the small towns have limited supplies and lack the lightweight backpacking meals and gear many long-distance trekkers prefer.

Sisters loaded up for their CT thru-hike.
PHOTO BY LINDA JEFFERS

Supplies also can be mailed ahead of time. Address parcels to yourself in care of "General Delivery," and send to the post offices listed in this guide. Or arrange to meet someone at points where the CT crosses a convenient access point. Bring along extras of any small, unique items that are crucial parts of your kit.

Also, please note that there are some long, remote stretches of the CT where convenient resupply is not possible.

Trail Adopter Harriet Patton teaches safety to other volunteers.
PHOTO BY DAVID ZALONE

Equipment

The Colorado Trail traverses a wide range of life zones from the hot, dry foothills of the Front Range to the harsh alpine tundra of the high mountains, where cold and wind can challenge anyone's gear. Effective, good-quality clothing and other gear can spell the difference between a safe, enjoyable day in the mountains and an unpleasant, or even potentially disastrous, experience.

When preparing for a hike on the CT, always start with the "ten essentials" as your foundation (see Equipment Checklists). Lightweight but sturdy shoes or boots are fine for most day trips. Backpackers carrying traditional weight loads will want heavier, stiffer boots for good ankle support. Others carrying lighter loads find trail shoes adequate. For clothing, modern synthetics, such as polypropylene and pile, are lightweight, insulate well, and dry quickly. But traditional wool clothing also is effective, even when damp. Avoid cotton entirely because it loses its insulating ability when wet. Rain gear should be water-proof and breathable.

Study the recommended equipment lists for both day and thru-hikes. Increasingly, long-distance backpackers are discovering lighter-weight gear that is as effective as their older gear without sacrificing safety or comfort. With its long segments and strenuous climbs, the CT lends itself well to this "going lighter" philosophy. An article on pages 26–29 offers tips and suggestions for the weight-conscious packer.

Equipment Checklists

The Ten Essentials

Have Packed

- [ ] [ ] Food
- [ ] [ ] Water
- [ ] [ ] Emergency shelter
- [ ] [ ] Extra clothing
- [ ] [ ] First-aid kit

Have Packed

- [ ] [ ] Flashlight
- [ ] [ ] Map and compass or GPS
- [ ] [ ] Matches/fire starter
- [ ] [ ] Pocketknife
- [ ] [ ] Sunglasses/sunscreen

For Day Hikes

- [ ] [ ] **Daypack**: 1,500 to 3,000 cubic inches
- [ ] [ ] **Insulating layer**: synthetic or wool tops and bottoms
- [ ] [ ] **Shirt or sweater**: synthetic or wool
- [ ] [ ] **Pants**: synthetic or wool
- [ ] [ ] **Parka shell**: waterproof and windproof

- [ ] [ ] **Pants shell**: waterproof and windproof
- [ ] [ ] **Hat**: stocking cap or balaclava
- [ ] [ ] **Gloves**: synthetic or wool
- [ ] [ ] **Shoes**: broken in
- [ ] [ ] **Extra socks**: ones that dry quickly

For Backpacking

- [ ] [ ] **Backpack**: 3,500 cubic inches or more
- [ ] [ ] **Insulating layer**: synthetic or wool tops and bottoms
- [ ] [ ] **Shirt or sweater**: synthetic or wool
- [ ] [ ] **Pants**: synthetic or wool
- [ ] [ ] **Parka shell**: waterproof and windproof
- [ ] [ ] **Pants shell**: waterproof and windproof
- [ ] [ ] **Hat**: stocking cap or balaclava
- [ ] [ ] **Gloves**: synthetic or wool
- [ ] [ ] **Shoes**: sturdy and broken in
- [ ] [ ] **Extra socks**: ones that dry quickly
- [ ] [ ] **Waterproof pack cover**

- [ ] [ ] Sleeping pad
- [ ] [ ] Stove and fuel
- [ ] [ ] Cooking gear
- [ ] [ ] Eating utensils
- [ ] [ ] Food and food bags
- [ ] [ ] Tent, tarp, or bivy sack
- [ ] [ ] Waterproof ground cloth
- [ ] [ ] Personal toiletries
- [ ] [ ] Camp shoes
- [ ] [ ] Headlamp
- [ ] [ ] Repair kit and sewing kit
- [ ] [ ] Water filter and/or iodine tablets
- [ ] [ ] Plastic trowel for catholes
- [ ] [ ] Plastic bags for garbage
- [ ] [ ] Rope or cord

Optional

- [ ] [ ] Pillow
- [ ] [ ] Camera gear
- [ ] [ ] Reading material and/or journal
- [ ] [ ] Fishing gear

- [ ] [ ] Binoculars
- [ ] [ ] Camp chair
- [ ] [ ] Radio
- [ ] [ ] Cell phone or satellite messenger
- [ ] [ ] Walking stick/hiking poles

Why and How to Go Light by Paul Magnanti

One sunny summer day in 1998, I summited Mount Katahdin in Maine. I not only had climbed one of the most majestic mountains in the East, but I had finished a thru-hike of the 2,175-mile Appalachian Trail. It was memorable day, and one I look back on fondly. A week or so later, though, my knees were in pain. I was twenty-four years old, muscular, fit, and in terrific shape, but I was hobbling up and down stairs like an elderly man. It would take almost a month for my body to fully recover.

So, why did I suffer so much discomfort? Blame much of it on my weight—my pack weight.

Why Lighten Up?

Many people say the Appalachian Trail is more physically demanding than any other long-distance hiking trail. Parts of the AT are indeed steeper than anything found on The Colorado Trail, the Pacific Crest Trail, or Continental Divide National Scenic Trail. Nevertheless, when I later thru-hiked the 300-mile Benton MacKaye Trail, which has more difficult grades than on the nearby AT, I was steadily and comfortably hiking about 25 miles per day.

What changed? I was more a more experienced hiker, for one. I also was in better shape mentally and physically than I was when I did my AT hike. And, finally, my gear was lighter.

After my AT hike, I vowed never to carry 50 pounds up and down mountains again. Over the next year, I read articles on how to reduce my backpack's weight. I went to a smaller pack. I made my own alcohol stove. I cut the size of my sleeping pad.

I did the physically demanding 273-mile Long Trail in Vermont in 1999 and felt great. The AT thru-hikers I met that year were a little surprised by my small pack. By the time I hiked the 2,650-mile Pacific Crest Trail in 2002, my base pack weight, or BPW (gear weight minus food, water, and fuel), was half that as on my AT hike.

The adventure of hiking the PCT was fantastic—incredible vistas, experiences I will not forget—and I felt great at the end of the journey. With lighter gear, the climbs were easier, I wasn't as tired at the end of the day, and the overall experience was much more enjoyable.

When I hiked The Colorado Trail, with its high elevations, big climbs, and long stretches far from resupply points, my lighter kit really came into its own. I was able to carry more food because of my lighter BPW. Inclement weather or shortened days could be dealt with because of my faster pace. The trail was not something to survive, but an experience to revel in and enjoy.

My gear continues to evolve, but my basic setup has not changed since the PCT: frameless pack, trail runners instead of boots, a good down bag, a simple shelter in lieu of a tent, a cut-down foam pad, and so on. (See complete list at PMags.com.) I would not go on another hike with my Appalachian Trail gear.

Nearing completion of the CT, two hikers are exuberant about their accomplishment and lightweight gear.
PHOTO BY JULIE VIDA AND MARK TABB

The Ultra-light Philosophy

In the process of lightening my load, I've come to look more at why I should take a particular piece of gear rather than what I should take. I do not consider myself an "ultralighter." That term, to me, evokes too technical an image, one where the emphasis is on gear and not on enjoying the trail itself. While gear is important, I think it is the least important part of hiking. I use gear to hike, not hike to use gear.

What I consider before going out are personal safety, comfort, and fun. On three-season solo hikes, my gear list is pretty scant. A simple tarp and thin pad are part of my kit. The stove is left behind. On social backpacks (more camping, less hiking), I'll take the stove, along with a book, and perhaps a small libation to enjoy at night.

Why do I advocate this approach? Because it simplifies things; there is little to come between me and my enjoyment of the outdoors. The simple act of walking can be enjoyed without worrying about how heavy the gear is on my back. A backpacker who isn't exhausted at the end of the day can better appreciate the sunset over the mountains, the sound of the wind in the trees, and the hike just completed.

Over the years my gear has changed and evolved. There has been a gradual decline in my BPW. I am now at a point where I can get lighter only by spending more money to shave ounces rather than pounds. I then have to ask myself how much is it worth to lose that weight in my pack? Or, as one thru-hiker friend said to me, "Losing pounds is cheap; losing ounces is expensive." To me, that can refer to money, time, or comfort. Each hiker has to find that balance for themselves.

Some Simple Changes

There is more than one way to lighten one's load. Most backpackers can easily get to the 15- to 20-pound BPW range without making any radical changes in their hiking or camping styles. Today, there is lighter gear available that is functionally equivalent to more traditional equipment.

A good friend of mine is a prime example of how anyone can benefit from a lighter kit. Backpacking had become for him a trudge rather than a pleasure. He'd be achy, sore, and exhausted at the end of the day. He wanted to enjoy hiking again, but also feel comfortable in camp. He asked me to look over his gear and give him some recommendations. That led to the purchase of a new frame pack, along with a good down sleeping bag and light synthetic jacket. A small pot, canister stove, lightweight two-person tent, and relatively light Therm-a-Rest sleeping pad completed the kit. We chose the gear based on his backpacking style, not mine.

The end result of this makeover? His BPW is now 17 pounds. Most people, if they are in the position to buy new gear, do not have to carry any more than that. His gear is functionally the same as his older, more traditional gear, but without the weight. It is not any less safe, nor does it require any more knowledge regarding its use, nor has he had to sacrifice any comfort. Actually, his comfort level is better now because he is no longer as tired and sore.

Going Even Lower?

As other experienced hikers have noted, it is difficult to go below 15 pounds BPW. The gear becomes more expensive and/or you need to become more of a minimalist. If you are the type of person who hikes all day and spends little time in camp, a minimalist kit may be for you. A cut-down foam pad instead of a Therm-a-Rest, a lined windshirt instead of a heavier jacket, and so on, might work well for you. But if you want more camp comforts and a more traditionalist setup, go for the 15- to 20-pound BPW range.

Remember, there is no such thing as the "best" gear, only what works best for you.

Below 10-pound BPW? You had better be comfortable, knowledgeable, and experienced in a wide range of outdoor situations to go that light. As more than one hiker has found out, it is one thing to read about the joys of going below 10 pounds, but it is something entirely different in real-world situations. What is your experience level? Are you honestly capable of handling whatever Mother Nature may throw at you with only a very minimal kit?

It's best to find that out on a shorter trip before venturing out on a longer trek. Discovering that you do not know how to set up your tarp, that you hate going stoveless, or that you wish you'd brought a thicker sleeping pad is easier to deal with on a weekend outing than in a fall snowstorm deep in the San Juans.

My kit is at about 8 pounds, 12 ounces now. (Lose the camera equipment and it's right at 8 pounds.) I've pretty much reached my limit, and I'm comfortable with it.

Hiking all or part of The Colorado Trail is a wonderful experience. With lighter gear, hiking the CT can be an even more enjoyable experience. You'll have fewer aches and pains and find it less tiring. Buy gear that works for you, go out on some backpacking trips, adjust accordingly, and have fun on your journey!

Other Resources

Lighten Up!, by Don Ladigin: A good "meat and potatoes" guide for traditional backpackers who want to lighten their load. Not as detailed as other guides, but sometimes too many details get in the way of the overall goal. It's a good guide for the why of going lightweight rather than the specific what. Start with this book if you want to go from a 30-pound BPW to 15 pounds.

Lightweight Backpacking and Camping, edited by Ryan Jordan: A detailed, gear-oriented workshop in book form. This book is aimed more toward high-end gear for lightening your load. But if you want diverse opinions from many different sources and wish to fine-tune your techniques, this book is a great guide. The editor is the publisher of backpackinglight.com.

Pmags.com: My website offers my take on the basics of backpacking and going light. Articles include: "Beginners Backpacking Primer," "Lightweight Backpacking 101," and "My Evolving Gear List."

It took many miles, many years, and much tweaking to get to my current level of gear. What I've learned may be instructive as you put together your own kit.

An old-style CT marker shows the way.
PHOTO BY AARON LOCANDER

Signs, Publications, and Navigating

The Colorado Trail is reasonably well marked. Alert trail users can generally navigate using the CT signs (the double-peaked triangular logo markers on posts and trees) alone. Nevertheless, things happen. Signs fall down, markers sometimes become souvenirs, and bad weather can cause travelers to lose their way. It is not uncommon for a CT user to veer off the trail unintentionally. The Colorado Trail Foundation strongly recommends that each user carry additional aids to help them navigate the trail.

Whether out for just the day or committed to completing the entire route in a single trip, all

CT users should carry the right tools to help them stay on the trail. These include *The Colorado Trail Guidebook, The Colorado Trail Databook, The Colorado Trail Map Book,* or other pertinent maps, plus a compass and/or GPS device to assist with orientation.

Many users have reported that the *Guidebook,* or portions of it, and a compass were adequate to navigate the trail. Others prefer carrying the *Databook,* partly because it is lighter and fits in a pocket. It includes mileages and GPS info, plus mini maps that indicate where water and campsites can be found. Still others appreciate the detail provided on topographic maps and choose the *Map Book* instead. A GPS unit can be invaluable to those proficient in its use, especially when the trail is covered by snow.

Over the years since The Colorado Trail was developed, a variety of signage has been used to mark the trail, from simple creosote posts to triangular plastic markers, from expensive redwood signs to reflective metal markers, and even to blazes on tree trunks. All have one thing in common: They display the instantly recognizable, mountain-shaped Colorado Trail logo.

In some segments, the CT's path coincides with another developed trail and shares signage with that trail. For instance, the markers and signs for the Continental Divide National Scenic Trail may be as conspicuous as that of the CT along the 200 or so

A hiker checks the *CT Databook* for what lies ahead.

PHOTO BY MORGAN AND ROBYN WILKINSON

miles where the two trails are co-located. In other sections, routes marked with blue diamonds denote cross-country ski trails that join the CT for (usually) short distances before veering off.

Unfortunately, both the tread itself and the signs marking it are susceptible to the elements, encroaching vegetation, downed trees, avalanches, and vandals. With the CT's many confusing intersections, indistinct or spotty tread in places, and the sporadic placing of trail signs, it is important to use the navigational aids available to the CT hiker.

Volunteer trail surveyor Jerry Brown embarks on his fifth CT thru-trip.
PHOTO BY CARL BROWN

Using GPS

A small, lightweight GPS receiver is a great tool for navigating The Colorado Trail. A GPS receiver can be loaded with waypoints, either manually or by electronic data transfer. Waypoints organized sequentially serve as a series of invisible cairns along the trail. Since a GPS receiver always knows exactly (to within a few meters) where it is, it can automatically calculate the bearing and distance to any

Columbines in bloom along the trail.
PHOTO BY LUCI STREMME

waypoint stored in its memory. As a result, you can easily determine how far it is to a campsite, which fork should you follow, or what the bearing and distance are to a reliable water source.

This guidebook lists the waypoints for 453 features along the CT, including trail and road intersections, stream crossings, and other important features. You can load these manually into your GPS unit or purchase the CT waypoint database from bearcreeksurvey.com. The waypoints are also listed in tables in both *The Colorado Trail Databook* and *The Colorado Trail Map Book*, which are available through The Colorado Trail store at ColoradoTrail.org/store.

Data for the trail was obtained using professional survey-grade GPS equipment. The data, collected at five-second intervals as the trail was hiked, was subsequently processed and errant points culled from the database. Whenever a feature such as a trailhead, stream, or intersection was encountered, the GPS receiver was positioned at the feature and data collected for 60 to 90 seconds, providing a high level of accuracy. Note that consumer-grade GPS units will generally not be as accurate as the mapmaking units, but are very close.

When you first turn on your GPS, it probably will be set up in WGS84 (World Geodetic System 1984). The data in the guidebook, however, uses NAD83 (North American Datum 1983) with UTM (Universal Transverse Mercator) coordinates. If you already have loaded some points in your GPS and didn't get satisfactory results, delete the data before proceeding. Your GPS must be set up for the correct units and coordinate system before you load any waypoint data. Here's how to do that:

1. Find and select the "Setup" menu on your GPS.
2. Find and select the "Units" menu.
3. Set the "Positions Format" to UTM Zone 13.
4. Set the "Map Datum" to either NAD83 or WGS84. Not all GPS receivers have a setting for NAD83. For recreational purposes, WGS84 and NAD83 can be considered to be the same.
5. Load the data, either electronically or manually.

Remember, whenever you load data into a GPS, the data entered must match the format the GPS is configured for—or you could end up miles off.

The waypoint database for The Colorado Trail is currently around 1,250 points. In the Features Table on each map page of this guide, mileage entries include a descriptive phrase, approximate elevation, plus waypoint data in UTM (NAD83).

UTM is a rectangular, straight-line system of X-Y coordinates, not unlike a checkerboard. Many trail users report it to be the easiest system to use and that it makes more sense than trying to decipher latitude-longitude pairs. Most trail maps now show UTM, enabling trail users to pinpoint their position on the map using the UTM coordinates in the Guidebook. GPS users can manually enter a UTM coordinate to verify where they are.

Be certain to follow the instructions for your particular GPS manufacturer. Before entering UTM data into the GPS unit, set the GPS position format to UTM/UPS and set the datum (may be called spheroid) to either NAD83 or WGS84. Once the UTM waypoint has been entered, GPS users can easily convert to latitude-longitude, if desired, by switching the coordinate format. Waypoint users need to be aware that the UTM zone switches in Segment 27 from UTM Zone 13 to Zone 12 at the 108-degree longitude line. It returns to Zone 13 early in Segment 28. Most GPS receivers will make this transition automatically. If for some reason your GPS doesn't, turning it off, then on again, will usually do the trick.

A hiker relaxes, refreshes, and replenishes his water supply at a creek along the trail.

PHOTO BY AARON LOCANDER

Water Along the Trail

Drinking water is readily available along most segments of The Colorado Trail, and the text and features tables in this guide point out many potential sources. On the first page of each segment, a symbol indicates whether water sources are scarce, abundant, or scattered in a typical year. There are some segments where careful water use is strongly advised. In these cases, reliable sources may be up to 20 miles apart, especially during drought years or in late summer when many seasonal streams have dried up.

Except for water available at campgrounds, picnic areas, and the like that is clearly marked as potable, water from all sources should be purified before drinking. In addition to the abundance of wild critters in the backcountry, grazing livestock, mostly sheep and cattle, is very common, even at higher elevations. All can introduce protozoa and bacterial organisms to water sources. You should treat all drinking water by one of four recommended methods: boiling, filtration, chemical disinfectant, or ultraviolet water purifier.

In addition, always practice Leave No Trace principles to safeguard the water supply for other users. That includes camping at least 100 feet from any stream, lake, or spring.

Chemically treating water obtained along the trail is one way to make it safe for drinking.

PHOTO BY ROGER FORMAN

Safe Drinking Water

In times past, one of the great outdoor pleasures for a hiker was to dip a Sierra cup into a fast-flowing stream for a long drink of ice-cold water. Today, hikers know that this can be an invitation for a nasty pathogen to invade your system.

While day-hikers on the CT typically carry adequate water for their needs, it is a constant daily chore for thru-hikers to meet their need for safe drinking water. Most likely possibilities for contamination in the Colorado backcountry include —*Giardia lamblia, Cryptosporidium,* and occasionally, some strains of bacteria and viruses in areas closer to towns.

While agricultural runoff is seldom a backcountry problem, chemical discharge from old mines is common in Colorado. The rule of thumb is to look in the stream for plants, insects, and other ample signs of life.

There are four proven methods for treating water to make it safe, and trail users will want to learn before deciding which method they choose:

▲ Boiling is the simplest, if you have adequate fuel, and kills most pathogens. While there is debate about boil times, a minimum of 5 minutes at a rolling boil is recommended.

▲ Chemical disinfection (including iodine, chlorine-based halazone tablets, and silver ion/chlorine dioxide tablets) is not as reliable as boiling, but provides some protection against *Giardia* and most bacteria, but not *Crypto.* Tablets are light and easy to carry, but don't reduce sediment from sources that are murky. Very cold water should be left to treat overnight.

▲ Filters are popular for backcountry water purification because they're relatively quick/easy and they remove sediments. Check the specifications for individual devices before buying one, and choose a filter with small enough pores to eliminate *Giardia* and *Crypto.* Many filters won't eliminate viruses, but some systems will. An advantage of filters is you can drink immediately after filtering and fill your containers again, which can reduce carried weight.

▲ Ultraviolet water purifiers are relatively new on the scene and they treat water quickly. These battery-powered devices use UV light rays instead of chemicals or filters. They are effective when used in relatively clear water and can work well to eliminate *Giardia* and *Crypto* but don't always kill viruses. Pre-filtering can be required to reduce turbidity.

Hygiene is also worth mentioning. Backcountry experts agree, "Besides proper treatment of water, basic sanitation will help prevent gastro-intestinal illnesses hikers sometimes experience. After any bowel movements and before eating, be sure to wash your hands. Alcohol gel sanitizer is lightweight, effective, inexpensive and requires no water."

Biking

Mountain biking is popular in Colorado, including along the stretches of The Colorado Trail where it's allowed. Particularly popular are the Buffalo Creek bicycle trails in the Pike National Forest around Segment 3, the CT west of Kenosha Pass in Segment 6, the dramatic ride over Searle and Kokomo passes in Segment 8, the nationally known Monarch Crest ride along the Continental Divide in Segments 15 and 16, the pedal through flower-filled meadows west of Molas Pass in Segment 25, and Segment 28 near Durango. In addition to the day-trippers, there are some intrepid cyclists who "bikepack" the trail, carrying or towing gear for multiday trips.

Cyclists need to be aware that portions of the trail that pass through federally designated wilderness areas are off-limits to cyclists and their bicycles. These include the Lost Creek Wilderness in Segments 4 and 5, the Holy Cross and Mount Massive areas in Segments 9 and 10, the Collegiate Peaks in Segments 12 and 13, La Garita in Segments 19 through 21, and the Weminuche Wilderness in Segment 24. Riders are strongly urged not to violate these prohibitions—it is illegal and a real hot-button issue among trail users.

Cyclists roll atop Elk Ridge between Searle and Kokomo passes in Segment 8.
PHOTO BY DAN MILNER

Mountain bikers face many technical challenges.

PHOTO BY JESSE SWIFT AND BILL TURNER

This guide notes the mandatory bicycle wilderness detours and describes carefully chosen detour routes around these wilderness areas. While small portions of the detours involve riding on busy highways, the majority of the miles are spent on little-used back roads and jeep trails through country every bit as scenic as the main CT route.

Most mountain bicyclists are responsible trail users and their thoughtfulness is appreciated. Also appreciated are the efforts by cyclists to be courteous to other trail users and to slow down when encountering hikers and riders and to pass responsibly. It is especially important that cyclists converse with horse riders well in advance of passing to keep from spooking their animals. Cyclists who avoid skidding are also appreciated. Skidding tires gouge the tread, which fosters erosion and can create significant repair work for volunteer trail crews.

Those cycling on the CT, as on other trails, are cautioned to be properly prepared. Make sure your bike is in good working order before leaving and that you are capable of making basic repairs on the trail.

Riders enjoy the scenery while their horses focus on the trail.

PHOTO BY BILL MANNING

Horseback Riding

The Colorado Trail is open to horses for the entire 486 miles, with a few restrictions in wilderness areas, usually regarding group size and the need to use certified, weed-free feed. Check with the appropriate ranger district for specific regulations for each wilderness area.

While many riders have completed the CT without problems and have thoroughly enjoyed their trip, others have reported some difficulties to The Colorado Trail Foundation. The CTF's maintenance guidelines call for the trail corridor to be cleared of vegetation 4 feet on either side of the centerline of the tread and to a height of 10 feet. While we strive to meet these guidelines, 8 feet wide and 10 feet high has not been achieved everywhere.

Low branches can usually be avoided without too much trouble and downed trees bypassed. However, riders may need to remove obstructions and should carry some sort of saw, such as one of the handy pocket chainsaws available from the CT store at ColoradoTrail.org/store. There may be some places, however, where the trail corridor is too narrow for a heavily loaded packhorse to pass. Tight spots can typically be passed by off-loading the pack animal, proceeding through the narrow section, and reloading.

Off-loading pack stock might be necessary at the Gudy Gaskill Bridge across the South Platte River at the beginning of Segment 2. Although the CTF expended considerable effort building a well-designed crossover, the heavy steel guardrail at the east end of the bridge can prove challenging for a pack animal to pass.

There are several barriers on segments at the Denver end of the CT to remind people that the trail is not open to motorized use. These typically consist of a steel pipe spanning the trail at a height of about 18 inches. Most horses have no trouble stepping over these, but some become panicky when encountering the barriers. Be aware of this potential problem and familiarize your horse with such obstacles.

Similarly, some horses become upset when encountering hikers and backpackers. Most hikers, if asked, are happy to move well clear of the trail while the horse passes.

Roundup Riders on one of their group's Colorado Trail rides.
PHOTO BY ROY BERKELEY

Most of the streams that cross the CT have a suitable ford around the footbridges. A few of the larger streams have sturdy wooden bridges suitable for horses. Some horses become agitated, though, at the sound of their steel shoes on a wooden bridge. Familiarization, again, with these types of obstacles can reduce problems on the trail.

The Colorado Trail has proved to be much harder on horseshoes than one might suspect. In a group of twenty horses on a weeklong ride on the CT, at least one horse required shoe repair every evening for loose or lost shoes. Carrying repair tools is essential.

Photography on the Trail

There are a multitude of scenic opportunities along the trail, as well as fantastic mountain lighting that can make carrying a camera worthwhile. Camera equipment is a personal choice generally based on a favored format—digital or film, SLR or point-and-shoot—and how much weight one is willing to carry. We recommend keeping your camera accessible in a case affixed to your backpack's chest strap or waist belt, or in a shirt or pants pocket if it's small enough. Also worth considering is that brightly colored clothes or backpack will often enhance your photos. For example, a red shirt or pack will sometimes really make a photo pop.

On longer excursions, it is easy to forget where each picture was taken. Keeping notes helps, of course, as can the chronological sequence of photos. We recommend shooting photos of signs or other landmarks along the way that will help identify the photos.

The trail is a photographer's delight.

PHOTO BY ELLIOT FORSYTH

In addition to sharing photos with friends and family, some trail users burn a disk (full-resolution image files) and send it to The Colorado Trail Foundation. This has been a great help to the CTF, which uses the images for newsletters and other publications, such as this guidebook.

Safety

Along the more isolated portions of The Colorado Trail, assistance may be many hours, even days, away. Travelers should keep the following things in mind:

▲ *Be aware of weather conditions:* Watch the sky and be alert. Hypothermia, dehydration, and lightning are all potential hazards.

▲ *Start early:* Summer afternoon thunderstorms are common in the high country. Start early and plan to be off exposed ridges before storms brew.

▲ *Don't travel alone:* It's safest to hike with companions; at the very least, make sure you leave a detailed itinerary with others.

▲ *Be in shape:* Get in condition and acclimatize to altitude before beginning your trek.

▲ *Use sun protection:* The UV radiation in Colorado can be very intense. Wear sunscreen and/or a long-sleeve shirt and pants and wide-brimmed hat. Sunglasses are strongly recommended.

▲ *Carry and use your map/guide/GPS:* Although the CT is generally well marked, travelers should always carry a guide or map, compass or GPS, and know how to use these tools.

To activate a rescue group, contact the nearest county sheriff. See page 282 for a list of contact numbers. Counties and other jurisdictions may pass along the costs of a search and rescue, which can often reach thousands of dollars, to the people involved. To protect oneself and to keep search-and-rescue efforts at a high standard, The Colorado Trail Foundation recommends purchasing a Colorado Outdoor Recreation Search and Rescue card. Proceeds go to the state's Search and Rescue Fund, which reimburses teams for the costs incurred in searches and rescues. Funds remaining at the end of the year are used to help pay for training and equipment. Anyone with a current hunting or fishing license is already covered by the fund. The CORSAR card costs $3 for one year or $12 for five years. Cards are available at 300 Colorado retailers or online at dola.colorado.gov/dlg/fa/sar/.

It should be noted that the CORSAR card is not insurance and does not reimburse individuals or pay for medical transport such as helicopter flights or ground ambulance. If an aircraft is used in a search, those costs can be reimbursed by the fund. If the aircraft becomes a medical transport due to a medical emergency, that portion is not covered.

Be aware that cell phones are not likely to operate in the backcountry and satellite phone service is limited in valley bottoms. Recent technological advances have produced

A hiker assesses the weather to determine whether to proceed or stay put for a while.
PHOTO BY CHRIS SZCZECH

satellite messengers such as Spot, which have been touted by many CT travelers and can bring peace of mind to both users and loved ones. This small device transmits a hiker's GPS location to facilitate a rendezvous or to bring aid in case of emergency.

Backcountry Ethics

The Colorado Trail runs almost entirely through national forest lands. In some areas, the trail crosses or is adjacent to private property or patented mining claims. Keep in mind that if problems arise, private landowners could withdraw rights. Please respect private property and no trespassing signs.

Remember also that federal law protects cultural and historic sites on public lands, such as old cabins, mines, and American Indian sites. These assets are important to us all and should not be scavenged for personal gain or enjoyment.

Practicing the Leave No Trace principles listed on pages 283–285 will ensure that our public lands remain pristine well into the future. It is your responsibility to be aware of rules and regulations on public lands crossed by the CT. Contact the agencies listed on page 285 for more information.

Additional Resources

In addition to *The Colorado Trail Guidebook, Map Book,* and other available maps, the following resources may be helpful to those wishing to hike all or part of The Colorado Trail:

▲ The Colorado Trail Foundation's website, ColoradoTrail.org, is the first place anyone interested in the CT should go. It answers many common questions and offers trail updates, including recent reroutes.

▲ *The Colorado Trail Databook* is a concise, inexpensive, pocket-sized guide that contains essential information such as mileage, water sources, and road crossings. After planning their trip using the *Guidebook,* many users choose to carry the lighter *Databook* on the trail. The *Databook* is available on the CTF website and at many retailers.

▲ Trailforums.com and Whiteblaze.net have an active base of users who are familiar with the logistics of planning a hike on The Colorado Trail. Each website has a forum specific to the CT.

▲ Many hikers post their stories on Trailjournals.com, which has a section specifically for The Colorado Trail.

▲ Pmags.com is the website of Paul Magnanti, a veteran long-distance hiker and friend of the CTF. The site features a Colorado Trail "End to End" Guide, kept up to date and concisely summarizing resupply options, transportation, resources, and other useful information.

Cascade Creek in Segment 25.
PHOTO BY AARON LOCANDER

Wilderness Area Regulations

Colorado has forty-three designated wilderness areas, encompassing more than 3.7 million acres. The Colorado Trail passes through six of them. From north to south they are the Lost Creek, Holy Cross, Mount Massive, Collegiate Peaks, La Garita, and Weminuche wilderness areas. Colorado Trail users may find a register at wilderness boundaries and may be asked to fill out a simple form and display their copy while passing through.

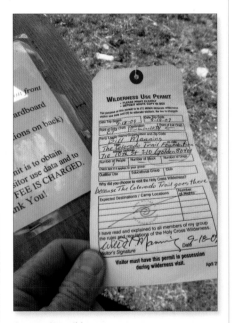

On entering wilderness areas, users encounter a register where they are asked to fill out a permit that helps the Forest Service gather usage information.

PHOTO BY BILL MANNING

Trail enthusiasts can minimize their impact by adhering to the Leave No Trace principles outlined on pages 283–285, and by following these general rules governing wilderness areas:

▲ Camp at least 100 feet from lakes and streams
▲ Use a stove rather than building a fire
▲ Bury human waste 6 inches deep and 200 feet from water sources
▲ Pack out toilet paper and trash
▲ Keep dogs leashed or under voice control
▲ Detour around the area if you are on a bike. It is prohibited to ride or even carry (possess) a bicycle in a wilderness area

Each wilderness area may have additional rules specific to that area. Check with the appropriate Forest Service office for other regulations that may apply.

Groups are limited to fifteen humans. The maximum number of "heartbeats" in a group, which includes horses and dogs, is twenty-five. Again, check with the appropriate Forest Service office for details.

THE HERITAGE OF THE COLORADO TRAIL

Early morning light in Segment 27. PHOTO BY ROGER FORMAN

FOR THOUSANDS OF YEARS, this land was their land—the towering peaks, the expansive intermountain parks full of game, the cool mountain streams. The southern Rockies were home to a succession of cultures that left little impact upon the land other than the paths through the mountains that defined their seasonal wanderings, some of which we still travel on today as part of The Colorado Trail.

By the 1600s, the Ute Indians, whose forebears probably arrived from the Great Basin a few centuries earlier, had established themselves in the mountains of west-central Colorado. Perhaps the first tribe to acquire horses, they pursued a nomadic existence following the movement of game, seeking spiritual guidance on mountaintop vision quests, and engaging in sporadic warfare with other tribes—the Arapahos, Navajos, and Comanches—who encroached on their mountain territory.

By the time white settlers arrived in the nineteenth century, two tribes of the several bands of Utes dominated western Colorado, the Tabegauche and the Uncompahgre. A succession of mostly failed treaties were signed that eventually would exile these bands to a small corner in the southwest part of the state and a reservation in Utah.

One of those treaties, negotiated in 1858, prohibited the Utes from entering areas where valuable minerals had been discovered, in effect limiting them to western and southern Colorado. Soon after, as miners continued to push west, conflicts erupted, resulting in the so-called Kit Carson Treaty of 1868. It was negotiated by a delegation of Utes, including Chief Ouray, who were led to Washington, D.C., by Carson, the famed scout and American Indian fighter. This treaty pushed the Utes farther into an area corresponding with the San Juan Mountains, west of the Continental Divide.

Two agencies were set up to distribute goods to the Indians: the White River Agency to the north and the Los Pinos Agency west of Cochetopa Pass. But blatant trespassing continued as prospectors probed the mineral-rich lands of the San Juans. The infamous

Brunot Treaty of 1873, once again facilitated by Chief Ouray, assisted by his friend Otto Mears, tried to settle the matter. The precious San Juans were ceded to the eager miners and the Utes were settled on reservations, where they were expected to shift from their traditional nomadic lifestyle to an agrarian one.

Many resisted the change, however, continuing with their age-old ways. Coupled with continued pressure from white settlers who coveted land north of the San Juans, the Brunot Treaty began to unravel. The conflict boiled over, culminating in the Meeker Massacre of 1879 at the White River Agency that left eleven white men dead. A final treaty forced on the Utes by an enraged white populace banished the Uncompahgre band to a new reservation in Utah, and the long occupation of Colorado's mountain region by the Utes ceased.

Chief Ouray, who had attempted to walk a fine line between two clashing cultures, never saw the heartbreaking removal of Utes from Colorado. He died while traveling to confer with other tribal leaders and is commemorated by a mountain peak bearing his name along the Continental Divide near Marshall Pass.

The First Explorers

The Spanish, whose knowledge of the vast region north of their empire was limited, were the first whites to explore the area that became Colorado. In 1765, Juan Maria de Rivera explored the San Juan country on his way to Utah, describing to his backers the mineral wealth of the region. Two friars, Fathers Dominquez and Escalante, followed in 1776. Charged with finding a route to California, their journeys throughout the Southwest, including the present-day

A small, pristine lake west of Rolling Pass in Segment 25.
PHOTO BY LISA TURNER

Durango area, and the detailed maps they produced had a great influence on subsequent travelers.

A few years later, an expeditionary force led by Juan Bautista de Anza entered the region in pursuit of raiding Comanche bands. They traveled through the San Luis Valley, noting the topography of the eastern flank of the San Juan Mountains and the Cochetopa

Hills, and crossed over Poncha Pass, viewing the skyscraping Sawatch Range. Others came after, and by the early 1800s the Spanish Trail wound through southwest Colorado as caravans carried goods from Santa Fe to California.

With the completion of the Louisiana Purchase in 1802 and the Treaty of Guadalupe Hidalgo following the war with Mexico in 1848, exploration of the region shifted to American interests. Trappers and mountain men penetrated the southern Rockies, following the ancient American Indian trails and using the same low passes over the Continental Divide that would later see wagon roads, railways, highways, and The Colorado Trail.

Government-sponsored expeditions set out to discover the character of this new land—destined, many believed, to become part of the country—and what lay beyond the seemingly impenetrable barrier known then as the "Shining Mountains." An 1820 expedition led by Major Stephen Long crossed the plains and tentatively explored along the Rocky Mountain front, including present-day Waterton Canyon (the start of today's Colorado Trail), as it investigated the source of the South Platte River.

Scouting the Way

Soon after the conclusion of the Mexican War, Congress planned five expeditions to study proposed routes for a transcontinental railroad. Thomas Hart Benton, an influential senator and strong proponent of Manifest Destiny, provided financial backing for several subsequent expeditions led by his son-in-law, Captain John C. Fremont, already known for his trailblazing in California. His ill-fated fourth expedition in the winter of 1848 attempted to cross the Continental Divide at the Cochetopa Hills and ended in disaster in the snowy mountains.

Despite that setback, Benton and others pushed to find a feasible rail route through the southern Rockies. In 1852, Captain John W. Gunnison, an officer with considerable experience in exploring and surveying the West, was dispatched to explore a mid-latitude rail route that would cross the Sangre de Cristo Mountains, pass through the San Luis Valley, cross the Continental Divide via one of the low passes in the Cochetopa Hills, and continue on to Utah and the Great Basin.

After great difficulty hacking a wagon road over Cochetopa Pass from a scant Indian trail—felling trees, moving huge rocks, and lowering wagons on ropes down the steep, western side—Gunnison's party emerged only to find the way blocked by an impassable gorge, now known as the Black Canyon of the Gunnison. Convinced that a rail route through the area was not practical, Gunnison nevertheless pushed on into Utah, only to be killed with several of his companions by a band of Piutes. His second-in-command, Lieutenant E. G. Beckwith, continued westward, completing the survey the following year.

While the Gunnison Expedition met with tragedy, it was to have an important impact, providing information about the country that would influence future settlement. Eventually, rails would cross the Divide at Marshall Pass, just a few miles east of Gunnison's crossing.

Following the Civil War, the government turned its attention to the settlement of the West. It sent out surveys to explore the country's resources and produce maps that would be useful to the miners, farmers, ranchers, and town builders who were clamoring for information. The two most important of these in Colorado were the War Department–led Wheeler and civilian-based Hayden surveys.

Both surveys ranged widely over the Colorado mountains, scaling summits to set up triangulations stations, naming topographic features, analyzing the geology and mineral deposits, and studying the agricultural potential. Many of the prominent features encountered today by Colorado Trail users, including scores of peaks, rivers and streams, and mountain passes, bear names recorded by the men of these surveys. Though Colorado was already well on its way to development as a result of a mining boom, the maps and reports completed by these surveys in 1879 were valuable in guiding the ensuing wave of railroad builders, water project developers, and entrepreneurs.

Land of Riches

Most of The Colorado Trail through the southern Rockies winds along the so-called "Mineral Belt," a geologic band trending from the northeast to southwest that contains the riches that attracted early prospectors and miners. After gold was discovered in Colorado in 1858, boom towns sprang up overnight and many, just as quickly, faded as the next big strike occurred.

By the early 1870s, when big silver finds began to stabilize

An old miner's cabin in Elk Creek in Segment 24.
PHOTO BY PETE KARTSOUNES

the mining industry in the state, more permanent towns and cities began to thrive. And although the eventual collapse of silver prices in the late 1890s threatened the economy of these young settlements, many live on to this day—places like Breckenridge, Leadville, Creede, Lake City, and Silverton—offering resupply points to The Colorado Trail hiker. Others left their rusting relics behind for the CT hiker to explore and ponder, things such as dilapidated cabins and hulking steam boilers. What was fortuitous in the eventual creation of The Colorado Trail was the network of footpaths, wagon roads, and rail lines built through the mountains as lifelines linking the remote communities together.

One of the most successful of the road builders was Otto Mears, a Russian immigrant who after drifting into the San Luis Valley following the Civil War, decided to go into road building on the advice of Territorial Governor William Gilpin. Mears' initial venture, over Poncha Pass, was the first toll road in southwestern Colorado. It launched his career as the "Pathfinder of the San Juans." Mears also built roads over Cochetopa Pass and to Ouray, and went on to construct railroads throughout the San Juan Mountains.

Railroads Come and Go

Railroads quickly became the key to the development of the state's mining towns and cities, and entrepreneurs vied to be the first to penetrate the mountain barriers and reach the new diggings.

The competition was fierce in the early 1880s between two narrow-gauge lines, John Evans' Denver South Park & Pacific and General William J. Palmer's Denver & Rio Grande Western, to reach the quickly growing Gunnison and San Juan mining districts. Today's CT hiker follows the original path of the DSP&P as

A rusting steam boiler and windlass sit next to an abandoned mine near Carson Saddle in Segment 22.

PHOTO BY ANDREW SKURKA

it once chugged into Waterton Canyon, then catches up with it again at Kenosha Pass. Colorado Trail users also encounter the old roadbed left behind at Chalk Creek, where the line once snaked up the valley to bore under the Continental Divide through the famous Alpine Tunnel. Likewise, users cross the old roadbed of the D&RGW at Tennessee and Marshall passes.

While these lines are long gone, a remnant of the D&RGW, rechristened the Durango & Silverton Narrow Gauge Railroad, still crosses the CT in the scenic Animas Canyon as a tourist train. The Colorado Midland Railroad was another short-lived line whose remains the CT visits near Mount Massive, where the Hagerman Tunnel once took the rails under the Continental Divide at 11,500 feet.

With the waning of mining in the first half of the twentieth century as a dominant industry in the state, the rails were torn up and a colorful time in the state's history vanished forever. Many of those abandoned railbeds and old wagon roads have become the roads and highways that today serve as the CT access routes.

In the 1930s, workers from the Civilian Conservation Corps and other Depression-era programs began a wave of trail building in the state that lasted into the 1950s, providing the tread for many miles of the current CT. These trails were constructed primarily for fire management, often paralleling mountain ranges and sending off numerous side trails. The Main Range Trail, which coincides with large sections of The Colorado Trail on the eastern slope of the Sawatch Range, is one example. Other trails were built to facilitate fish stocking of high country lakes and streams.

With the spectacular growth in backpacking, hiking, and other recreational pursuits, starting in the 1960s, these forgotten Indian trails, wagon roads, logging tracks, abandoned railbeds, and fire trails became the new highways into Colorado's spectacular backcountry. Linked by miles of new tread built by thousands of dedicated volunteers, The Colorado Trail has become part of this rich heritage.

Here is a sampling of historical highlights found along each of the five sections of The Colorado Trail.

WATERTON CANYON TRAILHEAD TO KENOSHA PASS (SEGMENTS 1–5)

In the first few miles of Waterton Canyon, The Colorado Trail follows the roadbed of the Denver South Park & Pacific Railroad. Just downstream of the Gudy Gaskill Bridge sits the shuttered South Platte Hotel, once a busy stopover for travelers on their way to the mines of Leadville and Gunnison. The DSP&P is encountered again at Kenosha Pass, where an interpretive display notes where the switchyard and maintenance shops once stood in the meadows atop the pass. The tracks over the pass were torn up in the 1930s. The DSP&P lost its famous race to reach Gunnison to the Denver & Rio Grande Western, and achieved its loftier goal of reaching the Pacific only after it was sold in foreclosure to the Union Pacific Railroad.

KENOSHA PASS TO MOUNT MASSIVE TRAILHEAD (SEGMENTS 6–10)

In 1942, a new city sprang up practically overnight in the mountain wilderness of Colorado. Camp Hale was established in the East Fork Valley as a winter and mountain training site for soldiers during World War II. The large flat valley, surrounded by steep hillsides, proved ideal for teaching skiing, rock climbing, and cold weather survival skills. The famed 10th Mountain Division trained here. Little known is that from 1959 to 1965, when the camp was deactivated, the site was used by the CIA to secretly train Tibetan rebels. Though there's little remaining of the camp to see today, its legacy is commemorated by a monument and display atop Tennessee Pass and at nearby Ski Cooper, as well as with the 10th Mountain Division hut system.

MOUNT MASSIVE TRAILHEAD TO MARSHALL PASS (SEGMENTS 11–15)

Three distinct peaks frame the view on the route to Marshall Pass: Mount Ouray, named for Chief Ouray; Chipeta Mountain, named for Ouray's wife; and Pahlone Peak, named after their son. From this point west, The Colorado Trail largely travels through the ancestral lands of the Utes, whose story is one of great freedom and loss, as whites ignored treaties and eventually pushed them out and onto reservations. Ouray attempted to straddle a middle path between the conflicting cultures, but in the end mostly gave in to white demands. Today he is considered one of Colorado's pioneers, remembered with a portrait at the State Capitol and the lofty peak that bears his name.

MARSHALL PASS TO SAN LUIS PASS (SEGMENTS 16–20)

Winding along the long section of the Continental Divide known as the Cochetopa Hills, The Colorado Trail crosses several historic passes. For centuries, these low points on the continent's backbone were used by both American Indians and animals. "Cochetopa" means buffalo, presumably because the beasts migrated to and from the San Luis Valley through here. Whites also were attracted to these easier crossings, sometimes with bad results. Explorer John C. Fremont's expedition to cross the Divide in the winter of 1848 led to disaster, with rumors of cannibalism—not the last time that charge was heard in these mountains. In 1874, a party of miners disappeared in nearly the same area. Months later, only Alfred G. Packer emerged. Packer was later convicted of murdering and dining on his companions.

SAN LUIS PASS TO JUNCTION CREEK TRAILHEAD (SEGMENTS 21–28)

You'll hear it long before you reach the bottom of Elk Creek and the Animas River Canyon in Segment 24—the long, mournful whistle of the Durango & Silverton Narrow Gauge Railroad. Completed in 1881, only nine months after construction began out of Durango, the railroad, then known as the Denver & Rio Grande Western, carried passengers and freight to the booming silver mines at Silverton. Through the years, slides, floods, snow, war, and financial instability threatened the line. Tourism saved it, and it continues to operate today, carrying passengers in vintage railcars pulled by historic steam locomotives.

THE NATURAL HISTORY OF THE COLORADO TRAIL

BY HUGO A. FERCHAU, Past Thornton Professor of Botany, Western State College

Meadow napping in Segment 25.
PHOTO BY TIM PITSCHKA

A marmot encounter.
PHOTO BY ERNIE NORRIS

THIS BRIEF LOOK AT ROCKY MOUNTAIN ECOLOGY is intended for both those new to Colorado Trail country and those locals who have rarely ventured into its vastness. Veterans of these wilds could probably write an equally good account. Regardless, there is no question that the natural history of this region is the prize, the reward for making the effort to hike the trail, and I would underscore the value of walking, not running, as you pass through it.

Over many years of leading groups of students through the Rockies, it has been my experience that those who reach camp well ahead of the rest can rarely relate any interesting observations. They might as well have worked out in a gym.

To get the most out of your Colorado Trail experience, take the time to look, to sit, to let nature present itself to you, and to soak up all that it has to offer. You may pass this way but once.

Observing Wildlife

For some reason, we commonly use the term "wildlife" to refer only to animals. Plants, evidently, are considered to be somewhat trapped or tamed, or at least subdued. There is less drama associated with plants because we can prepare for our encounters with them, whereas animals tend to take us by surprise—there all of a sudden, gone just as quickly. As a botanist, I recognize that most people would rather talk about a bear than about the bearberry.

Having been over most of The Colorado Trail, I cannot think of a single day that did not reveal much about the Rocky Mountain fauna. By the same token, I have seen students hike for days without seeing a single animal. This apparent contradiction can be explained by the fact that native animals are not in a zoo. They have instinctual and learned behaviors that enable them to avoid potential or perceived threats, such as hikers.

To see these animals, you must meet them on their own terms. Several general rules apply:

▲ Dawn and dusk are when animals tend to be most active, so rise early and get on the trail ahead of other hikers.

▲ Animals require water regularly, so look to their sources.

▲ Many animals will ignore you if you become part of the scenery, which means being quiet and still.

▲ Familiarizing yourself with the behavior of the animal, or animals, you wish to observe will increase your chances for success. Nocturnal rodents, for example, can be spotted at night by a patient observer with a flashlight.

Early-season trail users should note that deer and elk give birth in June. Try to avoid being disruptive if traveling at this time of year.

Though some may be fearful of wildlife encounters, there is little need for concern. In years of student trips, we have experienced no attacks. I have seen mountain lion and bear from reasonable distances, and I am sure they have observed me from distances that would have excited me had I known about them. I have seen bear droppings on the trail on a cold morning that were so fresh that steam was still rising from them. My wife woke up from a nap one afternoon and found fresh bear claw marks on a tree above her head.

Good judgment will help you avoid being molested. An animal seeks food, not your company. If you have no food in your presence, you will generally not be bothered. If you choose to keep food, even nuts or a candy bar, in your tent, you may wake up to find a hole chewed in the floor and the steely eyes of a mouse or pack rat staring back. After arriving in camp, hang your food away from your sleeping area—75 to 100 yards is a good distance.

Lush flowering bluebells in Segment 24 sparkling with morning dew.

PHOTO BY ROGER FORMAN

Plants

The highly variable topography of the central Rocky Mountains hosts a kaleidoscopic variety of vegetation. The accompanying diagrams indicate the types of vegetation encountered on The Colorado Trail, as well as their relationship to each other. Note that the zones are not defined by elevation alone, but also depend on local climatic factors.

In the field, of course, things can be more complicated. In areas that have been disturbed by fire or logging, for instance, different types of vegetation will exist in different relationships. Diagram 1 shows the relationship between various plant communities in a climax situation, that is, in an ecologically stable, undisturbed environment. When the land has been disturbed, the plants proceed through a succession phase before eventually evolving back into a climax state.

Diagram 2 shows the relationship between various types of vegetation during succession. Because of the severe climate and short growing season in the Rockies, successional vegetation patterns may persist for more than a hundred years. In addition, a single hillside may be covered with successional vegetation in one place and climax vegetation in another.

Riparian Vegetation: This is the vegetation found along streambanks, and it plays a variety of important roles, such as controlling erosion and providing cover and feed for wildlife. On the Western Slope, the area of Colorado on the western side of the Continental Divide, lower-elevation streambanks are dominated by a variety of trees, primarily cottonwood, alder, maple, and red osier dogwood.

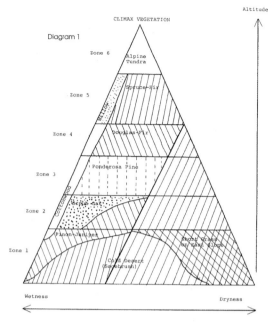

Diagram 1

Ferchau, 1970

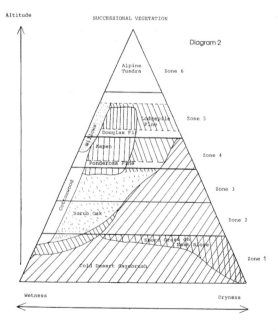

Diagram 2

Ferchau 1970

With increasing elevation, the cottonwoods become less evident, while the shrubs persist, eventually becoming dominated by willows. East of the Divide, cottonwoods are not as evident, but, as on the Western Slope, a mixture of shrubs prevails, becoming increasingly dominated by willows at higher elevations.

Moose with calf spotted near a trail crew camp.
PHOTO BY ERNIE NORRIS

Despite what appears to be very aggressive growth by riparian species, they are among the most sensitive to human activity. And because of their proximity to water, they are typically among the most threatened and endangered.

Sagebrush: Sagebrush, common to the cold, dry desert scrubland of the Rockies, is found from low to surprisingly high elevations. Interspersed with grasses, it predominates the primary grazing land of central and western Colorado.

Scrub Oak and Piñon-Juniper Woodland: This dryland plant community is most evident on The Colorado Trail where it climbs through the foothills above Denver. It also is seen occasionally at higher elevations, on the driest and most stressed sites, as the trail approaches Kenosha Pass. Junipers tend to be widely spaced, interspersed by grasses, while scrub oak tends to clump together so closely as to be almost impenetrable.

This vegetation makes for good game habitat, and hikers should be prepared for deer to pop up almost anywhere, particularly in early June. In late summer, this woodland is prone to wildfire, which can move rapidly through dry terrain. Such fires are often started by lightning strikes, and occasionally by hikers, who are reminded to pay attention to their campfires.

Ponderosa Pine: This is the lowest-elevation timber tree. Because of its good lumber quality and proximity to civilization, it has been the most extensively cut. Thus you may see large old ponderosa stumps among woodland vegetation, indicating a logged ponderosa forest where the tall pines have not yet returned. These long-needled pines tend to grow well spaced, with grasses flourishing in between. As a result, ranchers like to graze their stock among ponderosa, particularly in early spring. On the East Slope, ponderosa pine is found on less-stressed south-facing hillsides. On the Western Slope, it is encountered above the open, arid countryside of the sagebrush community.

Douglas Fir: Though related, this predominant tree is not to be confused with the giant firs of the Pacific Northwest. In the Rockies, these are the runts of the litter.

The Douglas fir occupies moist, cool sites. East of the Divide, these trees are found on the slopes opposite of ponderosa pine, and on the Western Slope they grow above the level of the ponderosa. In both regions, Douglas fir tend to grow closer together, with little ground cover underneath. Because Douglas fir is the tree type most likely to burn, much of its habitat is occupied by successional vegetation.

Spruce-Fir Forest: This, the highest-elevation forest, is composed of Engelmann spruce and subalpine fir. Because of the late snowmelt, moist summertime conditions, and early snowfall, this vegetation has been the least altered by fire. Many of the spruce-fir forests in the Rockies are 400 years old. These dense forests tend to contain many fallen logs, which can be a real deterrent to hiking. The logs are typically moist, and hikers walking over them may be surprised when the bark slips off and they lose their footing. Ground cover may be lacking and a thick humus layer may be present.

Approaching timberline, the spruce-fir stands tend to be more open. The trees are clustered, with grasses and beautiful wildflowers interspersed between. These clusters provide refuge for elk at night. At timberline, the trees are bushlike, weather-beaten, and windshorn. They often grow in very dense clumps, which can provide ideal refuge for hikers. Winds of 50 mph can whistle by virtually unnoticed as you sit in a clump of timberline

Deer, like this one in Waterton Canyon, are common along the trail.
PHOTO BY JULIE VIDA AND MARK TABB

trees. Animals are aware of this, too, and thus, while waiting out a storm, you may have the pleasure of observing a great deal of small mammal activity.

Lodgepole Pine and Aspen: These are ordinarily successional species that can occupy a given site for up to 200 years. The lodgepole pine often succeeds disturbed Douglas fir and spruce-fir communities and grows on the driest sites. Its seeds are opened by fire. A wildfire will cause the deposition of thousands of seeds, and, a few years later, dense stands of seedlings and saplings appear. These pine stands are often referred to as "horsehair." There is virtually no ground cover in the deep shade beneath the saplings and competition is fierce between the closely spaced trees. The dryness of such sites encourages repeated fires.

Aspens occupy moister sites. A clump of aspen among lodgepole pines suggests a potential source of water. Aspens reproduce from root suckers, and any ground disturbance such as a fire causes a multitude of saplings to appear. On drier sites aspens are typically interspersed with Thurber fescue, a large bunch-grass. In moderately moist sites, the ground cover will consist of a multitude of grasses, forbs, and shrubs. In wet aspen sites, ground cover is often dominated by bracken fern. Aspen groves can be attractive for camping, but during June and July may be infested with troublesome insects.

Alpine Tundra: Though it strikes many people as odd, the tundra can be likened to a desert because it sees only minimal precipitation. During

Elk herd above tree line on Cataract Ridge in Segment 23.
PHOTO BY PETE TURNER

winters, fierce winds prevent snow from accumulating in depth anywhere except in depressions. During summers, the snowmelt drains quickly off the steeper slopes, leaving the vegetation to depend on regular afternoon showers for survival.

Despite the harsh conditions, alpine tundra is quite diverse, and includes such different environments as meadows, boulder fields, fell fields, talus, and both temporary and permanent ponds. The cushionlike meadows are a favorite site for elk herds. Boulder fields are home to pikas, marmots, and other animals, and the protected spaces between the boulders can produce some of the most beautiful wildflowers. Fell fields are windswept sites from which virtually all mineral soil has been blown away, leaving behind a "pavement" that, despite its austerity, can produce some interesting plants. Talus fields consist of loose rock, and also host some interesting plants and animals. Tundra ponds often teem with invertebrates and are good sites for observing the fascinating bird known as the ptarmigan.

Wildflowers

Who can resist the elegant grace of Colorado's state flower, the blue columbine, or not be moved by nature's showy display blanketing the slopes astride The Colorado Trail in mid-summer? There are hundreds of species of flowering plants of conspicuous varieties (actually thousands, including inconspicuous plants such as grasses and sedges) along the CT as it winds its way through all five of the major Colorado lifezones.

Lifezones are delineated by elevation and are defined by their unique ecosystems and plant communities. Beginning on the margin of the high plains at 5,800 feet at Waterton Canyon (Segment 1), The Colorado Trail climbs to a lofty 13,271 feet on the slopes of Coney Summit (Segment 22). In the process, it ascends through these lifezones: plains (3,500–6,000 feet), foothills (6,000–8,000 feet), montane (8,000–10,000 feet),

A trekker identifies wildflowers in Segment 20.
PHOTO BY DON WALLACE

subalpine (10,000–11,500 feet), and alpine (11,500–14,400 feet). An alert hiker will notice the progression of plant communities along the way, which is driven by changes in climate, soil chemistry, seasonal snow accumulation, and other factors.

As the season unfolds, the colorful pageantry climbs up the slopes along with The Colorado Trail hiker. A Durango-bound thru-hiker starting among late-May blooming cactus and the bright, spring-green slopes in Waterton Canyon will reach tree line at Georgia Pass still blanketed by snow. But by the time he climbs atop Indian Trail Ridge near the end of his trek in mid-July, he will stroll through the tundra carpeted with an incredibly colorful display of alpine flowers.

The next two pages offer a sampling of some of the more common wildflowers prevalent in each of the five sections of The Colorado Trail delineated in this guide. In general, each section has characteristics that dictate the types of flowering plants a trail user may encounter. However, most of these plants are not unique to any one portion of the CT and may be found in any suitable habitat along the trail. (For instance, the many species and subspecies of Indian paintbrush, a common plant whose colorful bracts nearly any hiker can identify, exist throughout the state in a variety of habitats.)

Each plant listed here is identified by one of its common names, along with its scientific name. A plant can have several different common names, often varying by region, and the existence of a myriad of subspecies can frustrate precise identification for the amateur. You'll need to get a good hand lens for close examination of biological features as well as an excellent flower guide for Colorado plants. *Rocky Mountain Flora* by James Ells (Colorado Mountain Club Press) is an excellent field guide with more than 1,200 color photos of plants likely to be found along the CT.

PHOTO BY JOE BRUMMER

WATERTON CANYON TRAILHEAD TO KENOSHA PASS (SEGMENTS 1–5)

Most of this section is at lower elevations. Plants from the plains zone merge in Platte Canyon with foothills zone residents. Blooms begin as early as late April and extend well into June. Look for prickly pear cactus (*Opuntia macrorhiza*), yucca (*Yucca glauca*), tiny filaree (*Erodium caepitosa*), and showy prickly poppy (*Argemone polyanthemos*). The dry, gravelly soils beyond the canyon support sand lily (*Leucocrinum montanum*), while you may find **pasqueflower (*Anemone patens*)** in the damp ravines. Close to Kenosha Pass, wild iris (*Iris missouriensis*) bursts forth in the meadows of South Park.

KENOSHA PASS TO MOUNT MASSIVE TRAILHEAD (SEGMENTS 6–10)

Most thru-hikers cross the high passes of the Continental Divide and Tenmile Range too early for most flowers to appear. Look, however, for sweet-smelling alpine forget-me-not (*Eritrichium elongatum*) and alpine springbeauty (*Claytonia megarhiza*) in the fell fields and rock crevices. As the snow melts along the trail, snow buttercup (*Ranunculus adoneus*) and **globeflower (*Trollius albiflorus*)** spring out of retreating snowbanks. Once in the shadow of Mount Massive, alpine wallflower (*Erysimum capitatum*) and Ryberg penstemon (*Penstemon rydbergii*) are common.

PHOTO BY LORI BRUMMER

MOUNT MASSIVE TRAILHEAD TO MARSHALL PASS (SEGMENTS 11–15)

In this section, The Colorado Trail runs largely through thick montane forests, alternating between rather barren lodgepole stands and some lovely aspen forests. In aspen glens and forest clearings, tall heart-leaved arnica (*Arnica cordifolia*), larkspur (*Delphinium nuttallianum*), **red columbine (*Aquilegia elegantula*)**, and monkshood

PHOTO BY LORI BRUMMER

PHOTO BY JOEL BRUMMER

PHOTO BY LORI BRUMMER

(*Aconitum columbianum*) rise above the under-growth. Sharing the sunny benches above reservoirs with the ubiquitous sage are shrubby cinquefoil (*Pentaphylloides floribunda*) and rabbit-brush (*Chrysothamnus nauseosus*). The latter is a late bloomer and harbinger of fall.

MARSHALL PASS TO SAN LUIS PASS (SEGMENTS 16–20)

On this high, lonely section along the Divide, the mid-summer wildflowers are a cheerful companion to the CT hiker. Grasses and sedges dominate the sweeping ridgetop panoramas, punctuated by **alpine sunflower (*Rydbergia grandiflora*)**, with its huge heads turned to the rising sun, and the more understated American bistort (*Bistorta bistortoides*). Farther west, the Divide rises to true alpine tundra near San Luis Peak, and the slopes are carpeted with dwarf plants like alpine avens (*Acomastylis rossii turbinata*), alpine phlox (*Phlox condensata*), and moss campion (*Silene acaulis subacaulescens*).

SAN LUIS PASS TO JUNCTION CREEK TRAILHEAD (SEGMENTS 21–28)

For the thru-hiker, the best is saved for last. West of Molas Pass, The Colorado Trail enters a verdant landscape of rolling mountains, rising above lush subalpine meadows and culminating in mid-July in spectacular displays on Indian Trail Ridge. Blue columbine (*Aquilegia coerulea*), wild geranium (*Geranium caespitosum*), and silky phalecia (*Phaecelia sericea*) nod in the breeze. Along the rushing streams, monkeyflower (*Mimulus guttatus*), Parry primrose (*Primula parryi*), and **kingscrown (*Rhodiola integriflia*)** dip roots in cold melt water.

THE ROCKS ALONG THE COLORADO TRAIL

BY JACK REED

IN ITS 486-MILE COURSE from the outskirts of Denver to Durango, The Colorado Trail winds through some of the most diverse and spectacular scenery in the southern Rocky Mountains. It passes through forested valleys, spectacular canyons, alpine meadows; across uplands, high plateaus, and grassy parks; and skirts many of Colorado's most magnificent high peaks.

The diverse collage of landscapes the CT traverses has been shaped by the complex geologic history of the region through which it passes. At first the ages and types of rocks along the trail seems almost random, but if we study them carefully

Typical outcropping of Pikes Peak granite in Segment 3.
PHOTO BY JULIE VIDA AND MARK TABB

and try to decipher their stories, we find that they record a fascinating chronicle of geologic events beginning approximately 1.8 billion years ago and still continuing today. They tell of the slow shift of continents, the rise and destruction of mountain ranges, the ebb and flow of ancient seas, and the tireless work of wind, water, and glacial ice in shaping the ever-changing landscape. The geologic story of the rocks along the trail can be condensed into eight major chapters.

The Basement Rocks

The oldest rocks in the Colorado mountains are metamorphic and igneous rocks, the oldest of which formed between 1.8 and 1.6 billion years ago, during the consolidation of the part of the North American continental plate that would ultimately include Colorado. The metamorphic rocks are chiefly gneiss and schist derived from volcanic and sedimentary rocks when they were subjected to high temperatures and enormous pressure during burial to depths of as much as 8 miles. These metamorphic rocks were intruded by

Eroded formations of volcanic air-fall ash near Snow Mesa in Segment 21.

PHOTO BY AARON LOCANDER

extensive bodies of granite at several times; once during the times that they were being metamorphosed, then again about 1.4 billion years ago, and once again about 1.1 billion years ago. All of these rocks are collectively called basement rocks because they formed first and underlie all of the other rocks of the region. They are extensively exposed along the CT, particularly in the Front Range, the Tenmile Range, the Sawatch Range, and the Needle Mountains.

Rocks of the Western Seas

Following their formation, the basement rocks were uplifted and eroded to a nearly flat land surface. About 515 million years ago, during the early part of the Paleozoic era, eastward onto the continent the seas ebbed and flowed across the Colorado region for about the next 150 million years. These seas deposited extensive, relatively thin layers of sandstone, shale, and limestone. The CT crosses these beds in only a few places, one in Segment 9 just before Tennessee Pass, and another in Segments 24 and 25 near Molas Pass.

The Mountains No One Knew

About 320 million years ago, in the late Paleozoic, plate tectonic movements brought North America together with South America and Africa. One of the results of this collision was the uplift of great mountain ranges in the Colorado region. As these ancient mountains rose, the early Paleozoic sedimentary rocks that once blanketed the basement were stripped by erosion, and debris from

Sloping beds of sedimentary rocks at Section Point along Segment 26.

PHOTO BY NATE HEBENSTREIT

the rising mountains was swept into basins between the ranges, where thousands of feet of material accumulated. The ranges of the Ancestral Rockies are now completely gone, but the thick deposits of red conglomerate, sandstone, and shale (collectively known as redbeds) deposited in the flanking basins are now widely exposed, and make up some of the most spectacular of the modern ranges. These rocks are exposed near the start of The Colorado Trail on the eastern flank of the Front Range as red slabby flatirons, in Segment 8 between Copper Mountain and Tennessee Pass, and in Segments 25 through 28 between Molas Pass and Junction Creek.

The Great Cretaceous Seaway

With the erosion of the Ancestral Rocky Mountains, about 270 million years ago extensive layers of sandstone and shale were deposited across their eroded stumps. These deposits were laid down on land as wind-blown desert sands and deposits of sand and mud along sluggish meandering streams or shallow lakes. About 115 million years ago, in the Cretaceous period of the Mesozoic era, a great seaway that covered much of central North America began to spread westward across the future site of Colorado. Sand deposits along the advancing beaches formed what is now called the Dakota Sandstone. As the water deepened, deposits of black mud, now preserved as thousands of feet of black shale, were laid

Chalk Cliffs at the south end of Segment 13. The cliffs are not actually chalk, but 34 million year old granite altered by hot springs.
PHOTO BY CARL BROWN

down on top of the Dakota. Deposits of the seaway are exposed along The Colorado Trail only on the ridges north of Swan River in the western part of Segment 6. Some of the deposits that immediately pre-date the seaway cap the high ridge that the CT follows in Segments 27 and 28.

Conglomerate boulder in CT Segment 25.
PHOTO BY LINDA JEFFERS

The Laramide Orogeny

As the Cretaceous Seaway was beginning to withdraw about 70 million years ago, the first stirrings of the episode of mountain building that laid the foundations of most of the present mountain ranges began. Deformation related to plate movements along the western edge of the continent began to buckle the earth's crust, raising domes and elongate welts, most of which were bounded by folds or by faults along which slabs of rock were moved several miles with respect to the rocks beneath them. This episode of mountain building is called the Laramide Orogeny. During the orogeny, extensive bodies of granite and porphyry (a light-colored, fine-grained igneous rock studded with large rectangular crystals of feldspar) intruded both the basement rocks and the overlying sedimentary strata.

Erosion began to attack the uplifts as soon as they started to rise, carving mountain ranges from the more resistant rocks and depositing debris in the intervening basins. Except for the San Juans, all of the major ranges that the CT crosses have been carved by erosion from Laramide uplifts. Uplift continued for as much as 30 million years, but as it waned, erosion largely reduced the Laramide mountains to low rounded hills and occasional low mountains separated by flat sediment-filled basins. Parts of this post-Laramide landscape are preserved today, notably along parts of the trail in Segments 2 and 3.

The Great Volcanic Flare-Up

Igneous activity dwindled after the Laramide orogeny, but about 36 million years ago, during development of a subdued post-Laramide landscape, it resumed with a vengeance. Volcanoes spewed out huge volumes of lava, volcanic ash, and related deposits over large parts of the post-Laramide landscape. These eruptions continued for about 10 million years and built an extensive volcanic field, much of which has been removed by subsequent erosion. However, most of the San Juan Mountains are carved from a remnant of this volcanic field. Most of the ridges and peaks along The Colorado Trail in Segments 16 through 23 are formed by these volcanic rocks. Many bodies of granite and porphyry also were emplaced during this chapter of geologic history.

Uplift and Erosion

The final episode in the shaping of the present mountain landscape began about 26 million years ago, during the Oligocene Epoch of the Tertiary Period, when tectonic forces that had compressed and shortened the earth's crust during the Laramide changed direction and began to pull the crust apart. As the crust extended, a number of faults developed, the most significant of which are the faults bounding the Rio Grande rift, the series of fault-bounded basins that extend southward from Leadville through the Upper Arkansas and San Luis valleys, and through New Mexico all the way to El Paso. Some of the faults are still active today. Development of the faults was accompanied by regional uplift of the post-Laramide landscape, which originally stood only a few thousand feet above sea level, to its present elevation of 8,000 to more than 10,000 feet. During this uplift, which may be still continuing, all of the major canyons were incised into the post-Laramide surface, and the present mountain ranges were carved from the uplifted roots of the Laramide mountains and from the volcanic rocks of the San Juan volcanic field. During erosion the more resistant rocks, such as the basement rocks, some of the sedimentary rocks from the Ancestral Rocky Mountains, young granite and porphyry, and some of the volcanic rocks, tended to form mountains, while softer, less resistant rocks formed valleys and basins.

Redbeds along Indian Trail Ridge in Segment 27.
PHOTO BY JESSE SWIFT AND BILL TURNER

Red Mountain and neighboring peaks in the Lake City caldera near Segment 22.
PHOTO BY ROGER FORMAN

The Ice Ages

Most of the erosion of the uplifted roots of the Laramide mountains was the work of rock weathering and removal of material by streams and rivers. However, in the last 2 million years glaciers played a major role in shaping the mountain landscape. While there were several earlier periods of glaciation in the Colorado mountains, the principal glacial advances that shaped the present landscape were the Bull Lake glaciation between about 170,000 and 120,000 years ago, and the Pinedale glaciation between about 30,000 and 12,000 years ago. These were the glaciers that shaped the spectacular glacial amphitheatres, carved the U-shaped glacial valleys, deposited the conspicuous moraines, and shaped the basins that hold many of the jewel-like mountain lakes. Most of the accumulations of talus and the many rock glaciers in the high mountains formed after retreat of the last great glaciers.

Sources and Additional Reading

Blair, Rob. "Origins of landscapes," *in* Blair, Rob, et al., *The Western San Juan Mountains, Their Geology, Ecology, and Human History.* Boulder: University of Colorado Press, 1996.

Chronic, Halka, and Felicie Williams. *Roadside Geology of Colorado* (2nd ed.). Missoula: Mountain Press, 2002. 398 p.

Hopkins, Ralph L., and Lindy B. Hopkins. *Hiking Colorado's Geology.* Seattle: The Mountaineers, 2000. 235 p.

Mathews, Vincent. *Messages in Stone* (2nd ed.). Denver: Colorado Geological Survey, 2009. 163 p.

Raup, Omer B. *Colorado Geologic Highway Map.* Denver: Colorado Geological Survey, scale 1:1,000,000, 1991.

Reed, Jack, and Gene Ellis. *Rocks Above the Clouds - A Hiker's and Climber's Guide to Colorado Mountain Geology.* Golden: Colorado Mountain Club Press, 2009. 240 p.

Tweto, Ogden. *Geologic Map of Colorado.* U.S. Geological Survey, scale 1:500,000, 1979.

View of Lake San Cristobal and Slumgullion Slide showing the curved river valley that follows the outer wall of the Lake City caldera. At left, Red Mountain is in a lava dome within the caldera.

COURTESY OF COLORADO MOUNTAIN EXPEDITIONS

Waterton Canyon Trailhead to Kenosha Pass (Segments 1–5)

Segment 1: Waterton Canyon Trailhead to South Platte Canyon

Waterton Canyon and the South Platte River.
PHOTO BY JULIE VIDA AND MARK TABB

Distance: 16.8 miles

Elevation gain: Approx. 2,830 feet

The Elevation loss: Approx. 2,239 feet

USFS maps: Pike National Forest, pages 72–73

The Colorado Trail Databook 4/e: pages 8–9

The CT Map Book: pages 9–10

National Geographic Trails Illustrated map: No. 135

Latitude 40° map: Summit County Trails

Jurisdiction: South Platte Ranger District, Pike National Forest

Access from Denver end:

Access from Durango end:

Availability of water:

Bicycling:

"A broken toggle or cotter pin may be difficult to replace along the trail, as sporting good stores are far apart. Make sure your backpack is in excellent condition before setting off."

If you are a thru-hiker, you need to make sure your gear is in top shape. Although this guide points out towns along the way for resupply, they are few and far between. Carry spares of small, critical items.

Gudy's TIP

ABOUT THIS SEGMENT

The first segment of The Colorado Trail begins at the Waterton Canyon Trailhead on the South Platte River. The trail follows a well-maintained dirt road for the first 6.7 miles, climbing an average of 40 feet per mile. There are mileage signs every half-mile. Enjoy the moderate walking and biking—it won't last for long! The canyon was carved in 1.7 billion-year-old metamorphic rocks from the Front Range uplift during the Laramide Orogeny.

Bighorn sheep are often seen in Waterton Canyon, where their habitat is protected.

PHOTO BY JULIE VIDA AND MARK TABB

Because of its proximity to the Denver metro area, this is by far the busiest section of The Colorado Trail. In spite of its popularity, this portion of the trail is very enjoyable, offering the potential for spotting deer and bighorn sheep that scramble along the canyon walls. Since this road is used by the Denver Water Board to access Strontia Springs Dam, there are several restrictions: Motor vehicle access is limited to official vehicles, no dogs are allowed on this stretch of trail, and there is no camping until after the single-track trail begins at 6.7 miles. The road is open from a half-hour before sunrise to a half-hour after sunset.

Lenny's Rest at mile 7.9 is a great place to stop for lunch or a snack after the first challenging climb on the CT. There are nice displays of wildflowers, including Colorado's state flower, the blue columbine, along the small creeks and in the drainages the trail passes.

The best camping in Segment 1 is found along Bear Creek (mile 8.7). There are several good spots available there. Once past the creek, however, there are few good sites. Plan your day with this in mind. If you do plan to continue beyond this point, be aware that the next reliable water source is more than 8 miles away when you reach the South Platte River again.

! Camping is NOT permitted within sight of the river along the first 7 miles of Segment 1. Dogs are also prohibited on the Denver Water Board Road, which serves as the first 6.7 miles of The Colorado Trail.

Trail users who want to travel with their dogs will be happy to know that the first 6.7 miles of Segment 1 is the only stretch of the CT where dogs are prohibited. You can maximize your CT "dog miles" by choosing an alternate starting point at the east end of Segment 1. Begin instead at the Indian Creek Trailhead and Campground, which is accessible via CO Hwy 67, approximately 10 miles west of Sedalia. From the parking lot, proceed through the equestrian campground to the west for a quarter-mile and join the Indian Creek Trail. Proceed for about 6 miles until the trail intersects the CT at mile 7.9.

There is additional information on The Colorado Trail Foundation website, ColoradoTrail.org, including a map titled "Singletrack & Dogs Route" (click on Trip Planning, then Dogs). Another option is to arrange for someone to bring your dog to the start of Segment 2 at the South Platte River Bridge Trailhead.

TRAILHEAD/ACCESS POINTS

Waterton Canyon Trailhead: Take I-25 south out of Denver to the C-470 exit. Go west on C-470 for 12.5 miles and take the Wadsworth Boulevard (CO Hwy 121) exit. Go left (south) on Wadsworth for 4.5 miles, then turn left onto Waterton Canyon Road. Continue 0.3 mile to the large trailhead parking area on the left. If this parking area is full, there is another parking area a quarter-mile north up the road. It is connected to the lower parking lot by a trail.

South Platte River Trailhead: See Segment 2 on page 74.

SERVICES, SUPPLIES, AND ACCOMMODATIONS

Denver and its suburbs have a full array of services.

TRAIL DESCRIPTION

The Colorado Trail begins across the road from the parking lot on Waterton Canyon Road at mile **0.0** (5,522 feet) Continue past the interpretive display and through another parking area that is closed to the public. Bear right at a fork in the road at **mile 0.4** (5,522), staying on the main dirt road for the next 6.2 miles. There is no camping permitted along this stretch of trail and dogs are not allowed.

At **mile 6.2** (5,786), there is a turnoff on the right for Strontia Springs Dam. The CT bears to the left. At **mile 6.6** (5,840), where there is a trail junction, stay to the right. At **mile 6.7** (6,024), there is an intersection. Bear to the left and follow the single-track trail. The trail begins to climb more steeply from here.

The first campsite is at **mile 7** (6,180), but it is small and does not have a nearby water source. The trail continues climbing, following a series of switchbacks until reaching a bench known as Lenny's Rest in honor of Eagle Scout Leonard Southwell, at **mile 7.9** (6,543). There is an intersection here with Indian Creek Trail #800, a singletrack sometimes used as an alternate to Waterton Canyon. The trail then descends, crossing Bear Creek at **mile 8.7** (6,177). This is the last reliable water source until the end of Segment 1 at the South Platte River. There are several good campsites in this area.

The trail bends to the right and begins another climb. At **mile 9.6** (6,641), the CT joins an old motorcycle trail that is now very much overgrown. The only remaining evidence of that trail is the "Closed to Motor Vehicles" signs that remain. At **mile 9. 8** (6,689) the CT begins to parallel and then occasionally cross West Bear Creek. More remnants of the old motorcycle trail are found at miles **10.2** (6,900) and **10.8** (7,206).

The trail continues climbing to a ridge at **mile 12.6** (7,517), the segment's highest point. From here, the CT descends for 4.2 miles before reaching Douglas County Rd 97 and the South Platte River Trailhead, the end of Segment 1, at **mile 16.8** (6,117). From here, the trail continues over the river on the Gudy Gaskill Bridge.

A volunteer improves a water diversion to stem trail erosion.
PHOTO BY BILL MANNING

Waterton Canyon

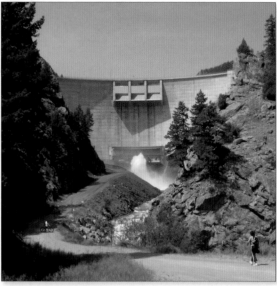

Strontia Springs Dam.
PHOTO BY LAWTON "DISCO" GRINTER

📷 A favorite with day-hikers, bike riders, anglers, birders, and others, Waterton Canyon can be a sometimes crowd-filled beginning to a 486-mile trek through the heart of the Colorado Rockies. The Colorado Trail follows a Denver Water Board service road for the first 6.7 miles, itself once a roadbed for the Denver, South Park & Pacific Railroad, built in 1877.

Water was the driving force in the development of the canyon. Explorer Stephen Long, an Army major charged with finding the headwaters of the Platte River, camped here in 1820. Years later, the town of Waterton sprang up, serving as headquarters for the Denver Water Board's decades-long effort to harness the resource for the thirsty city that was developing on the plains nearby. Near the mouth of the canyon is the Kassler Treatment Plant, a national landmark noted for its technologically advanced (for 1912) slow-sand filtration system. Farther up the road, you can see the original diversion dam for the 130-year-old High Line Canal, a 65-mile irrigation canal that snakes its way through the Denver metro area. Other diversion dams also take water from the Platte to Marston Reservoir, a few miles to the north.

At mile 6.4 on the trail, the 243-foot-high Strontia Springs Dam soars above the river. Finished in 1983, its 1.7-mile-long lake and extensive tunnel system tie together elements of the huge metro-area water delivery network.

If water developers had had their way, an even more immense reservoir, Twin Forks, would have been built upstream, threatening the canyon and inundating a portion of the CT. The proposal was beaten back in 1990, and for now, once past the dam, civilization is left behind and the canyon remains much as Stephen Long must have found it, with fir and pine sheltering the slopes and elusive bighorn sheep frolicking on the crags.

Viewing Bighorn Sheep

The Rocky Mountain bighorn sheep, the state mammal, is a fitting symbol of Colorado. With their massive curving horns, rams present a majestic silhouette that matches the grandeur of their rugged surroundings. Waterton Canyon is home to a band of bighorn that has been increasingly threatened by encroaching human activities.

The Waterton band is unusual because of its existence at such a low elevation and so close to a major city. Before human settlement, however, bighorns often wintered in the foothills and even ventured out onto the plains. Today, they are found mostly at higher elevations, often near or above tree line, usually avoiding forested country and civilization.

Bighorn are susceptible to lungworm and pneumonia, the spread of which appears to be tied to the stress of human pressure. Also, traditional routes to salt licks, important to the animals' mineral requirements, are being cut off. The construction of the Strontia Springs Dam in the 1980s severely impacted the Waterton band, which has recovered somewhat since then.

Visitors frequently spot the sheep, sometimes right along the service road. CT users should not harry, startle, or attempt to feed the animals. Thru-hikers have several chances to view this magnificent animal along the CT, usually near or at tree line in open, rolling terrain, such as along the Continental Divide in Segments 15 and 16, and then again in the high fastness of the La Garita and Weminuche wilderness areas.

Bighorns in Waterton Canyon present an opportunity for photographers.
PHOTO BY MIKE BOLLINGER

SCALE: Squares in grid approx. 1 Mile x 1 Mile

- CT (current segment)
- CT (adjacent segment)
- CT Bicycle Wilderness Detour
- 1.8 CT Feature Mileage & Location
- Trail
- Paved Road
- Improved Road
- Unimproved Road
- 4WD Unimproved Road and 4WD
- National Forest Boundary
- Wilderness Boundary
- Continental Divide
- Trailhead
- P Parking
- A Camping
- lighter greens = National Forest
- darker greens = Wilderness Area
- orange or tan = BLM Land
- purples = State Land
- white = Private Land

SEGMENT 1 FEAURES TABLE Pike National Forest

Mileage	Features & Comments	Elevation (feet)	Mileage from Denver	Mileage to Durango	UTM-E	UTM-N (NAD83)	Zone
0.0	Begin Segment 1	5,522	0.0	485.8	491,827	4,371,302	13
6.2	Pass Strontia Springs Dam	5,786	6.2	479.6	489,428	4,365,023	13
6.6	Turn right at intersection	5,840	6.6	479.2	489,774	4,364,575	13
6.7	Begin single track	6,024	6.7	479.1	489,711	4,364,357	13
7.9	Lenny's Rest and intersection Tr. 800	6,543	7.9	477.9	489,598	4,363,840	13
8.7	Cross Bear Creek	6,177	8.7	477.1	489,297	4,363,337	13
9.6	Join FS Rd 692	6,641	9.6	476.2	489,178	4,362,657	13
9.8	Cross West Bear Creek	6,689	9.8	476.0	489,063	4,362,460	13
10.2	Diverge from FS Rd 692	6,900	10.2	475.6	488,822	4,362,057	13
10.8	Go straight at intersection	7,206	10.8	475.0	488,452	4,362,417	13
12.6	High point on ridge	7,517	12.6	473.2	486,841	4,361,820	13
16.8	End Segment 1	6,117	16.8	469.0	485,565	4,361,212	13

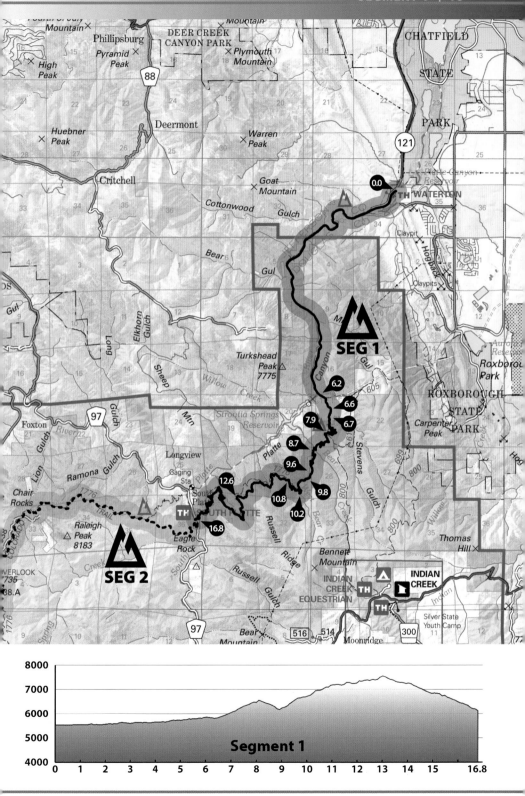

Segment 2: South Platte Canyon to Little Scraggy Trailhead

The evening sun illuminates Raleigh Peak as viewed from a recent CT reroute near Top of the World.

PHOTO BY BILL BLOOMQUIST

Distance: 11.5 miles

Elevation gain: Approx. 2,482 feet

Elevation loss: Approx. 753 feet

USFS map: Pike National Forest, pages 78–79

The Colorado Trail Databook 4/e: pages 10–11

The CT Map Book: pages 10–11

National Geographic Trails Illustrated map: No. 135

Jurisdiction: South Platte Ranger District, Pike National Forest

Access from Denver end:

Access from Durango end:

Availability of water:

Bicycling:

"When you reach the South Platte River (at the end of Segment 1), fill up on water because it is a long, dry climb to Top of the World ridge."

This segment is relatively low in elevation and shade is scarce due to a wildfire in 1996. As a result, it can be brutally hot. Use your water carefully and hike early in the day when it is cooler.

Gudy's TIP

ABOUT THIS SEGMENT

As it crosses the South Platte River the trail passes from metamorphic basement rocks into coarse-grained 1.1 billion-year-old Pikes Peak granite. This granite erodes to form spectacular spires, rounded domes, and smooth rocky faces. It decomposes into coarse porous mineral soil that holds little water. Forests that grow on this dry loose soil are especially prone to wildfires.

The effects of the 1996 Buffalo Creek Fire are the dominating feature of Segment 2 and provide a great learning opportunity. The fire burned more than 12,000 acres and the impacts are still obvious. There are long stretches of the segment that have no shade because all of the trees were burned. The landscape is revegetating nicely, however, and many plants that love disturbances such as fire have taken hold. Keep your eyes open for paintbrush, buckwheat, yucca, and sunflowers, which bloom extensively in the summer.

There is EMERGENCY drinking water available at an unmanned fire station a short walk north of where the CT first approaches Jefferson County Rd 126. There is a water faucet at the rear of the building. Fill your water bottle, TURN OFF THE WATER, and leave the area immediately.

ONE OTHER CAUTION: Property owners along this segment tend to zealously guard their privacy. Don't trespass or park your vehicle on private land.

It is imperative to be well prepared when heading into Segment 2. There is no reliable water source after leaving the South Platte River until reaching mile 1.3 of Segment 3. That's a distance of 12.8 miles. The lack of trees exposes trail users to the direct sun, making the temperature feel much warmer than in a shaded forest. In addition, there is no camping allowed along the South Platte River, so it is likely that any campsite in Segment 2 will be dry. Keep this in mind when beginning the section. Carry plenty of water and hike early or late to avoid the heat of the day.

TRAILHEAD/ACCESS POINTS

South Platte River Trailhead: From Denver, drive southwest on US Hwy 285 for about 20 miles to the mountain town of Conifer. One-quarter mile past the end of town, exit the highway to your right. At the stop sign turn left, proceed under the highway, turn right, proceed a few feet to the stop sign, and turn left. This is Jefferson County Rd 97, better known as Foxton Road. Proceed about 8 miles on Foxton Road to a stop sign at an intersection with Jefferson County Rd 96. Turn left on 96 and go 5.5 miles to the boarded-up South Platte Hotel. Cross the bridge and the road becomes Douglas County Rd 97. Seven-tenths of a mile on, you will see the 141-foot-long Gudy Gaskill Bridge on the right. This is the South Platte River Trailhead, the start of Segment 2 of The Colorado Trail.

This trailhead also can be reached from the south via Woodland Park and north on CO Hwy 67 to Deckers (a one-store town). Follow the river via Douglas County Rds 67/97 to the trailhead.

Little Scraggy Trailhead on FS Rd 550: See Segment 3 on page 80.

TRAIL DESCRIPTION

Segment 2 begins by crossing the South Platte River on the Gudy Gaskill Bridge, **mile 0.0** (6,117 feet). The trail turns to the right, heads down to the river, then turns back to the right and goes under the bridge. Soon after, the trail begins a steady climb on several switchbacks above the river. At **mile 1.1** (6,592), pass an abandoned quartz mine and enter the Buffalo Creek Fire area. Note how the forest is beginning to regenerate.

At **mile 2.5** (6,841), the trail passes a distinct outcrop of pink granite and continues through rolling terrain until reaching an old jeep road at **mile 4.3** (7,357). There are several good campsites along this stretch of the trail, including a site between boulders at the top of a ridge at **mile 5.2** (7,745). From this spot, the Chair Rocks are visible to the west. Raleigh Peak (8,183) is about a mile to the southeast and Long Scraggy Peak (8,812) is about 4 miles to the south.

After a slight downhill, The Colorado Trail crosses Raleigh Peak Road at **mile 6.0** (7,691 At **mile 7.3** (7,613), cross an old jeep road and continue through the burned area. Approachin; mile 10.1 is a metal building on the right, the unmanned fire station with emergency water spigot on the northeast corner. Turn left at **mile 10.1** (7,600), where the trail parallels Jefferson County Rd 126 for 0.3 mile. Cross Jefferson County Rd 126 at **mile 10.4** (7,650) and follow the Forest Service dirt road as it bends to the south.

Segment 2 ends when the trail reaches a large parking area at the Little Scraggy Trailhead on FS Rd 550 at **mile 11.5** (7,834). There is a toilet and an information display here. This trailhead is a Forest Service fee area. The fee to park is $5. Camping is not allowed in the parking area, but is permissible outside this area in the vicinity of The Colorado Trail.

SERVICES, SUPPLIES, AND ACCOMMODATIONS

The town of **Buffalo Creek**, on Jefferson County Rd 126, is 3.2 miles north of the trail at mile 9.5. Once a whistle stop on the Denver, South Park & Pacific Railroad, the town survives with a few cabins, a small general store (unique!), a pay phone, and a Forest Service work center.

Distance from CT: 3.2 miles
Elevation: 6,750 feet
Zip code: 80425
Area code: 303

Buffalo Creek Services

Groceries/Post Office
J. W. Green Mercantile Co.
17706 Jefferson County Rd 96
(303) 838-5587

Fire!

📷 On May 18, 1996, the human-induced Buffalo Creek Fire burned nearly 12,000 acres of the Pike National Forest, including most of the western half of Segment 2, and nearly destroyed the small mountain community of Buffalo Creek. Following the wildfire, several torrential rainstorms swept the area, including one on July 12 that dumped almost 5 inches of rain on the denuded slopes, causing severe flash flooding. Two people died and millions of dollars in property damage occurred. Downstream, some 300,000 cubic yards of sediment were swept into Strontia Springs Reservoir and miles of habitat were lost along area creeks and rivers.

The fire torched the Top of the World Campground and other features along the CT, dramatically changing the character of the landscape. Once a walk through pleasant pine forests, the CT in Segment 2 now has expansive views. Today, grasses and small plants are well established, but few trees survived the inferno, and it will be centuries before the area recovers to become a mature forest again.

It's little consolation to the victims, but a wildfire can be a good thing. Before human settlement, such fires occurred on a frequent basis, clearing out debris, rejuvenating the soil with nutrients, and keeping the amount of fuel low, which meant that rarely would a fire burn large or hot enough to destroy mature trees. Decades of fire suppression, and perhaps a decrease in logging, contributed to a disaster

A hiker passes through landscape recovering from fire. PHOTO BY ANDREW SKURKA

in the making. The Buffalo Creek area, in fact, is part of an almost continuous 2,500-square-mile swath of ponderosa pine forest that is primed for catastrophic fires, as was borne out only a few years later by the even more apocalyptic 138,000-acre Hayman Fire, which struck only a few miles to the south.

If there is an unintended boon for the CT hiker or rider, it is the vistas that have opened up in the area. The weathered domes of rough Pikes Peak granite—including the Cathedral Spires, Raleigh Peak, and Long Scraggy Peak—are striking sights from the trail. Early-season CT users are rewarded with acres of wildflowers in the opened-up slopes, including sand lily and paintbrush in the dry, gravelly areas and pasqueflower and spring beauty in the damper ravines.

Pincushion cactus in bloom.
PHOTO BY BILL BLOOMQUIST

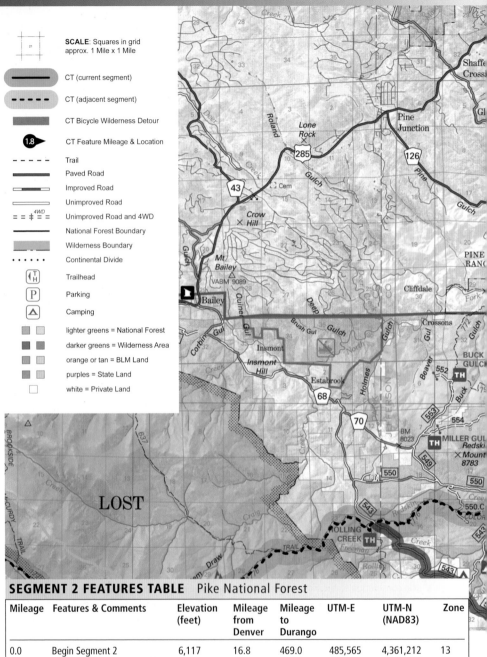

SCALE: Squares in grid approx. 1 Mile x 1 Mile

— CT (current segment)

- - - CT (adjacent segment)

■■■ CT Bicycle Wilderness Detour

(1.8) CT Feature Mileage & Location

- - - - Trail

━━━ Paved Road

▭▬▭ Improved Road

▭▭▭ Unimproved Road

= = ‡ = = 4WD Unimproved Road and 4WD

━━━ National Forest Boundary

▨▨▨ Wilderness Boundary

• • • • • • Continental Divide

(TH) Trailhead

(P) Parking

(A) Camping

■ □ lighter greens = National Forest

■ ■ darker greens = Wilderness Area

■ □ orange or tan = BLM Land

■ □ purples = State Land

□ white = Private Land

SEGMENT 2 FEATURES TABLE   Pike National Forest

Mileage	Features & Comments	Elevation (feet)	Mileage from Denver	Mileage to Durango	UTM-E	UTM-N (NAD83)	Zone
0.0	Begin Segment 2	6,117	16.8	469.0	485,565	4,361,212	13
1.1	Pass abandoned quartz mine	6,592	17.9	467.9	485,160	4,360,758	13
2.5	Pass large granite outcrop	6,841	19.3	466.5	483,612	4,361,244	13
5.2	Chair Rocks visible to west	7,745	22.0	463.8	480,693	4,361,700	13
6.0	Cross dirt road	7,691	22.8	463.0	479,996	4,361,244	13
7.3	Cross old jeep road	7,613	24.1	461.7	479,319	4,359,731	13
10.1	Turn left	7,622	26.9	458.9	478,845	4,356,741	13
10.4	Cross road	7,675	27.2	458.6	478,666	4,356,299	13
11.5	End Segment 2	7,834	28.3	457.5	477,783	4,355,124	13

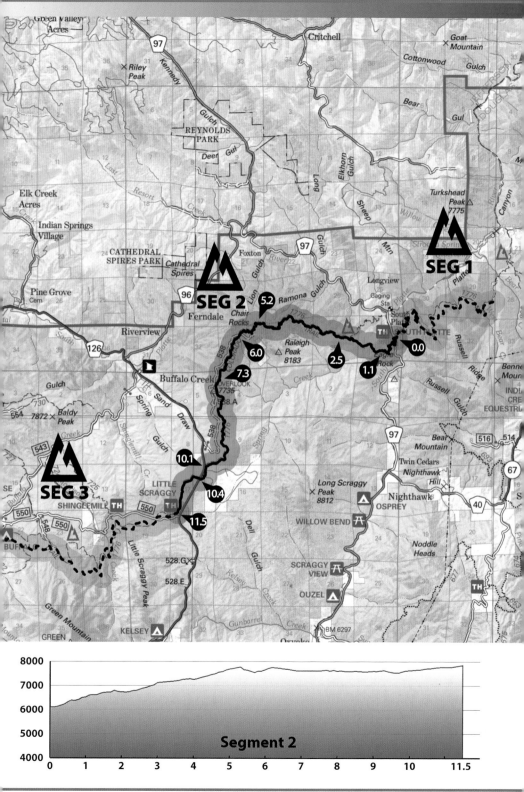

Segment 3: Little Scraggy Trailhead to FS Rd 560 (Wellington Lake Road) Trailhead

Granite outcrops good for camping and photo ops.

PHOTO BY BILL MANNING

Distance: 12.2 miles

Elevation gain: Approx. 1,975 feet

Elevation loss: Approx. 1,549 feet

USFS map: Pike National Forest, pages 84–85

The Colorado Trail Databook 4/e: pages 12–13

The CT Map Book: pages 11–13

National Geographic Trails Illustrated maps: Nos. 105, 135

Jurisdiction: South Platte Ranger District, Pike National Forest

Access from Denver end:

Access from Durango end:

Availability of water:

Bicycling:

"The trailhead on FS Rd 550 now charges a parking fee, so plan for that."

This has become a popular trailhead, especially on weekends and with mountain bikers. For the $5 daily use fee, a toilet and picnic tables are provided, but there is no water available.

Gudy's TIP

ABOUT THIS SEGMENT

Segment 3 is very popular with mountain bikers and day-hikers due to its proximity to Denver. The pine and fir forests, along with many small creeks, make this segment quite inviting. In addition, winter snow usually melts by early spring, allowing for this segment to be accessible earlier than many of the higher portions of the CT. Thru-hikers will appreciate the plentiful water sources and shaded portions of the trail after making it through the previous segment, which is very dry and often brutally hot. While most of this section is relatively flat, the climbs should not be taken for granted, especially considering the trail eclipses the 8,000-foot mark at the end of the segment.

The beginning of Segment 3 has a parking lot and bathroom. There is a parking fee.

PHOTO BY JULIE VIDA AND MARK TABB

TRAILHEAD/ACCESS POINTS

Little Scraggy Trailhead on FS Rd 550:
Drive southwest from Denver on US Hwy 285 for approximately 32 miles to Pine Junction (it has a traffic light). Turn left (southeast) on Jefferson County Rd 126 (Pine Valley Road) and proceed through the hamlets of Pine and Buffalo Creek. Continue 4 miles past the bridge over the South Platte River in Buffalo Creek to the intersection with FS Rd 550. This intersection is also 1 mile past Spring Creek Road. Turn right (west) on FS Rd 550 and drive 0.1 mile to the parking area. The Colorado Trail trailhead is at the northwest end of the parking area. To park you must pay a fee.

FS Rd 560 Trailhead: See Segment 4 on page 86.

SERVICES, SUPPLIES, AND ACCOMMODATIONS

These amenities are available in Buffalo Creek, see Segment 2 on page 74, and in Bailey, see Segment 4 on page 86.

TRAIL DESCRIPTION

Segment 3 begins at the Little Scraggy Trailhead next to the interpretive display at the northwest end of the parking area, **mile 0.0** (7,834 feet). At **mile 0.6** (7,855), the trail crosses FS Rd 550, then rolls before dropping slightly to a small intermittent stream at **mile 1.3** (7,813). For thru-hikers, this water source is a nice relief after making it through

Segment 2 and the Buffalo Creek Fire area. There is a small campsite just past the stream on the left side of the trail.

The trail crosses the Shingle Mill Trail at **mile 1.9** (7,795), then crosses another small intermittent stream with marginal camping at **mile 2.1** (7,746). At **mile 2.8** (7,709), where there's an abandoned jeep trail, cross a stream, then cross another stream at **mile 3.4** (7,760). Cross Tramway Creek at **mile 5.1** (7,797), where there are some good campsites, and take a left at the Tramway Trail at **mile 5.6** (7,681). Intersect the Green Mountain Trail and take a right at **mile 6.3** (7,645). Cross a small stream at **mile 6.4** (7,592). From here, the trail descends slightly to an intersection at **mile 7** (7,516) with a trail that leads to Buffalo Creek Campground, a fee area about a quarter-mile north. Go straight through this intersection and continue on to another intersection at **mile 7.5** (7,441), this time following the CT to the right.

At **mile 7.6** (7,405), cross Meadows Group Campground Road, then go through a gate and veer left at **mile 7.7** (7,364). After a nice walk up Buffalo Creek, cross it and FS Rd 543 at **mile 8** (7,391). Turn left at an intersection at **mile 8.2** (7,480) and head up the hill. Ahead is a rifle range and it's common to hear shots; it is best to stay on the trail. The trail climbs to **mile 9.6** (7,920), where it crosses Buffalo Creek Gun Club Road. At

Aspen alight in the early morning.
PHOTO BY MORGAN AND ROBYN WILKINSON

mile 11.9 (8,145), cross a small stream, which offers good camping. After a short but steep climb, arrive at FS Rd 560 and the end of Segment 3 at **mile 12.2** (8,279).

Mountain Biking

Bicyclists, the trail user group that travels the fastest, have sometimes been singled out, especially for their potentially startling interaction with other users. IMBA, the International Mountain Bicycling Association, has been a leader in making recommendations for responsible riding, including these useful tips:

▲ **Yield to Others and Pass with Courtesy:** Mountain bikers should yield to hikers and equestrians. Slow down when approaching other trail users and respectfully make others aware you are approaching. Pass with care and be prepared to stop if necessary.

▲ **Equestrians:** Because horses can spook easily and the chance for injury is high, use extra caution around equestrians. If you want to pass a horse, establish voice contact with the rider. Begin speaking with something like, "cyclists here, may we pass?" Your voice can calm both horse and rider, helping prevent horses from being spooked. Be prepared to stop until asked to proceed.

▲ **Ride Slowly on Crowded Trails:** Just like a busy highway, when trails are crowded you must move slowly to ensure safety for all trail users.

▲ **Say No to Mud:** Riding a muddy trail can cause unnecessary trail widening and erosion that may lead to long-lasting damage.

▲ **Respect the Trail, Wildlife, and Environment:** Be sensitive to the trail and its surroundings by riding softly and never skidding. Skidding through turns or while braking loosens trail soil and fosters trail erosion.

Trail users and the Forest Service have collaborated to establish a network of trails popular with cyclists on and around Segment 3 of the CT. The trail system is called the Buffalo Creek Recreation Area. For information and trail map, see the website for the Front Range Mountain Bike Patrol, frmbp.org. For information on IMBA, visit its website at imba.com or phone (303) 545-9011.

Cyclists enjoy an extensive network of side trails in Segment 3.

PHOTO BY PETER MORALES

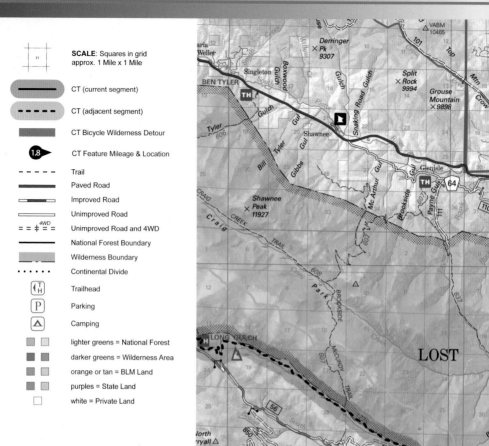

SCALE: Squares in grid approx. 1 Mile x 1 Mile

CT (current segment)

CT (adjacent segment)

CT Bicycle Wilderness Detour

1.8 CT Feature Mileage & Location

Trail

Paved Road

Improved Road

Unimproved Road

4WD Unimproved Road and 4WD

National Forest Boundary

Wilderness Boundary

Continental Divide

Trailhead

Parking

Camping

lighter greens = National Forest

darker greens = Wilderness Area

orange or tan = BLM Land

purples = State Land

white = Private Land

SEGMENT 3 FEATURES TABLE   Pike National Forest

Mileage	Features & Comments	Elevation (feet)	Mileage from Denver	Mileage to Durango	UTM-E	UTM-N (NAD83)	Zone
0.0	Begin Segment 3	7,834	28.3	457.5	477,783	4,355,124	13
0.6	Cross FS Rd 550	7,855	28.9	456.9	477,117	4,354,829	13
1.9	Cross Shingle Mill Trail	7,795	30.2	455.6	475,591	4,354,778	13
2.8	Cross stream	7,709	31.1	454.7	475,402	4,353,638	13
5.1	Cross Tramway Creek	7,645	33.4	452.4	473,709	4,353,530	13
5.6	Take sharp left at Tramway Trail	7,681	33.9	451.9	473,322	4,353,875	13
6.3	Go right at Green Mountain Trail	7,645	34.6	451.2	472,598	4,353,856	13
7.0	Intersect trail to Buffalo Creek Campground	7,516	35.3	450.5	471,694	4,354,181	13
7.5	Stay right	7,441	35.8	450.0	471,187	4,354,505	13
7.6	Cross Meadow Creek Campground Road	7,405	35.9	449.9	470,946	4,354,572	13
8.0	Cross FS Rd 543	7,391	36.3	449.5	470,682	4,354,577	13
8.2	Go left at intersection	7,454	36.5	449.3	470,526	4,354,688	13
9.6	Cross dirt road	7,930	37.9	447.9	468,473	4,354,753	13
11.9	Cross small stream	8,145	40.2	445.6	465,855	4,354,444	13
12.2	End Segment 3	8,279	40.5	445.3	465,429	4,354,406	13

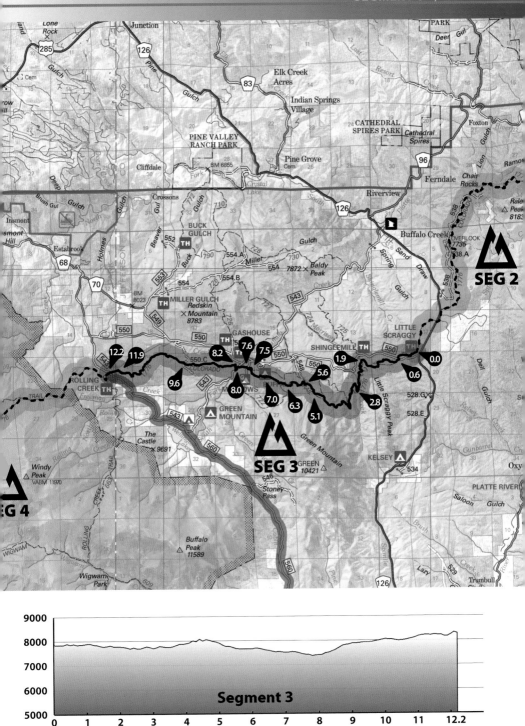

Segment 4: FS Rd 560 (Wellington Lake Road) Trailhead to Long Gulch

Looking east down Long Gulch.
PHOTO BY JULIE VIDA AND MARK TABB

Distance: 16.6 miles

Elevation gain: Approx. 3,271 feet

Elevation loss: Approx. 1,373 feet

USFS map: Pike National Forest, pages 92–93

The Colorado Trail Databook 4/e: pages 14–15

The CT Map Book: pages 13–15

National Geographic Trails Illustrated map: No. 105

Jurisdiction: South Park and South Platte Ranger Districts, Pike National Forest

Access from Denver end:

Access from Durango end:

Availability of water:

Bicycling: See pages 90–91

"Segments 1 through 3 and Segment 5 see heavy use by day-hikers and cyclists. You'll find peace and solitude in the Lost Creek Wilderness Area."

This is the first of six designated wilderness areas the CT passes through on its 486-mile route. Review the wilderness regulations on page 42; especially note that bicycles are prohibited and dogs should be leashed.

Gudy's TIP

ABOUT THIS SEGMENT

Segment 4 enters the Lost Creek Wilderness Area shortly after the trail leaves the main parking area and trailhead. Because of that, mountain bikers have to begin the long, mandatory detour to Rock Creek. At mile 1.5 the trail passes out of Pikes Peak granite and back into metamorphic rocks. There are abundant water sources and a lot of potential campsites along this section. The meadows along the North Fork of Lost Creek are great places to spot wildlife, including deer and bears. Be sure to keep your eyes and ears open! Many volunteers have helped build bridges and fill in boggy sections of the trail near the head of the meadow system. If you see a trail crew in the area, please thank them for their efforts.

TRAILHEAD/ACCESS POINTS

FS Rd 560/Rolling Creek Trailhead: Drive west from Denver on US Hwy 285 for about 39 miles to Bailey. Turn left and head southeast on Park County Rd 68 (the main intersection in town) that eventually turns into FS Rd 560 (Wellington Lake Road). After about 5 miles, you come to a Y in the road. Take the right branch, which continues as FS Rd 560. Two miles farther on, take the right fork again (still FS Rd 560). Continue another mile to a small parking area on the right. Drive slowly; it is easy to miss. A small road goes a short distance southwest to another small parking area.

North Fork Trailhead: This trailhead is remote and the last 4 miles of the road are seldom used (except during hunting season). It is suitable only for four-wheel-drive vehicles with high clearance. Drive southwest from Denver on US Hwy 285 for 58 miles to Kenosha Pass. Continue another 3.2 miles to a gravel side road on the left marked Lost Park Road (Jefferson County Rd 56 and later FS Rd 56). Proceed a little more than 16 miles to a side road (FS Rd 134) that branches to the left and starts to climb. Follow it about 4 miles to its end. The CT is just a

Aptly named, Long Gulch is an open meadow that extends for nearly seven miles.

PHOTO BY CARL BROWN

short walk across the valley on the other side of the stream. The Brookside-McCurdy Trail comes into the trailhead from the southeast and joins the CT, going northwest along it for a couple of miles, then exiting to the north.

Lost Park Campground Access: 🚗 An alternate way to the North Fork Trailhead in a two-wheel-drive vehicle is to continue on FS Rd 56 for 20 miles to its end at Lost Park Campground and walk north on the Brookside-McCurdy Trail for 1.7 miles, joining the CT at the North Fork Trailhead.

Long Gulch Trailhead: 🚗 See Segment 5 on page 94.

SERVICES, SUPPLIES, AND ACCOMMODATIONS

Bailey, west of Denver on busy US Hwy 285 (approximately 8 miles west of the Rolling Creek Trailhead using FS Rd 560 and Park County Rd 68), has a small business center supported by dispersed mountain residences.

Distance from CT: 8 miles
Elevation: 7,750 feet
Zip code: 80421
Area code: 303

Bailey Services

Dining, several places including:
Coney Island
10 Old Stage Coach Rd.
(303) 838-4210

El Rio
60006 US Hwy 285
(303) 816-9345

**Gear
(including fuel canisters)**
Knotty Pine
60641 US Hwy 285
(303) 838-5679

**Groceries
(convenience-store type)**
Conoco Bailey Self-Service
US Hwy 285
(303) 838-5170

Info
Chamber of Commerce
PO Box 477
(303) 838-9080

Laundry
Sudz Laundromat
Near US Hwy 285
(303) 838-4809

Lodging
Glen Isle Resort
US Hwy 285
(303) 838-5461

Bailey Lodge
US Hwy 285
(303) 838-2450

Post Office
Bailey Post Office
24 River Dr.
(800) 275-8777

TRAIL DESCRIPTION

Segment 4 begins at FS Rd 560, **mile 0.0** (8,279 feet). Follow the road to a parking area at **mile 0.3** (8,354), where there is an information display and trail register. The Colorado Trail is on the right side of the parking area and heads in a northwesterly direction. At **mile 1** (8,527), take a left when the trail joins an old logging road. After passing a

Volunteers improve one of many boggy sections in Long Gulch.

PHOTO BY CHUCK LAWSON

fence, where there is a possible dry campsite, continue uphill to **mile 1.9** (9,016), where the trail enters the Lost Creek Wilderness Area. As with all wilderness areas, bikes and motorized vehicles are not permitted.

There are several small seasonal streams and potential campsites in the next two miles. Intersect the Payne Creek Trail on the right at **mile 3.3** (9,307) and continue straight ahead. Cross the headwaters of Craig Creek at **mile 4.6** (9,380). There are good campsites nearby. At **mile 5.6** (9, 897), reach an intersection where the trail leaves the old road. Take a left onto the single-track trail and begin a steep climb. At **mile 7.4** (10,483), the trail rejoins old Hooper Road, crosses a small spring at **mile 8** (10,343), then leaves the wilderness area at **mile 8.2** (10,314). After entering a large, grassy valley, follow the North Fork of Lost Creek upstream. There are many potential campsites along the way.

The Brookside-McCurdy Trail joins The Colorado Trail at **mile 8.9** (10,199) by a trail register. At **mile 11.3** (10,428), the Brookside-McCurdy Trail goes to the right, while the CT bears to the left. Leave the valley at **mile 14.5** (10,929) and enter the forest at the head of the North Fork of Lost Creek. The trail descends steeply from here. After crossing a small stream at **mile 16.5** (10,200), hike a short distance to **mile 16.6** (10,176) and the end of Segment 4.

Mules are loaded with heavy culverts that volunteers will install to help keep the trail dry.

PHOTO BY CHUCK LAWSON

The Hayman Fire

Beginning in a campfire circle on the morning of June 8, 2002, the Hayman Fire quickly escaped to become the largest wildfire in Colorado's recorded history. Drought conditions, high winds, and record hot weather spurred the blaze, which burned nearly 138,000 acres over three weeks. The fire destroyed 133 homes and cost nearly $40 million. The fire leapt highways, clear-cuts, and prescribed burn areas, pushing into the heavy underbrush and timber in the southern portion of the Lost Creek Wilderness Area, stopping just a few miles short of the CT. Thus, CT hikers will see little evidence of this catastrophe. But mountain bikers, who have to bypass to the south of the wilderness on Forest Service roads, will see firsthand nature's fury. Campers in the wilderness are reminded to use a stove and forgo building fires.

Lost Creek Wilderness Bicycle Detour

This long, mandatory bike detour in Segments 4 and 5 bypasses the Lost Creek Wilderness Area. It follows several dirt roads, skirting the wilderness to the south, and rejoining the CT at the Rock Creek Trailhead at mile 8 of Segment 5. The detour passes through the area devastated by the Hayman Fire. This lengthy detour skips 24.4 miles of the CT.

Taken from *The CT Map Book* (pages 68–71), the detour begins at the end of Segment 3 at FS Rd 560 (Wellington Lake Road). Turn left and follow the road southeast for 2.8 miles to an intersection next to Wellington Lake (8,040 feet). Continue straight ahead and cross a stream at **mile 3.8** (8,080). Continue uphill to **mile 5.2** (8,575) and cross Stoney Pass (8,562). Cross streams at **mile 8.1** (7,920) and **mile 8.6** (7,920). Ignore a fork to the right at

mile **9.7** (8,224) and continue to another intersection with FS Rd 51 at **mile 12** (7,495). Stay on FS Rd 560 to the left. Reach FS Rd 211 at **mile 13.6** (7,475). Follow it to the right (west) and cross a creek at **mile 18.8** (7,555) to reach an intersection just beyond at **mile 19** (7,620). Take the right fork, continuing on FS Rd 211. Pass Goose Creek Campground at **mile 21.8** (7,720). (The campground was closed after the Hayman Fire, but water can be filtered from the creek there.)

Riders in Segment 3 prior to the Lost Creek detour.
PHOTO BY JESSE SWIFT AND BILL TURNER

Continue on FS Rd 211. Pass a private campground at **mile 35.4** (8,290) and hit Park County Rd 77 at **mile 35.9** (8,230). Follow the paved road to the right (northwest). Pass through the small community of Tarryall at **mile 41** (8,700) and by the Outpost Wilderness Adventure camp at **mile 49.4** (8,751). (Camp officials have offered to provide low-cost, bunkhouse-style lodging and cafeteria meals to thru-bikers, but contact them first at owa.com to check on availability.)

Approaching FS 560 and the Lost Creek detour.
PHOTO BY BILL MANNING

Continue on Park County Rd 77 past Tarryall Reservoir at **mile 54.1** (8,886) to **mile 63** (9,227), where it intersects with Park County Rd 39. Turn right onto Park County Rd 39 and proceed to **mile 68.6** (9,560), where it intersects with Lost Park Road (FS Rd 56). Turn right (east) on Lost Park Road and ride to **mile 70.7** (9,526). Turn left on FS Rd 133 at The Colorado Trail/Rock Creek Trailhead sign. Turn left and pedal a little less than a mile to rejoin The Colorado Trail at **mile 71.6** (9,730).

SCALE: Squares in grid approx. 1 Mile x 1 Mile

CT (current segment)

CT (adjacent segment)

CT Bicycle Wilderness Detour

1.8 CT Feature Mileage & Location

Trail

Paved Road

Improved Road

Unimproved Road

4WD Unimproved Road and 4WD

National Forest Boundary

Wilderness Boundary

Continental Divide

TH Trailhead

P Parking

A Camping

lighter greens = National Forest

darker greens = Wilderness Area

orange or tan = BLM Land

purples = State Land

white = Private Land

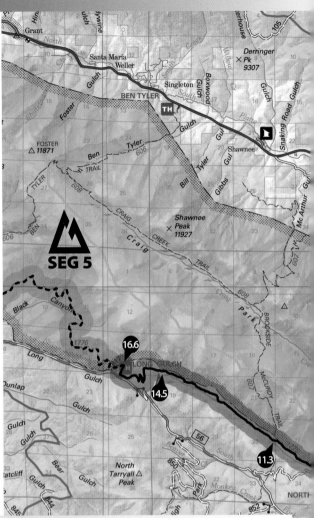

SEGMENT 4 FEATURES TABLE   Pike National Forest

Mileage	Features & Comments	Elevation (feet)	Mileage from Denver	Mileage to Durango	UTM-E	UTM-N (NAD83)	Zone
0.0	Begin Segment 4	8,279	40.5	445.3	465,429	4,354,406	13
0.3	Go right onto trail	8,354	40.8	445.0	465,294	4,354,122	13
1.0	Go left on old logging road	8,527	41.5	444.3	464,474	4,354,588	13
1.9	Enter Lost Creek Wilderness Area	9,016	42.4	443.4	463,618	4,353,766	13
3.3	Intersect Payne Creek Trail	9,307	43.8	442.0	461,803	4,353,395	13
5.6	Turn left onto single-track trail	9,897	46.1	439.7	459,175	4,351,669	13
7.4	Rejoin old Hooper Road	10,483	47.9	437.9	457,542	4,350,771	13
8.2	Exit Lost Creek Wilderness Area	10,314	48.7	437.1	456,422	4,351,041	13
8.9	Brookside-McCurdy Trail joins CT for the next 2 miles	10,199	49.4	436.4	455,590	4,350,933	13
11.3	Brookside-McCurdy Trail exits CT to the right	10,428	51.5	434.3	452,524	4,352,903	13
14.5	Head of North Fork of Lost Creek	10,929	55.0	430.8	448,413	4,355,450	13
16.6	End Segment 4	10,176	57.1	428.7	446,882	4,355,620	13

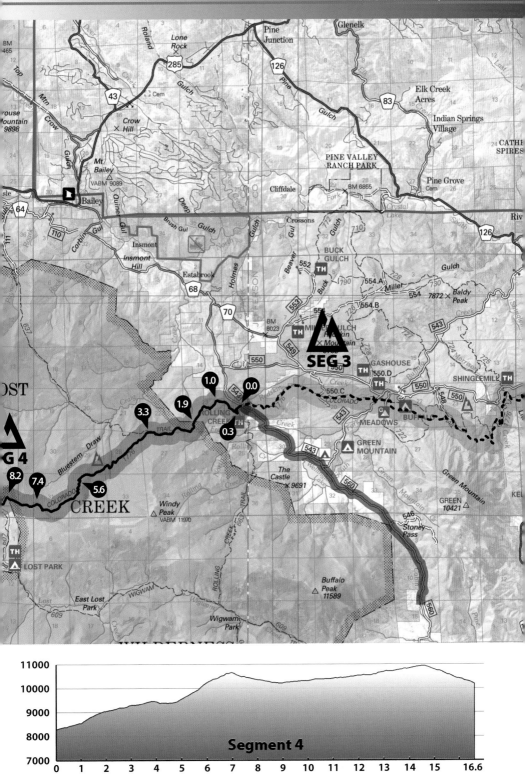

Segment 5: Long Gulch to Kenosha Pass

South Park near the west end of Segment 5 offers expansive views and fall color.

COURTESY OF THE COLORADO TRAIL FOUNDATION

Distance: 15.1 miles

Elevation gain: Approx. 2,109 feet

Elevation loss: Approx. 2,302 feet

USFS map: Pike National Forest, pages 98–99

The Colorado Trail Databook 4/e: pages 16–17

The CT Map Book: pages 15–17

National Geographic Trails Illustrated map: No. 105

Jurisdiction: South Platte and South Park Ranger Districts, Pike National Forest

Access from Denver end:

Access from Durango end:

Availability of water:

Bicycling:
See page 90–91

"Between Black Canyon and Kenosha Pass, stop to take in the incredible vistas of South Park and the mountainous backdrop."

South Park is a fault-bounded basin filled with sedimentary rocks that date from the time of the Ancestral Rocky Mountains and Cretaceous seaway. These rocks are overlain with younger sediments deposited during erosion of the mountains formed during the Laramide Orogeny. In this segment, you get your first look at the Continental Divide, dominated by a lofty pyramid, Mount Guyot (pronounced gee-oh). Note Georgia Pass, the low point to the right of Mount Guyot, where the CT first enters the alpine ecosystem before crossing the Great Divide in Segment 6.

Gudy's TIP

ABOUT THIS SEGMENT

The trees are one of the highlights of Segment 5. The trail passes through several spectacular stands of aspen, a species that shares extensive root systems that produce colonies that can live thousands of years. The CT also passes by bristle-cone pines. This five-needled pine lives at high elevations, and despite the poor soil and long winters, hearty individual bristlecones can live up to 5,000 years. If you are not familiar with the trees along the CT, be sure to bring a guidebook specifically for this section. Toward the end of the segment, views of the Continental Divide open up, giving thru-hikers a good idea of the change in terrain to come.

! The last reliable water source in Segment 5 is at mile 8.3. Another steady water source doesn't appear until mile 2.8 of Segment 6.

TRAILHEAD/ACCESS POINTS

Long Gulch Trail Access: 🚗 Drive west from Denver on US Hwy 285 for about 60 miles to Kenosha Pass. Continue another 3.2 miles to a turnoff on the left side of the road marked Lost Park Road. Follow this road for 11 miles. Look for a gully on the left side and a road marked FS Rd 817. Drive or walk up this road for 0.2 mile to its end. Walk a short distance up the gully to the Forest Service register. Angle slightly to the right and follow the access trail to its intersection with the CT.

Rock Creek Trailhead (FS Rd 133): 🚗 Follow the aforementioned Long Gulch Trail instructions to Lost Park Road. Drive 7.5 miles on Lost Park Road to a primitive road that branches off to the left. Proceed on this primitive road for 1.2 miles to the intersection with the CT. There is limited parking here.

Kenosha Pass Trailhead: 🚗 See Segment 6 on page 100.

Mid-June snowpack lies ahead at Georgia Pass.
PHOTO BY BERNARD WOLF

SERVICES, SUPPLIES, AND ACCOMMODATIONS

The town of Jefferson is approximately 4.5 miles southwest of Kenosha Pass on US Hwy 285. See Segment 6 on pages 100–109.

TRAIL DESCRIPTION

NOTE: This description begins at the trailhead parking area and sign just off Lost Park Road. A side trail, marked as the Long Gulch Trail, goes 0.2 mile

A hiker in Segment 5 has a broad view of the Continental Divide to the west.

PHOTO BY ANDREW SKURKA

up the hillside to intersect The Colorado Trail. Thru-hikers will not encounter this trailhead unless they make a specific detour to it.

From the trailhead, cross the creek on a small bridge and go uphill for 0.2 mile to the CT, **mile 0.0** (10,176 feet). Westbound hikers will turn left at this well-marked intersection. There is a good campsite near here, with water available from a fast-moving creek. Cross the creek about 300 feet past the intersection. The trail enters the Lost Creek Wilderness Area at **mile 0.3** (10,261). Then at **mile 1.6** (10,380) it heads through a mixed aspen-fir forest with some bristlecone pines. Cross a seasonal stream at **mile 2.9** (10, 366). There is a good campsite nearby. Cross a marshy area at **mile 3.1** (10, 388) and streams at **mile 3.9** (10,347) and **mile 4.5** (10,258). There is another creek at **mile 5.3** (10, 185) with several good campsites.

The CT leaves the Lost Creek Wilderness Area at **mile 6.6** (9,815) and crosses Rock Creek at **mile 7.3** (9,534) where users should refill their bottles. Turn left when intersecting the Ben Tyler Trail at **mile 7.4** (9,521). Ranch buildings are visible ahead. Pass through a Forest Service gate at **mile 7.6** (9,556), continue to the Rock Creek Trailhead at **mile 8** (9,727), and cross the road. Cross Johnson Gulch and a small, seasonal stream at **mile 8.4** (9,570). This possible water source is the last until Kenosha Pass and there's room to camp.

Just past the stream, the CT crosses a jeep road and eventually passes through a stand of large aspen trees. The CT is very well marked as it passes two more jeep trails. There are great views of the mountains to the south and west and toward the town of Jefferson. The trail eventually reaches a parking area at **mile 14.9** (10,010). It continues to the left, and after crossing US Hwy 285, reaches the end of Segment 5 at **mile 15.1** (9,969).

Lost Creek Wilderness Area

The name Lost Creek conjures up an image of an enigmatic place. And indeed, this 119,790-acre wilderness area has a fascinating history of lost gold, vanished dreams, and hidden places.

Lost Creek begins in the open meadows of Lost Park, sandwiched between the granite knobs of the Kenosha and Tarryall mountains. The last native bison killed in Colorado fell in Lost Park in 1897. From here the creek descends into a deeply etched canyon, vanishing among tumbled boulders and underground tunnels, and reappearing nine times. The "lost" stream eventually re-emerges as Goose Creek at the southeast end of the wilderness area.

More than a century ago, the notorious Reynolds Gang terrorized nearby South Park, holding up stagecoaches and lone riders for their gold. The stories vary, but some say the gang stashed their lost cache in Handcart Gulch, north of Kenosha Pass, while others claim it is hidden among the strange granite outcrops that dot the hills above Lost Park, a frequent hideout for the gang.

Dreamers often vanished into the recesses of Lost Creek looking for riches. Both the Lost Jackman Mine and the Indian Mine were supposed to be fabulously rich in gold; but if they ever existed at all, they are lost forever to time.

Perhaps the most ambitious scheme was an early twentieth-century attempt to build an unusual subterranean dam on Goose Creek, which would have flooded a major

The entrance to the Lost Creek Wilderness Area near the beginning of Segment 5.

PHOTO BY LAWTON "DISCO" GRINTER

valley, to meet the water needs of Denver.

Fortunately, this effort failed, and Denver citizens have benefited more by having this magnificent wilderness preserved at their doorstep.

The Lost Creek Wilderness Area was established in 1980. Despite heavy use by recreationalists, there are still some unexplored corners and hidden places in the Lost Creek. In the early 1990s, prolific peak-bagger Bob Martin frequently visited the area in his quest to climb every peak in Colorado over 11,000 feet. He discovered a half-dozen remote "eleveners" tucked away in the wilderness area without signs of previous ascent. He reports that most were difficult scrambles, some requiring the assistance of a rope.

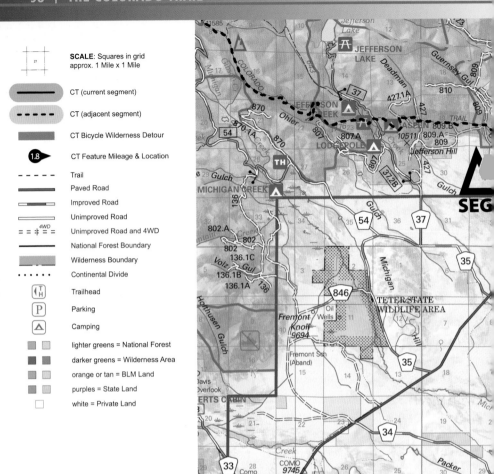

Legend

SCALE: Squares in grid approx. 1 Mile x 1 Mile

- CT (current segment)
- CT (adjacent segment)
- CT Bicycle Wilderness Detour
- 1.8 CT Feature Mileage & Location
- Trail
- Paved Road
- Improved Road
- Unimproved Road
- Unimproved Road and 4WD
- National Forest Boundary
- Wilderness Boundary
- Continental Divide
- Trailhead
- Parking
- Camping
- lighter greens = National Forest
- darker greens = Wilderness Area
- orange or tan = BLM Land
- purples = State Land
- white = Private Land

SEGMENT 5 FEATURES TABLE   Pike National Forest

Mileage	Features & Comments	Elevation (feet)	Mileage from Denver	Mileage to Durango	UTM-E	UTM-N (NAD83)	Zone
0.0	Begin Segment 5	10,176	57.1	428.7	446,882	4,355,620	13
0.3	Enter Lost Creek Wilderness	10,261	57.4	428.4	446,494	4,355,578	13
2.9	Cross seasonal stream	10,366	60.0	425.8	445,292	4,357,257	13
3.1	Cross marshy area	10,388	60.2	425.6	445,247	4,357,475	13
3.9	Cross seasonal stream	10,347	61.0	424.8	444,712	4,358,504	13
4.5	Cross seasonal stream	10,258	61.6	424.2	444,333	4,358,566	13
5.3	Cross creek	10,185	62.4	423.4	443,443	4,359,029	13
6.6	Exit Lost Creek Wilderness	9,815	63.7	422.1	441,738	4,357,965	13
7.3	Cross Rock Creek	9,534	64.4	421.4	441,104	4,357,452	13
7.4	Intersect Ben Tyler Trail	9,521	64.5	421.3	441,079	4,357,404	13
7.6	Pass through gate	9,556	64.7	421.1	441,333	4,357,157	13
8.0	Cross road at Rock Creek Trailhead	9,727	65.1	420.7	440,776	4,357,207	13
8.4	Cross Johnson Gulch	9,570	65.5	420.3	440,110	4,357,096	13
14.9	Go left at parking area	10,010	72.0	413.8	435,018	4,362,945	13
15.1	End Segment 5	9,969	72.2	413.6	434,724	4,362,829	13

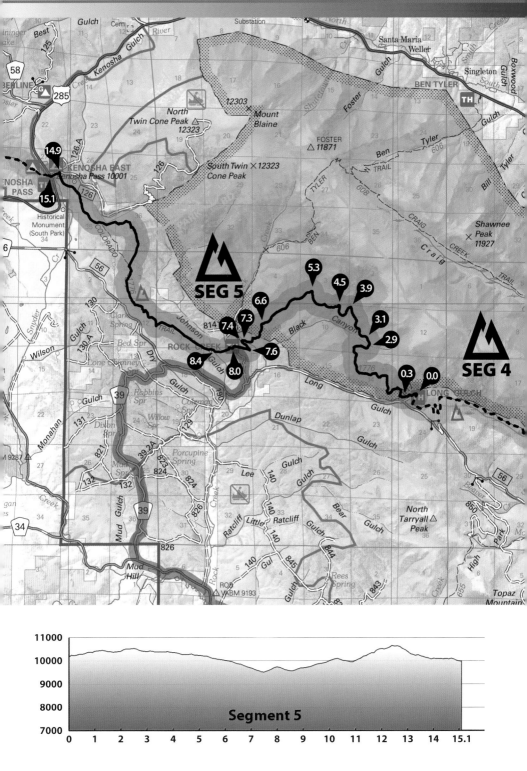

Kenosha Pass to Mount Massive Trailhead (Segments 6–10)
Segment 6: Kenosha Pass to Gold Hill Trailhead

Distance: 32.9 miles

Elevation gain: Approx. 5,196 feet

Elevation loss: Approx. 5,968 feet

USFS maps: Pike and White River National Forests, see pages 108–109

The Colorado Trail Databook 4/e: pages 18–19

The CT Map Book: pages 17–20

National Geographic Trails Illustrated maps: Nos. 104, 105, 108, 109

Latitude 40° map: Summit County Trails

Jurisdiction: South Park and Dillon Ranger Districts, Pike and White River National Forests

Access from Denver end:

Access from Durango end:

Availability of water: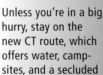

Bicycling: 🚲

A cyclist pedals through golden aspen west of Kenosha Pass.

PHOTO BY NICK WILDE

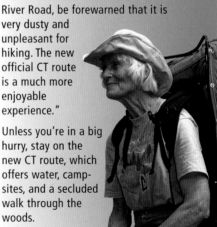

"If you decide to take the old, shorter CT route down the Swan River Road, be forewarned that it is very dusty and unpleasant for hiking. The new official CT route is a much more enjoyable experience."

Unless you're in a big hurry, stay on the new CT route, which offers water, camp-sites, and a secluded walk through the woods.

Gudy's TIP

ABOUT THIS SEGMENT

Segment 6 is the longest segment on The Colorado Trail. During its 32.9 miles, it reaches the Continental Divide, passes through several distinct watersheds, runs along a ridge near Keystone Ski Resort, and ends in the resort town of Breckenridge. There are lots of good places to camp near the major streams and many other potential campsites between water sources and near small streams.

There are great views to the south and north when crossing Georgia Pass atop the Divide, and southbound users first encounter the sometimes co-located Continental Divide National Scenic Trail (CDNST), with which the CT shares a total of 234.8 miles in two lengthy sections.

It is not uncommon to encounter snowdrifts above tree line well into July, so be prepared. In addition to snow, summer thunderstorms can move in quickly and catch people off guard. Keep track of the time and weather conditions when heading into alpine areas. At mile 25.3 the CT crosses from metamorphic basement rocks into black shale deposited in the Cretaceous seaway. The two types of rock are separated by the Elkhorn Mountain thrust, a Laramide fault along which the basement rocks have been carried westward more than 5 miles across the younger shale. The same fault forms the eastern margin of South Park.

The view toward Georgia Pass and the Continental Divide at the beginning of Segment 6.
PHOTO BY MORGAN AND ROBYN WILKINSON

The Middle and North forks of the Swan River have several great campsites, but this part of the trail is accessible to motor vehicles via the roads near the rivers. Keep this in mind when choosing campsites because there may be other folks there as well.

The last few miles of Segment 6 go through large forested areas that are being killed by mountain pine beetles. Fire suppression and relatively warm winters have allowed the beetles to proliferate and wreak havoc. Eventually, these trees will be blown down and the character of the area changed dramatically.

Evening light over South Park after a rainy day.
PHOTO BY MICK GIGONE

TRAILHEAD/ACCESS POINTS

Kenosha Pass Trailhead: From Denver, drive southwest on US Hwy 285 for about 58 miles to Kenosha Pass. Kenosha Pass Campground is on the right and the Kenosha Pass Picnic Area can be seen on the left side of the highway, back in the trees. Both are fee areas. You may park alongside the highway, however, without paying the fee. The beginning of Segment 6 is on the righthand (northwest) side of the highway, just past the turn-in to the campground. The CT is visible from the highway, proceeding into the forest in a northwesterly direction. Note that The Colorado Trail no longer goes through the campground. Water is available in the campground from a hand pump, after payment of the fee. If one proceeds through the picnic area and a short way into the forest, there is a meadow suitable for camping without fee payment.

Jefferson Lake Road Access: 🚗 This access requires a fee payment. From Kenosha Pass, continue southwest on US Hwy 285 for 4.5 miles to the town of Jefferson. Turn right on Jefferson Lake Road. Drive 2.1 miles to an intersection. Turn right and proceed about a mile to the fee collection point. Continue 2.1 miles to where the CT crosses the road. A small parking area is 0.1 mile farther on the left. Another larger parking area is 0.6 mile down the road, near the Jefferson Lake Campground.

Georgia Pass Trail Access: 🚗 Using the driving instructions for the aforementioned Jefferson Lake Road access, turn right on Jefferson Lake Road, which is also known as the Michigan Creek Road. After 2.1 miles, where Jefferson Lake Road turns right, continue straight on Michigan Creek Road for 10 miles to Georgia Pass. The last 2 miles are a little rough, but most vehicles with reasonable ground clearance can make it. From the pass, the CT crosses a jeep trail to the right. There is a parking area at the pass, but none at the CT crossing. The last 0.2 mile to the CT crossing is very rough.

One of many small, refreshing creeks in the segment.
PHOTO BY BERNARD WOLF

North Fork of the Swan River Access: 🚗 From Denver, travel west on I-70 for about 75 miles to exit 203 (Frisco/Breckenridge). Proceed south on CO Hwy 9 for 7 miles to a traffic light at Tiger Road. Turn left on Tiger Road and drive 7 miles to an intersection with the drainage of the North Fork of the Swan River. Turn left on a single-lane road for 0.5 mile to a nice open area, suitable for camping, just before the road enters the forest. The CT comes out of the forest about 100 yards up a drainage on the left side of the road and proceeds north out of the valley up a closed logging road.

Middle Fork of the Swan River Access: 🚗 Follow the aforementioned instructions for the North Fork access until the point where one turns left onto the single-lane road. Instead of turning left, continue straight for a little over a mile, then turn left up the Middle Fork of the Swan. Continue up the Middle Fork for 1.5 miles to the CT crossing. Stay alert because the CT crossing is not obvious.

Gold Hill Trailhead: 🚗 See Segment 7 on page 110.

SERVICES, SUPPLIES, AND ACCOMMODATIONS

The town of **Jefferson** is approximately 4.5 miles southwest of Kenosha Pass on US Hwy 285. Historically it was a train stop and now has a population of 18 with a tiny market in a 100-year-old building that doubles as the post office.

Distance from CT: 4.5 miles to Jefferson
Elevation: 9,499 feet
Zip code: 80456
Area code: 719

Jefferson Services

Basic Supplies/Post Office
The Jefferson Market
38600 US Highway 285
(719) 836-2389
(719) 836-2238 (post office)

White globeflower near Georgia Pass.
PHOTO BY DAVE JONES

TRAIL DESCRIPTION

Segment 6 begins on the west side of Kenosha Pass. There are large parking areas on both sides of the highway. After signing in at the trail register at **mile 0.0** (9,969 feet), continue into the forest where the trail passes under a power line and reaches a ridge shortly afterward with great views to the west. At **mile 1.5** (10,273), cross an old, unused jeep road. After passing through a stand of aspen trees and open meadows, the trail crosses an irrigation ditch at **mile 2.8** (9,920) and FS Rd 809 at **mile 3** (9,852). Just past the road, cross Guernsey Creek, a small stream at **mile 3.1** (9,828). There are several good campsites in this area.

The trail continues west toward the Continental Divide. Cross FS Rd 427 at **mile 4.4** (10,161) and Deadman Creek on a bridge at **mile 4.5** (10,164). Gain a saddle and pass through a Forest Service gate at **mile 5.2** (10,262). Cross Jefferson Lake Road at **mile 5.9** (10,014) and Jefferson Creek at **mile 6** (9,975). At **mile 6.1** (9,986) there is an intersection. Take a right on the West Jefferson Trail for 0.1 mile, then go left at the fork at **mile 6.2** (9,983). From here, the climb to Georgia Pass begins.

At **mile 7.8** (10,699), the CT intersects the Michigan Creek Trail. Stay to the right. After the trail leaves a subalpine fir forest and emerges above tree line, cross the Jefferson Creek Trail at **mile 11.7** (11,667) and another jeep road at **mile 12.1** (11,838). (This is the point where users first encounter the Continental Divide National Scenic Trail, which comes in from the north. The CT and CDNST are co-located for the next 99.6 miles into CT Segment 11 where they again diverge.) There are several good campsites in the forest, but be aware of changing weather patterns when above tree line. Reach the top of Georgia Pass and the Continental Divide at **mile 12.3** (11,874).

Descend in a northerly direction. Cross Glacier Creek Road at **mile 12.5** (11,798) and go right. After entering the trees, cross an ATV trail at **mile 15.4** (11,135). Keep descending, passing a pond, then a small stream just above the bottom of the canyon. There are many good campsites in this area. Cross the bridge over the Middle Fork of the Swan River and go right for 50 feet on Middle Fork Road at **mile 17.1** (10,203). The Colorado Trail veers to the left onto a single-track trail at a well-marked intersection.

Follow the trail in a northwesterly direction, crossing a small stream and eventually the North Fork of the Swan River at **mile 19.7** (9,981). There is good camping in this area too. After passing over the river on a good bridge, cross a road and then go right at an intersection at **mile 20.1** (10,067). From here, the trail begins to climb out of the drainage. Keystone Ski Resort eventually comes into view along the high point of the ridge to the northeast. When the trail comes to an intersection at **mile 22.6** (11,114), take a left. At another intersection at **mile 23.8** (11,022), head to the left again. After a long descent on a series of switchbacks, the trail reaches an intersection at **mile 26.1** (10,035) and goes to the left again.

After dropping into a small valley and passing a power line, take a right at the fork at **mile 27.5** (9,973). Cross Horseshoe Gulch at **mile 28.8** (9,458) and follow the trail as it heads north. There are a series of switchbacks during which Breckenridge comes into view. Take a left at an intersection at the bottom of the switchbacks, cross CO Hwy 9 at **mile 32.4** (9,203), and take a right on the bike path. Follow the bike path for 0.2 mile until reaching the Gold Hill Trailhead on the left and the end of Segment 6 at **mile 32.9** (9,197).

Snow remains through June on the high peaks. PHOTO BY BERNARD WOLF

Mountain Pine Beetles

On approaching the town of Breckenridge, it becomes apparent there is something amiss with the local forests. The needles of many of the pine trees are red, indicating the trees have died or are dying. Other pines have large popcorn-shaped masses of resin called "pitch tubes." On still others you can see wood dust from boring insects in the crevices of the bark or on the ground at the base of the tree. Some of the trees have foliage that is turning yellow, and eventually will turn red. These all are signs of infestation by the mountain pine beetle (*Dendroctonus ponderosae*), an insect native to Colorado's pine forests.

The beetle is only about the size of a grain of rice and has a one-year life cycle, but it has been able to kill approximately 2 million acres of forest as of 2008. The mountain pine beetle normally attacks trees that are under stress from injury, poor soil conditions, root damage, or old age. In addition to these problems, forests in Colorado and Wyoming have become overcrowded due to fire suppression, enabling the beetles to proliferate and move easily from tree to tree.

The beetle population is normally held in check by cold winter temperatures, but relatively warm winters in recent years have not killed off sufficient amounts of beetles to stop the outbreak, which has been building over the past decade. Now, nearly all of the pine trees in the area are dead or dying. The risk of fire in these tracts of forests is incredibly high and potentially devastating to local communities. Eventually, the dead trees will burn or be blown over in windstorms, thinning out the forests and beginning a new cycle of life in the region.

The Legacy of Two Passes

Sign points to Georgia Pass.
PHOTO BY ANTHONY SLOAN

📷 The Colorado Trail crosses two historic mountain passes in Segment 6. Kenosha Pass, which isn't especially high by Colorado standards, never reaching tree line, has been an important crossing for centuries. It was used by bands of Ute Indians, then white trappers, to reach hunting grounds in South Park. Explorer John C. Fremont crossed the pass in the 1840s. During the Colorado gold rush in the mid-1800s, prospectors used the pass to reach placer diggings around Fairplay.

When a toll road was built to the new diggings, it was stagecoach driver Clark Herbert who named Kenosha Pass after his Wisconsin hometown. The silver boom of the 1870s brought the narrow-gauge tracks of the Denver, South Park & Pacific Railroad through Kenosha Pass. A switchyard was built on its flat meadows. When the tracks were removed in 1937, a modern highway, essentially following the old rail route, was built and continues to bring visitors and commerce over Kenosha Pass into South Park.

With the discovery of gold in 1860 near present-day Breckenridge, miners poured over the Continental Divide at another relatively low point, christening it Georgia Pass. With the coming of the railroad, the wagon road over Georgia Pass fell into disuse, becoming the obscure jeep track that it is today.

Atop Georgia Pass with Mount Guyot behind.
PHOTO BY PETE TURNER

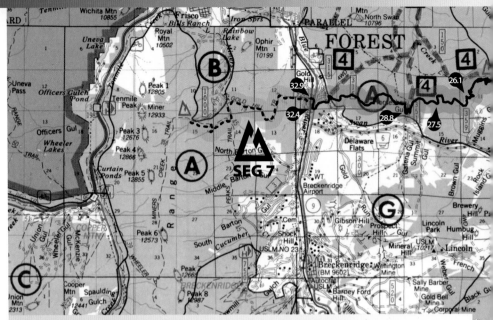

SEGMENT 6 FEATURES TABLE White River and Pike National Forests

Mileage	Features & Comments	Elevation (feet)	Mileage from Denver	Mileage to Durango	UTM-E	UTM-N (NAD83)	Zone
0.0	Begin Segment 6	9,969	72.2	413.6	434,724	4,362,829	13
1.5	Cross jeep road	10,273	73.7	412.1	432,603	4,363,668	13
3.0	Cross FS Rd 809	9,852	75.2	410.6	431,008	4,364,547	13
3.1	Cross Guernsey Creek	9,828	75.3	410.5	430,950	4,364,524	13
4.4	Cross FS Rd 427	10,161	76.6	409.2	428,883	4,364,683	13
4.5	Cross Deadman Creek	10,164	76.7	409.1	428,671	4,364,711	13
5.2	Gain saddle, pass gate	10,262	77.4	408.4	428,143	4,364,439	13
5.9	Cross Jefferson Lake Road	10,014	78.1	407.7	427,277	4,364,791	13
6.0	Cross Jefferson Creek	9,975	78.2	407.6	427,198	4,364,680	13
6.1	Go right on West Jefferson Trail	9,986	78.3	407.5	427,051	4,364,626	13
6.2	Go left at fork	9,983	78.4	407.4	426,967	4,364,744	13
7.8	Intersect Michigan Creek Trail	10,699	80.0	405.8	425,237	4,364,884	13
11.7	Cross Jefferson Creek Trail	11,667	83.9	401.9	422,370	4,367,556	13
12.1	Cross jeep track	11,838	84.3	401.5	421,847	4,367,858	13
12.3	Reach top of Georgia Pass	11,874	84.5	401.3	421,619	4,367,998	13
12.5	Cross Glacier Ridge Road, go right	11,798	84.7	401.1	421,696	4,368,342	13
15.4	Cross ATV trail	11,135	87.6	398.2	420,857	4,370,885	13
17.1	Go right for 50 feet on Middle Fork Road	10,203	89.3	396.5	420,411	4,372,426	13
19.7	Cross North Fork of Swan River	9,981	91.9	393.9	419,661	4,374,519	13
20.1	Go right	10,067	92.3	393.5	419,339	4,374,809	13
22.6	Go left at intersection	11,114	94.8	391.0	418,778	4,377,279	13
23.8	Go left at intersection	11,022	96.0	389.8	417,675	4,378,355	13
26.1	Go left at intersection	10,035	98.3	387.5	416,521	4,377,391	13
27.5	Go right at fork	9,973	99.7	386.1	415,356	4,377,124	13
28.8	Cross Horseshoe Gulch	9,458	101.0	384.8	414,089	4,376,884	13
32.4	Cross CO Hwy 9, go right	9,203	104.6	381.2	410,431	4,377,005	13
32.9	End Segment 6	9,197	105.1	380.7	410,455	4,377,354	13

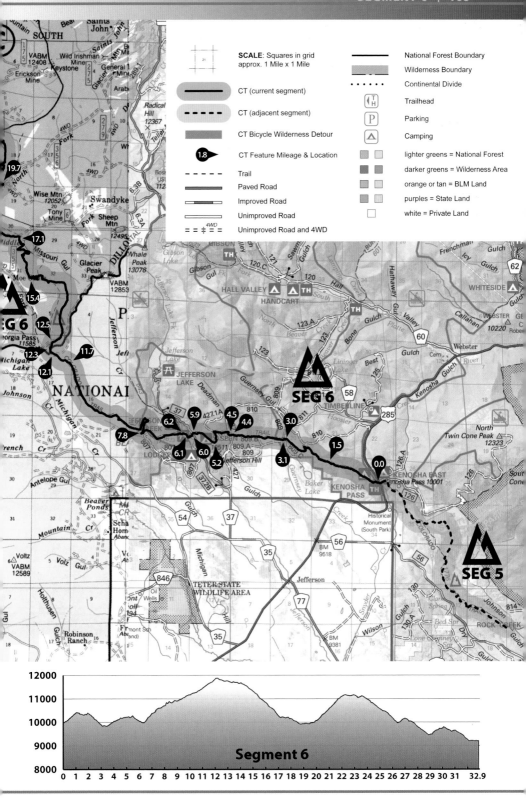

SCALE: Squares in grid approx. 1 Mile x 1 Mile

— CT (current segment)

- - - CT (adjacent segment)

CT Bicycle Wilderness Detour

1.8 ◤ CT Feature Mileage & Location

- - - Trail

═══ Paved Road

═══ Improved Road

═══ Unimproved Road

= = ╪ = = ⁴ᵂᴰ Unimproved Road and 4WD

—— National Forest Boundary

Wilderness Boundary

· · · · · Continental Divide

Ⓣ🇭 Trailhead

Ⓟ Parking

Ⓐ Camping

lighter greens = National Forest

darker greens = Wilderness Area

orange or tan = BLM Land

purples = State Land

white = Private Land

Segment 6

Segment 7: Gold Hill Trailhead to Copper Mountain

An exhilarating view of the Tenmile Range.

PHOTO BY BERNARD WOLF

Distance: 12.8 miles

Elevation gain: Approx. 3,674 feet

Elevation loss: Approx. 3,053 feet

USFS map: White River National Forest, pages 116–117

The Colorado Trail Databook 4/e: pages 20–21

The CT Map Book: pages 20–21

National Geographic Trails Illustrated maps: Nos. 108, 109

Latitude 40° map: Summit County Trails

Jurisdiction: Dillon Ranger District, White River National Forest

Access from Denver end:

Access from Durango end:

Availability of water:

Bicycling:

"The hanging glacial valley at 11,000 feet in the Tenmile Range supports a huge colony of pikas."

You are more likely to hear first, then see, these tiny creatures of the rock slides. The uninitiated may confuse their alarm calls with marmots, which are also numerous in these high cirques. Marmots make a high-pitched whistle, whereas the pika's call is a shrill bark.

Gudy's TIP

ABOUT THIS SEGMENT

A well-deserved rest at the top.
PHOTO BY PETE AND LISA TURNER

This segment of The Colorado Trail climbs 3,600 feet in 6 miles across 1.7 billion-year-old basement rocks to gain the crest of the Tenmile Range, then descends 3,000 feet in another 6 miles through similar rocks to the narrow valley below. This is the first time the trail is above tree line for several miles, rewarding those who reach the tundra with great views of the surrounding mountains and communities below. Take note of the alpine wildflowers in the summer—the blooms can be magnificent. There can be snow along the high parts of this segment until mid-July and summer thunderstorms can move in quickly. There are good water sources throughout, but camping is limited due to the thick forests and steep watersheds. The best camping is near Miners Creek. Plan ahead to avoid potential problems.

TRAILHEAD/ACCESS POINTS

Ross Avens are wonderfully colorful at high altitude.
PHOTO BY BILL MANNING

Gold Hill Trailhead: Drive west from Denver on I-70 for about 75 miles to exit 203 (Frisco/Breckenridge). Proceed south on CO Hwy 9 for about 6 miles. The trailhead is on the right side of the highway at the intersection with Gateway Drive. (If you cross the bridge over the Blue River, you have gone 0.25 mile too far.)

Miners Creek Access Point: The CT can be accessed via the Miners Creek four-wheel-drive road at about mile 4.8. Miners Creek Road departs south of Peak One Boulevard at the south edge of Frisco (just west of the Summit County government offices).

Wheeler Flats Trailhead: See Segment 8 on page 118.

SERVICES, SUPPLIES, AND ACCOMMODATIONS

Breckenridge is approximately 4 miles south of the Gold Hill Trailhead on CO Hwy 9. Frisco has comparable services and is located approximately 5 miles northwest of the trailhead. The Summit Stage provides free bus service between the towns. There is a bus stop on Hwy 9 about 0.2 miles south of the trailhead. Both towns are restored mining/railroad towns serving the popular Summit County resorts.

Distance from CT: 4 miles to Breckenridge (5 miles to Frisco)
Elevation: 9,605 feet
Zip code: 80424 (Frisco 80443)
Area code: 970

Breckenridge Services (also Frisco)

Bus
Summit Stage
(970) 668-0999

Gear (including fuel canisters)
Mountain Outfitters
112 S. Ridge St.
(970) 453-2201

Groceries
City Market
400 N. Park Ave.
(970) 453-0818

Info
Chamber of Commerce
311 S. Ridge St.
(970) 453-2913

Laundry
Norge Laundry
105 S. French St.
Breckenridge
(970) 547-4614

Frisco's Washtub Coin Laundry
406 Main
Frisco
(970) 668-3552

Lodging
Fireside Inn B&B and Hostel, 114 N French St. (970) 453-6456

Medical
Breckenridge Medical Clinic
555 S. Park Ave.
(970) 453-1010

Post Office
Breckenridge Post Office
311 S. Ridge St.
(970) 453-5467

Frisco Post Office
35 W. Main St.
(970) 668-0610

Showers
Breckenridge Recreation Center
880 Airport Rd.
(970) 453-1734

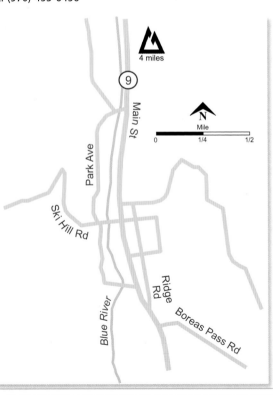

Atop the Tenmile Range at the end of June, when the snow has melted enough to pass over.
PHOTO BY BERNARD WOLF

TRAIL DESCRIPTION

Segment 7 begins at the Gold Hill Trailhead on the west side of CO Hwy 9. This segment is poorly marked in places. For the most part, markings consist of blue ski-trail markers.

From the parking area, head west toward the well-marked intersection, **mile 0.0** (9,197 feet). The trail climbs to **mile 1** (9,659), where there is a well-marked, three-way logging road intersection. Bear to the left. Cross a logging road at **mile 1.6** (9,990), passing an old clear-cut area that recently has been replanted. At **mile 2** (10,158) the CT turns to the right through a colonnade of young trees at another well-marked intersection. At **mile 2.8** (10,168) the CT crosses a road and continues to **mile 3.2** (9,952), where the trail turns left at the intersection with the Peaks Trail near some beaver ponds. There is water here and good camping.

At **mile 3.4** (10,018), turn right on the Miners Creek Trail. The trail sign here does not identify The Colorado Trail, but there are confidence markers on trees on both sides of the intersection. Over the next mile, cross and recross a small tributary to Miners Creek several times. There are good campsites in the vicinity of the crossings. At **mile 4.8**

Hikers on the ridge of the Tenmile Range.
PHOTO BY JEFF SELLENRICK

(10,555), the Miners Creek Trail reaches a parking area for jeep access to the trail. Continue on the Miners Creek Trail by bearing to the left after passing most of the parking area. There are campsites on both sides of the parking area. Cross Miners Creek at **mile 4.9** (10,583) and several more times in the next mile, most with potential campsites. The last crossing of Miners Creek before entering the tundra is at **mile 6** (11,281).

The trail continues in a southerly direction, climbing past Peak 3, Peak 4, and Peak 5 before reaching the crest of the Tenmile Range at **mile 8** (12,495). The views on a clear day are magnificent. Along the way up, Lake Dillon and the town of Dillon are visible to the north, Breckenridge sits stately to the east, and Copper Mountain lies 2,500 feet below to the west. After topping out, follow the ridge, passing just west of Peak 6.

A steep descent reaches tree line at **mile 9.9** (11,720). The trail then makes a sharp right turn at the Wheeler Trail at **mile 10.4** (11,249). Head downhill to the northwest, crossing several small seasonal streams before coming to Tenmile Creek and a good bridge at **mile 12.4** (9,767). After crossing the bridge, turn left and walk south along a parking lot. Continue to the south until reaching CO Hwy 91 and the end of Segment 7 at **mile 12.8** (9,820). There is no camping within the first 4 miles of Segment 8 while on Copper Mountain Resort property, so thru-hikers should take this into consideration.

Tundra Plants

In portions of Segments 6 and 7, the CT passes into the open realm of the tundra for the first time. In Colorado, this alpine zone varies from above an altitude of 10,500 feet in the northern part of the state to more than 12,000 feet near the border with New Mexico. Above tree line, a harsh environment exists—one where summer lasts a fleeting 30 to 40 frost-free days, and in winter, temperatures can fall to well below zero. In essence, the tundra is a cold desert with precipitation levels of 20 inches per year or less, mainly in the form of snow. How this snow is distributed by the wind dictates the distribution of hardy alpine plants.

Compared with other alpine regions in the lower 48 states, Colorado's alpine tundra is particularly rich in plant numbers and species, putting on a spectacular display beginning with the first alpine forget-me-nots (*Eritrichium elongatum*) in June and lasting until arctic gentians (*Gentiana algida*) in early September signal the rapid approach of fall. Most species are "cushion" plants or miniature versions of species common at lower altitudes—a concession to the severe environment. Their growth rate is slow, with some plants taking up to a century to produce a mat only a foot or so in diameter, and is all the more reason to stay on the trail to avoid damaging them.

As you progress westward on the CT, the display of wildflowers becomes even more striking in the deeper soils of the moister western ranges, reaching a climax in the high alpine basins of the San Juan Mountains.

Tiny blue alpine forget-me-nots.

PHOTO BY BILL MANNING

SCALE: Squares in grid approx. 1 Mile x 1 Mile

CT (current segment)

CT (adjacent segment)

CT Bicycle Wilderness Detour

1.8 CT Feature Mileage & Location

Trail

Paved Road

Improved Road

Unimproved Road

Unimproved Road and 4WD

National Forest Boundary

Wilderness Boundary

Continental Divide

Trailhead

Parking

Camping

lighter greens = National Forest

darker greens = Wilderness Area

orange or tan = BLM Land

purples = State Land

white = Private Land

SEGMENT 7 FEATURES TABLE White River National Forest

Mileage	Features & Comments	Elevation (feet)	Mileage from Denver	Mileage to Durango	UTM-E	UTM-N (NAD83)	Zone
0.0	Begin Segment 7	9,197	105.1	380.7	410,455	4,377,354	13
1.0	Go left at intersection	9,659	106.1	379.7	409,065	4,377,498	13
1.6	Cross logging road	9,990	106.7	379.1	408,702	4,376,653	13
2.0	Bear right	10,158	107.1	378.7	408,456	4,376,523	13
3.2	Turn left at Peaks Trail	9,952	108.5	377.3	407,049	4,376,983	13
3.4	Turn right onto Miners Creek Trail	10,018	108.8	377.0	407,121	4,376,548	13
4.8	Continue on Miners Creek Trail	10,555	109.9	375.9	405,670	4,376,507	13
8.0	Reach ridge crest	12,495	113.1	372.7	404,219	4,373,364	13
9.9	Encounter tree line	11,720	114.7	371.1	404,055	4,370,864	13
10.4	Turn right onto Wheeler Trail	11,249	115.5	370.3	404,066	4,370,149	13
12.4	Cross bridge	9,767	117.5	368.3	402,368	4,372,579	13
12.8	End Segment 7	9,820	117.9	367.9	402,335	4,372,046	13

Segment 7

Segment 8: Copper Mountain to Tennessee Pass

Forest Service workers pack in supplies for a volunteer crew. PHOTO BY BILL BLOOMQUIST

Distance: 25.4 miles

Elevation gain: Approx. 4,417 feet

Elevation loss: Approx. 3,810 feet

USFS map: White River National Forest, pages 126–127

The Colorado Trail Databook 4/e: pages 22–23

The CT Map Book: pages 21–24

National Geographic Trails Illustrated map: No. 109

Latitude 40° map: Summit County Trails

Jurisdiction: Holy Cross and Dillon Ranger Districts, White River National Forest

Access from Denver end:

Access from Durango end:

Availability of water:

Bicycling:

"Be sure to stop for a quick shower along Cataract Creek near Camp Hale. There's even a resting bench. But take note of all the shell holes made during World War II training at Camp Hale in the Tennessee Pass area. They're potential 'pitfalls' when walking at night or during an engrossing conversation."

Gudy's TIP

ABOUT THIS SEGMENT

The beginning of Segment 8 is much different from the preceding segments. The CT passes through Copper Mountain Resort, traversing ski slopes, edging along a golf course, and skirting the Copper Mountain Village Center, where there are restaurants, outdoor shops, lodging, and limited grocery shopping. While convenient for resupply, this area can be pricier than other resupply spots.

Somewhere on the slopes of Copper Mountain the CT crosses the Gore fault, a major fault active during uplift of the Ancestral Rockies. Rocks west of the fault were displaced downward 10,000 feet or more relative to basement rocks of the Tenmile Range.

Both the fault and the bedrock on either side are concealed beneath glacial deposits, but west of the fault redbeds deposited during rise of the Ancestral Rockies are exposed as the trail climbs toward Searles Pass. On the ridges near the pass, the redbeds are cut by irregular bodies and sheetlike layers of porphyry that were injected during the Laramide Orogeny.

Elk Ridge, the high point of Segment 8. Behind looms the Tenmile Range.

PHOTO BY DAN MILNER

The middle of this segment takes trail users back into the tundra after a long climb from the resort. Again, the views of the surrounding mountains are impressive. After crossing Searle Pass, there are many opportunities for side trips to nearby peaks. The descent to Eagle Park and Camp Hale provide an entirely different feel from Copper Mountain. This abandoned training ground for the 10th Mountain Division is steadily deteriorating under the extreme weather conditions, but retains its rich military legacy.

A trekker crosses Piney Gulch at mile 22.2.

PHOTO BY PETE TURNER

The CT passes the ruins of several coking ovens just before reaching Tennessee Pass, capping a scenic walk through a variety of eras that have left their mark on this stretch of the trail.

TRAILHEAD/ACCESS POINTS

Trailhead access to The Colorado Trail in this area is a bit unusual. In recent years, the CT was rerouted from the main street running through Copper Mountain Resort to the forested area south of the built-up portion of the resort. Parking is prohibited on the wide shoulders of CO Hwy 91 where the CT crosses. The official trail parking areas are the Wheeler Flats Trailhead and the Copper Mountain Chapel parking lot.

Wheeler Flats Trailhead: Drive west from Denver on I-70 for about 80 miles to exit 195 (Copper Mountain/Leadville/CO Hwy 91). Immediately after crossing over I-70 and exiting the interchange, take the

The view west from Kokomo Pass toward Camp Hale. In the distance is the Mount of the Holy Cross.

PHOTO BY PETE KARTSOUNES

first lefthand road. Continue down the side road for 0.4 mile to where it dead-ends at the Wheeler Flats Trailhead parking area. To get to the CT, hike south on the power line access road on the east side of Tenmile Creek for approximately 1 mile, joining the CT at a bridge that crosses Tenmile Creek. After crossing the creek, follow the CT south to a crossing of CO Hwy 91. Segment 8 begins on the west side of the highway. Use caution when crossing the highway; traffic comes very fast from both directions.

Chapel Parking Lot Access: From Denver, follow the aforementioned directions, but take the first right turn into Copper Mountain Resort after exiting I-70. Continue approximately 1 mile, then turn left into the chapel parking lot. Walk south and west to the Village Center Plaza in the area of the American Eagle chairlift. To intersect the CT, go about 150 yards diagonally southeast between the condos on the left and the American Eagle lift on the right. To go toward Searle Pass and Camp Hale, turn right and climb diagonally west-southwest under the American Eagle ski lift. Proceed left (east) for about 1.6 miles to get to the start of Segment 8 at CO Hwy 91.

Union Creek Ski Area Access: 🚗 Instead of parking at the chapel lot, continue through Copper Mountain Village to the Union Creek drop-off parking area. (Parking is permitted here during off-ski-season months.) Cross over the covered bridge, go past the ticket office and under the elevated walkway, turn right on a gravel road, pass under a ski lift, and go about 200 yards on the road. Turn left up the road, around a green security gate, and follow the road east uphill about 400 yards to a wide area in the road. Pick up the single track of the CT to the right, by a painted white rock.

Tennessee Pass Trailhead Access: 🚗 See Segment 9 on page 128.

SERVICES, SUPPLIES, AND ACCOMMODATIONS

The Colorado Trail passes through **Copper Mountain Resort** near the start of this segment. Copper Mountain is not a town, but rather a large ski resort. Overnight accommodations and restaurants may be pricey. There is a convenience store/gas station near Wheeler Flats Trailhead.

Distance from CT: 0 miles
Elevation: 9,600 feet
Zip code: 80443
Area code: 970

Copper Mountain Services

Bus
Summit Stage
(970) 668-0999

Groceries
McCoy's Mountain Market
Village Square
(970) 968-2182

Info
Copper Mountain Chamber of Commerce
Snow Bridge Square
(970) 968-6477

Lodging
Copper Mountain Lodging Services
(800) 458-8386

Medical
Closest services in Vail
(970) 476-2451

Post Office
West Lake Lodge
800 Copper Road
(970) 668-0610
(Self-service only; full service available in Frisco)

TRAIL DESCRIPTION

Begin Segment 8 at the edge of the Copper Mountain Golf Course on the west side of CO Hwy 91 at **mile 0.0** (9,820 feet). Enter the forest on a well-marked trail that skirts the golf course, follow a few switchbacks up the valley, cross a bridge, and pass under a power line. The CT then heads to the northwest, where it traverses two ski runs and goes under two ski lifts. Continue to follow the trail to **mile 1.6** (9,768), where it crosses under

The CT crosses beneath the ski lifts at Copper Mountain Resort. PHOTO BY JULIE VIDA AND MARK TABB

the American Eagle ski lift. There are restaurants, sporting goods shops, and some grocery shopping at the base of the ski hill. The trail is well marked and becomes a single track at **mile 2.1** (9,988), following a few roundabout switchbacks up the hill. There are two streams ahead, followed by great views of the Tenmile Range. There are numerous confidence markers in the trees to guide the way.

At **mile 3.4** (10,345), bear sharply to the right and leave the horse trail the CT was following. A cross-country ski trail merges from the left at **mile 5** (10,519), but the CT continues straight ahead. At **mile 5.2** (10,480), pass Jacque Creek, immediately followed by Guller Creek. There is a campsite just up the hill between the two. Janet's Cabin, a popular ski hut, comes into view as the trail climbs out of the canyon.

Leave the trees at **mile 8.7** (11,708) and continue to the top of Searle Pass at **mile 9.7** (12,043). The trail crosses several streams in the next few miles as it rolls through the tundra. There are frequent wooden posts with confidence markers through this area. Climb to the top of Elk Ridge at **mile 12.3** (12,282), then descend to Kokomo Pass at **mile 12.9** (12,023). From here, continue down to tree line at **mile 13.5** (11,639) on a series of switchbacks until reaching Cataract Creek. The trail crosses the creek several times in the next few miles. There are a few potential campsites along the way.

At **mile 16.5** (10,085), take a switchback to the left at a jeep road crossing and continue to **mile 17.1** (9,668), where the trail turns right at the intersection just above the road. Cross Cataract Creek on a bridge by Cataract Falls at **mile 17.2** (9,700). Camping is not allowed from this point until you reach the other side of Camp Hale in Eagle Park, a distance of about 2 miles. At **mile 17.9** (9,438), the trail comes to FS Rd 714. Take a right onto the road and walk 0.1 mile, picking up the trail again on the right. Rejoin the road at the Camp Hale Trailhead, where there is a small parking area at **mile 18.6** (9,362). Beyond the parking area, continue to the right on FS Rd 714, looking for the next road on the left. Turn left on an intersecting road at **mile 18.8** (9,349). The road ends at **mile 19.2** (9,326) near some old concrete bunkers. Here the trail resumes, crossing a footbridge and heading uphill. Cross FS Rd 726 at **mile 20.1** (9,671). There is a great campsite about 0.1 mile north of this intersection and water 0.1 mile farther north.

After re-entering the forest, the trail begins a steady climb, reaching a bench at an overlook at **mile 20.4** (9,778). Cross a jeep road at **mile 21.2** (9,863). There are several potential campsites in this area. Walk over a footbridge at Fiddler Creek, **mile 21.7** (9,967), then continue south until reaching US Hwy 24 at **mile 22.1** (9,966). Cross the highway, then a set of railroad tracks, followed by footbridges over three small creeks.

After leaving the swampy area, the CT turns to the southwest and follows Mitchell Creek in a wide grassy meadow, which features several potential campsites. At **mile 23.6** (10,180), the trail turns east and begins following an old railroad grade. After bending to the south, the trail crosses a footbridge over a seasonally wet area and a railroad bridge before reaching the remains of old coke ovens at **mile 25.2** (10,382). Reach the parking area for Tennessee Pass and US Hwy 24 at **mile 25.4** (10,424). This is the end of Segment 8.

Dense woods surround the trail between Copper Mountain and Guller Creek.
PHOTO BY CARL BROWN

Mount of the Holy Cross

From several vantage points on Segment 8, hikers have excellent views to the west of the photogenic Mount of the Holy Cross. Nearly a century ago, this was perhaps the most famous and revered mountain in America.

In the early 1800s, explorers brought back rumors of a great mountain in the West that displayed a giant cross on its side, but the exact location was shrouded in mystery. The search for the peak became one of the most intriguing in the history of the West. F. V. Hayden made it his top priority in the 1873 field session of his topographic survey. Hayden's team determined that the peak lay somewhere north and west of Tennessee Pass. After several arduous days of travel, Hayden reached the summit on August 22. From Notch Mountain across the valley, famed photographer W. H. Jackson captured an image of the immense snowy cross.

W. H. Jackson's famous image.

It's hard to imagine today the sensation Jackson's photo caused around the country. Henry Wadsworth Longfellow was moved to write a poem after viewing the image, and well-known artists such as Thomas Moran journeyed to Colorado to paint the peak. Hundreds of people made pilgrimages up Notch Mountain to view the cross, faith healings were reported, and Congress established it as a national monument in 1929.

The mountain was used for mountaineering training by troops from nearby Camp Hale during World War II, including a first-ever winter ascent of the 1,200-foot-high cross in December 1943. But as time passed, religious interest faded and the mountain's monument status was rescinded shortly after the war.

A later USGS survey determined that the 14,005-foot peak just barely qualified as a fourteener (Hayden had listed it at 13,999 feet), and today, Mount of the Holy Cross is a favorite with peak-baggers.

! Camping is NOT permitted between Cataract Creek and the South Fork of the Eagle River (due to undiscovered munitions). White arrows mark the travel corridor.

The Legacy of Camp Hale

Camp Hale bunkers.
PHOTO BY BERNARD WOLF

📷 In 1942, Camp Hale was established to train troops for mountain and winter warfare during World War II. The famed 10th Mountain Division learned techniques in winter survival, skiing, rock climbing, and campcraft, in addition to normal military training, before embarking for the European Theater to fight the Nazis.

Attached to the 5th Army, the 10th fought bloody battles up the spine of Italy's Apennine Mountains, culminating in the taking of the strategic Riva Ridge and Mount Belvedere. The division suffered nearly 25 percent casualties, one of the highest of any unit in the war.

After the war, many veterans of the 10th, intrigued by the powder snow they encountered in Colorado, returned to the state and were instrumental in developing the ski industry. Camp Hale itself was largely abandoned before being completely dismantled in 1963. Not much remains to be seen at the site (although ordnance continues to be found at times). A plaque on Tennessee Pass commemorates the sacrifices of the soldiers of the 10th.

Remnants of coking ovens used to transform raw coal into high-grade "coke" used in the production of steel are found near Tennessee Pass.

PHOTO BY JULIE VIDA AND MARK TABB

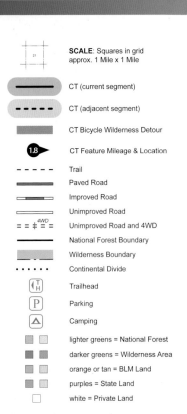

SCALE: Squares in grid approx. 1 Mile x 1 Mile

CT (current segment)

CT (adjacent segment)

CT Bicycle Wilderness Detour

1.8   CT Feature Mileage & Location

Trail

Paved Road

Improved Road

Unimproved Road

Unimproved Road and 4WD

National Forest Boundary

Wilderness Boundary

Continental Divide

Trailhead

Parking

Camping

lighter greens = National Forest

darker greens = Wilderness Area

orange or tan = BLM Land

purples = State Land

white = Private Land

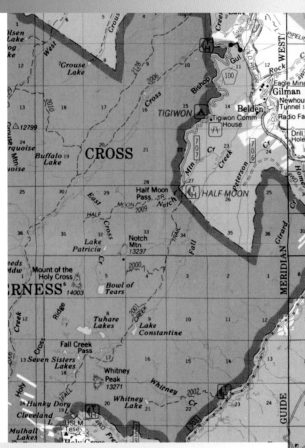

SEGMENT 8 FEATURES TABLE   White River National Forest

Mileage	Features & Comments	Elevation (feet)	Mileage from Denver	Mileage to Durango	UTM-E	UTM-N (NAD83)	Zone
0.0	Begin Segment 8	9,820	117.9	367.9	402,335	4,372,046	13
5.2	Cross Jacque Creek	10,480	123.1	362.7	397,633	4,371,608	13
8.7	Reach tree line	11,708	126.6	359.2	394,006	4,369,297	13
9.7	Searle Pass	12,043	127.6	358.2	394,332	4,368,348	13
12.3	Elk Ridge	12,282	130.2	355.6	395,116	4,365,436	13
12.9	Kokomo Pass	12,023	130.8	355.0	394,405	4,365,068	13
13.5	Tree line	11,639	131.4	354.4	393,632	4,365,845	13
16.5	Switchback left	10,085	134.4	351.4	390,731	4,364,642	13
17.1	Turn right at intersection	9,668	135.0	350.8	390,543	4,364,366	13
17.9	Go right on road	9,438	135.8	350.0	389,339	4,364,312	13
18.6	Camp Hale Trailhead	9,362	136.5	349.3	388,229	4,364,653	13
20.1	Cross road	9,671	138.0	347.8	386,859	4,363,442	13
20.4	Reach bench and overlook	9,778	138.3	347.5	386,799	4,363,011	13
21.2	Cross jeep road	9,863	139.1	346.7	386,601	4,361,960	13
21.7	Cross Fiddler Creek	9,967	139.6	346.2	386,751	4,361,352	13
22.1	Cross US Hwy 24	9,966	140.0	345.8	386,556	4,360,752	13
23.6	Turn left onto road	10,180	141.5	344.3	385,625	4,359,709	13
25.2	Pass by coke ovens	10,382	143.1	342.7	386,477	4,358,073	13
25.4	End Segment 8	10,424	143.3	342.5	386,983	4,357,913	13

Segment 9: Tennessee Pass to Timberline Lake Trailhead

Wetlands in the Holy Cross Wilderness Area.
PHOTO BY ROGER FORMAN

Distance: 13.6 miles

Elevation gain: Approx. 2,627 feet

Elevation loss: Approx. 3,004 feet

USFS map: San Isabel National Forest, pages 134–135

The Colorado Trail Databook 4/e: pages 24–25

The CT Map Book: pages 24–26

National Geographic Trails Illustrated maps: Nos. 109, 126

Latitude 40° map: Summit County Trails

Jurisdiction: Leadville Ranger District, San Isabel National Forest

Access from Denver end:

Access from Durango end:

Availability of water:

Bicycling: See page 132

"There is a fascinating tundra walk between Longs Gulch and the St. Kevin Lake Trail in the Holy Cross Wilderness Area."

There are several lakes and ponds, ideal for camping, situated just off the trail and glaciated headwalls of the Continental Divide, exemplified by Porcupine Lakes (mile 7.7), a beautiful spot for high-altitude camping.

Gudy's TIP

Mid-July snowpack on the Continental Divide.
PHOTO BY BERNARD WOLF

ABOUT THIS SEGMENT

In Segment 9, The Colorado Trail turns south, passing through gneiss and 1.4 billion-year-old granite that forms the eastern flank of the Sawatch Range. Alternating between ascents to passes and ridges and descents to creeks or rivers at the bottom of drainages, the segment typically stays between the 9,000- and 12,000-foot levels. Much of this section of the CT follows the path of the old Main Range Trail, which was built by the Civilian Conservation Corps in the 1930s for both recreation and fire protection. There are great views along the trail of the Arkansas River Valley and the Mosquito Range to the east. This part of the Arkansas Valley marks the northern end of the Rio Grande Rift. Equally dramatic are the views of the Sawatch Range peaks to the west. Toward the end of the segment, the CT passes through the southeast corner of the Holy Cross Wilderness Area. Here there are some great views of Mount Massive, the second-highest mountain in Colorado at 14,421 feet, to the south.

TRAILHEAD/ACCESS POINTS

Tennessee Pass Trailhead: 🚗 Travel north from Leadville on US Hwy 24 for approximately 9 miles to the top of Tennessee Pass. A parking area with bathrooms on the west side of the highway is the start of this segment.

Wurts Ditch Road Trail Access: 🚗 Drive north from Leadville on US Hwy 24 for about 7.5 miles to Wurtz Ditch Road (FS Rd 705). It's easy to identify by the old-fashioned yellow road grader parked beside the road. Proceed about 1 mile on the gravel road to an intersection. Turn right. Proceed 0.3 mile to the CT crossing. Parking space is limited.

Timberline Lake Trailhead: 🚗 See Segment 10 on pages 136.

Sunrise at Porcupine Lakes.
PHOTO BY AARON LOCANDER

SERVICES, SUPPLIES, AND ACCOMMODATIONS

These amenities are available in Leadville; see Segment 10 on pages 136–145.

TRAIL DESCRIPTION

Segment 9 begins at the Tennessee Pass parking area with bathrooms on the west side of US Hwy 24, **mile 0.0** (10,424 feet). From the trailhead sign, follow the CT into the forest in a southwesterly direction. At **mile 2.5** (10,422), cross Wurts Ditch and a creek (both often dry) on two bridges. Then pass over Wurts Ditch Road 0.2 mile farther on. There are good campsites in this area. (Mountain bikers should leave the trail at this intersection in order to bypass the wilderness area ahead.) Cross a jeep trail called Lily Lake Road at **mile 3.4** (10,396), then cross the North Fork of Tennessee Creek at **mile 3.5** (10,390) and West Tennessee Creek 0.2 miles after that. More campsites are nearby. At **mile 4.1** (10,502), the single track inconspicuously joins a very old jeep road.

Southbound in the Holy Cross Wilderness, looking toward the Continental Divide.
PHOTO BY BERNARD WOLF

After a gentle climb, there is a poorly marked intersection at **mile 4.9** (10,704). Take a right here. The trail enters the Holy Cross Wilderness Area at **mile 6.7** (10,875). There is a boundary sign and trail register. Climb to Porcupine Lakes at **mile 7.7** (11,451), where there are potential campsites. After a short descent, climb to a high point on the tundra at **mile 8.8** (11,702). Head downhill, ignoring an unmarked side trail heading down the valley to the left, and bear right at a sharp bend at **mile 9.6** (11,498). At **mile 10.5** (11,128), cross a small stream and turn right at the intersection with the trail to Bear Lake. Pass an unnamed lake to the right of the trail, then pass another unnamed lake to the right at **mile 10.9** (11,041). There are more good campsites here.

Climb to another saddle at **mile 11.4** (11,422). The trail goes above tree line briefly here, then descends steeply on a series of switchbacks, re-enters the trees, and passes two small seasonal streams. Leave the Holy Cross Wilderness Area at **mile 12.6** (10,561). Pass under a power line at **mile 12.9** (10,434) and a second power line at **mile 13.3** (10,141). Continue downhill to the parking area for the Timberline Creek Trailhead at **mile 13.6** (10,043) and the end of Segment 9.

Holy Cross/Mount Massive Wilderness Bicycle Detour

This detour bypasses both the Holy Cross and Mount Massive wilderness areas and 24.1 miles of the hiking route.

Leave the trail at **mile 2.5** (10,420 feet) of Segment 9, where the CT crosses the Wurts Ditch Road. Turn left on the road and follow it to an intersection with FS Rd 100 at **mile 0.3** (10,390). Turn left and follow the road to **mile 1.3** (10,150), where it intersects US Hwy 24. Turn right on the highway and ride south. Reach an intersection with CO Hwy 91 at **mile 8.4** (10,160) and bear right at the fork to Leadville. Leadville is a great place to stop and spend a night or two and resupply.

Continue south of Leadville on US Hwy 24 to **mile 14** (9,560) and turn right on CO Hwy 300. At **mile 14.8** (9,560), turn left on FS Rd 160 and follow it to a sharp right turn at **mile 16** (9,480). This is Halfmoon Creek Road (FS Rd 110). There are numerous campsites and Forest Service campgrounds along the way. Follow the road southwest to **mile 21.5** (10,060) and rejoin The Colorado Trail where it takes off to the left, just before a bridge on Halfmoon Creek. Segment 11 begins at this point.

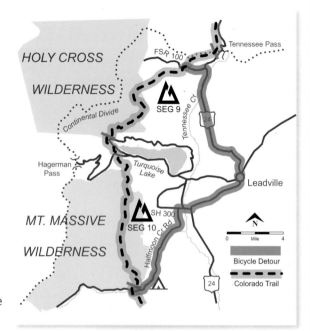

Sign at north end of detour.
PHOTO BY BILL MANNING

10th Mountain Division Hut System

For backcountry skiing, snowshoeing, and snowboarding enthusiasts, there are a number of winter access points to the CT, usually where the trail crosses a major pass at a regularly plowed highway. Undoubtedly, the best of these is the Tennessee Pass access, at the start of Segment 9, which is smack in the middle of a network of mountain huts run by the 10th Mountain Division Hut Association.

The hut association is a nonprofit founded in 1980 by a group of backcountry recreationalists, including several veterans of the U.S. Army's famed 10th Mountain Division, which trained at nearby Camp Hale in the 1940s.

PHOTO BY BILL MANNING

The hut system lies within a large triangle roughly formed by Vail, Leadville, and Aspen. In the style of traditional European hut-to-hut travel, twenty-nine huts provide overnight shelter for back-country skiers, snow boarders, snowshoers, mountain bikers, and backpackers. Six of the huts were built with donations from family and friends to honor individuals who died while serving in the 10th Mountain Division during World War II.

Janet's Cabin.

PHOTO BY BILL BLOOMQUIST

The huts are situated between 9,700 and 11,700 feet and are designed for experienced backcountry travelers. Most operate in the winter between late November and late April, and then again for three months in the summer.

Accommodations are best described as comfortably rustic, with bunks sleeping about fifteen people in a communal setting. Huts are equipped with wood stoves for heat, propane for cooking, photovoltaic lighting, mattresses, and utensils. You bring your own sleeping bag, food, and clothing. Users melt snow for water in winter and collect it from streams in summer.

More than 300 miles of trails link the huts and several are close to The Colorado Trail, including Janet's Cabin, Vance's Cabin, and Uncle Bud's Hut. Reservations are required. Contact the 10th Mountain Division Hut Association at (970) 925-5775 or visit its website at huts.org. Note that this website administers a system of huts, including those of the 10th as well as the Alfred A. Braun Huts and Friends Huts.

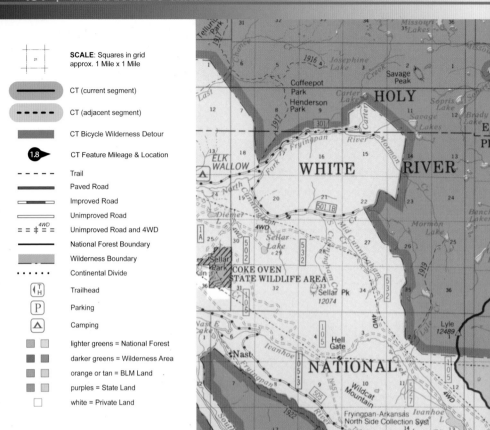

SCALE: Squares in grid approx. 1 Mile x 1 Mile

CT (current segment)

CT (adjacent segment)

CT Bicycle Wilderness Detour

1.8 CT Feature Mileage & Location

Trail

Paved Road

Improved Road

Unimproved Road

Unimproved Road and 4WD

National Forest Boundary

Wilderness Boundary

Continental Divide

Trailhead

Parking

Camping

lighter greens = National Forest

darker greens = Wilderness Area

orange or tan = BLM Land

purples = State Land

white = Private Land

SEGMENT 9 FEATURES TABLE   San Isabel National Forest

Mileage	Features & Comments	Elevation (feet)	Mileage from Denver	Mileage to Durango	UTM-E	UTM-N (NAD83)	Zone
0.0	Begin Segment 9	10,424	143.3	342.5	386,983	4,357,913	13
2.5	Cross Wurts Ditch	10,422	145.8	340.0	383,769	4,356,745	13
3.4	Cross Lily Lake Road	10,396	146.7	339.1	382,932	4,356,261	13
3.5	Cross North Fork of Tennessee Creek	10,390	146.8	339.0	382,809	4,356,185	13
3.7	Cross West Tennessee Creek on a bridge	10,365	147.0	338.8	382,825	4,355,876	13
4.1	Single track joins jeep trail	10,502	147.4	338.4	382,169	4,355,712	13
4.9	Turn right at intersection	10,704	148.2	337.6	381,244	4,355,702	13
6.7	Enter Holy Cross Wilderness	10,875	150.0	335.8	378,906	4,354,265	13
7.7	Pass Porcupine Lakes	11,451	151.0	334.8	378,148	4,353,381	13
9.6	Bear right	11,498	152.9	332.9	378,890	4,351,836	13
10.5	Go right at intersection	11,128	153.8	332.0	377,760	4,350,973	13
10.9	Pass second lake	11,041	154.2	331.6	377,200	4,350,635	13
11.4	Tree line	11,422	154.7	331.1	376,655	4,350,577	13
12.6	Leave Holy Cross Wilderness Area	10,561	155.9	329.9	375,610	4,350,011	13
13.6	End Segment 9	10,043	156.9	328.9	375,190	4,349,393	13

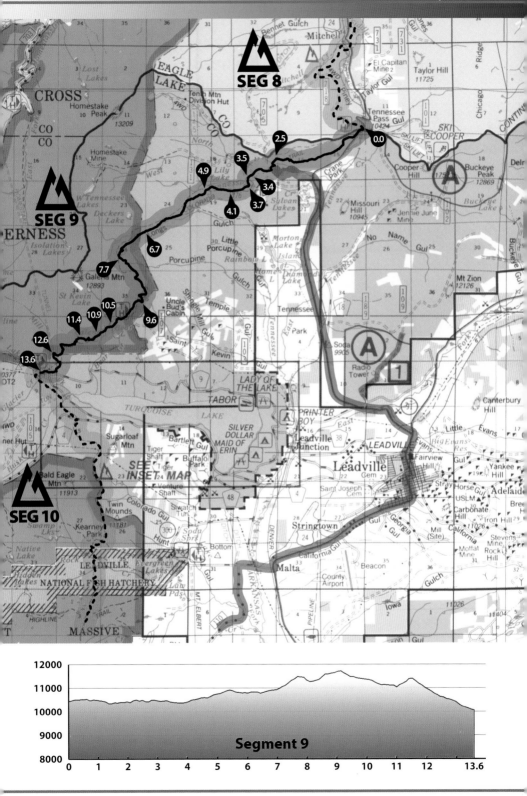

Segment 10: Timberline Lake Trailhead to Mount Massive Trailhead

Distance: 13.6 miles

Elevation gain: Approx. 2,690 feet

Elevation loss: Approx. 2,676 feet

USFS map: San Isabel National Forest, pages 144–145

The Colorado Trail Databook 4/e: pages 26–27

The CT Map Book: pages 26–28

National Geographic Trails Illustrated maps: Nos. 126, 127

Latitude 40° map: Summit County Trails

Jurisdiction: Leadville Ranger District, San Isabel National Forest

Access from Denver end: 🚗

Access from Durango end: 🚗

Availability of water: ☕

Bicycling: See page 132

A stout bridge crosses Busk Creek near the start of Segment 10.

PHOTO BY PETE TURNER

"If your goal is to climb Mount Elbert or Mount Massive, get a very early start. Thunderstorms and lightning can roll in by noon during the summer. By starting early, you'll also avoid the crowd of peak-baggers."

There is camping near the Mount Massive Trailhead, which serves as a good base camp for climbing both of these fourteeners.

Gudy's TIP

ABOUT THIS SEGMENT

This segment has seen many changes through the eight versions of *The Colorado Trail Guidebook*. The trailhead location has been changed and the trailhead and segment break is now at the Timberline Lake Trailhead, which has ample parking, water sources nearby, and potential campsites. It used to be called the Timberline Lake and CT Trailhead, but now has been simplified and shortened to the Timberline Lake Trailhead. The segment ends at the Mount Massive Trailhead, formerly known as the Halfmoon Creek Trailhead.

Airing out one's feet is delightful! PHOTO BY PETE TURNER

Segment 10 takes trail users into the Mount Massive Wilderness Area and features several long climbs and descents. At mile 6.4, the CT crosses the Leadville National Fish Hatchery, one of the oldest hatcheries in the federal system. It was established by Congress in 1889 and is still active. The hatchery buildings are about 2 miles east of where the CT crosses Rock Creek. At about mile 10.4, a side trail leads to the top of Mount Massive (14,421), the second-highest mountain in Colorado. For those interested in the side trip, it is 3.5 miles each way, with a little over 3,000 feet of climbing. This segment ends as you leave the wilderness area at the Mount Massive Trailhead.

Mt. Massive climbers diverge here.
PHOTO BY BILL MANNING

During the last ice age, the Sawatch Range was festooned with glaciers and icefields. Glaciers in the major valleys advanced beyond the mountain front and into the Arkansas Valley, leaving massive terminal moraines composed of glacial debris that accumulated as the ice melted at their snouts. Turquoise Lake lies behind one of these moraines. The valley of Halfmoon Creek was also occupied by a glacier that built a similar moraine.

TRAILHEAD/ACCESS POINTS

Timberline Lake Trailhead: This access road seems to have several names, depending or your source: Turquoise Lake Road, Lake County Rd 9, and FS Rd 104. Turquoise Lake Road seems to be the most comprehensive, since it applies to the road starting from the end of the 1000 block of West 6th Street in downtown Leadville, all the way around Turquoise Lake, and back to its starting point on West 6th Street. Access to the CT is at the westernmost point of Turquoise Lake Road. To get to the trailhead from US Hwy 24, which runs through the center of Leadville, turn west on West 6th Street and follow it to the end of the 1000 block. Curve right around the Lake County Recreation Center, then almost immediately turn left onto Turquoise Lake Road. Follow it to its westernmost point and turn west onto the access road for the 100-yard drive to the parking area. It makes no difference whether you drive around the north side of the lake or the south, but the south is a bit shorter.

Hagerman Pass Road Access (no parking): Follow the aforementioned instructions to Turquoise Lake Road. Follow it around the south side of the lake. After crossing Sugarloaf Dam, at mile 3.1, Hagerman Pass Road exits at a shallow angle to the left. The CT crosses 0.9 mile up this road. There is no parking space here.

Mount Massive Trailhead: See Segment 11 on page 146.

A green carpet of groundcover surrounds the path.
PHOTO BY ROGER FORMAN

SERVICES, SUPPLIES, AND ACCOMMODATIONS

Leadville, a historic mining and railroad town, is about 8 miles east of the trail access points by way of Turquoise Lake Road.

Distance from CT: 8 miles
Elevation: 10,152 feet
Zip code: 80461
Area code: 719

Leadville Services

Dining
Several locations in town

Gear (including fuel canisters)
Bill's Sport Shop
225 Harrison Ave.
(719) 486-0739

Sawatch Backcountry
480 Harrison Ave.
(719) 486-2271

Groceries
Safeway
1900 US Hwy 24 North
(719) 486-0795

Info
Chamber of Commerce
809 Harrison Ave.
(719) 486-3900

Laundry
Mountain Laundry
1707 Poplar Ave.
(719) 486-0551

Lodging (several)
Leadville Hostel & Inn
500 E. 7th St.
(719) 486-9334

Medical
St. Vincent General Hospital
4th and Washington Sts.
(719) 486-0230

Post Office
Leadville Post Office
130 W. 5th St.
(719) 486-9397

Showers
Lake County Aquatic Center
1000 W. 6th St.
(719) 486-6986

Shuttle
Leadville Hostel & Inn
500 E. 7th St.
(719) 486-9334

Looking north at peaks in the Holy Cross Wilderness Area.
PHOTO BY CARL BROWN

TRAIL DESCRIPTION

Segment 10 begins at the Timberline Lake Trailhead parking area above Turquoise Lake, **mile 0.0** (10,043 feet). Just after leaving the parking area, take a left at the well-marked intersection with the trail to Timberline Lake. Cross a small stream shortly after this intersection. Cross Glacier Creek at **mile 0.4** (10,115) on a good bridge with campsites nearby, then cross Busk Creek on another good bridge at **mile 1.2** (10,039). Ignore the small fishing trail that heads to the left and climb steeply to Hagerman Pass Road at **mile 1.8** (10,341). Just after the trail crosses Hagerman Pass Road, there is a good, dry campsite above the road. Continue climbing until reaching the Sugarloaf Mountain saddle at **mile 3.1** (11,094), where the trail crosses an old logging road. Great views of Mount Elbert open up when the CT reaches the high point on the ridge. Enter the Mount Massive Wilderness Area at **mile 3.3** (11,057). There is a trail register here. Several small streams and good camping lie just ahead.

Pass under the summits of Bald Eagle Mountain to the west, eventually reaching the Twin Mounds saddle at **mile 4.9** (11,009). After a short descent, bear to the right at the intersection at **mile 5.5** (10,644). There is a good, dry campsite here. There is a Forest Service sign identifying the CT and the Kearney Park Trail at **mile 5.7** (10,660). The Colorado Trail goes to the left (south) here, while the Kearney Park Trail heads east across the meadow. Cross Fish Hatchery Road then a bridge over Rock Creek at **mile 6.4** (10,269). Climb to the Highline Trail at **mile 8** (11,009). Continue in a southerly direction.

At **mile 9** (11,040), the CT crosses a bridge over North Willow Creek. There are potential campsites in this area. Climb to the top of a ridge at **mile 9.5** (11,310), where there is an exposed, dry campsite. Head downhill to **mile 10.4** (11,060), where the CT intersects the trail to Mount Massive. Shortly thereafter, cross Willow Creek at **mile 10.5** (11,030) and continue descending until crossing South Willow Creek at **mile 11.2** (10,804). Leave the Mount Massive Wilderness Area at **mile 13.4** (10,140) and reach the Mount Massive Trailhead parking area near Halfmoon Creek at **mile 13.6** (10,065), the end of Segment 10.

Rock Creek in the Mount Massive Wilderness Area.
PHOTO BY BILL MANNING

The Fourteeners and Climbing
Mount Elbert and Mount Massive

Of the 54 peaks in Colorado that rise above 14,000 feet, nearly two-thirds are within 20 miles of The Colorado Trail. They are a common and inspiring sight from many a ridgetop along the trail. The CT's closest encounter with a fourteener, however, comes when it passes San Luis Peak (14,014 feet) in Segment 20.

All of Colorado's fourteeners lie within a radius of 120 miles, centered in the Sawatch Range near Buena Vista. None of the other Rocky Mountain states has even one fourteener, despite their related geologic history. The reason why may rest with two geological features unique to Colorado: the Colorado Mineral Belt and the Rio Grande Rift. The Colorado Mineral Belt is a northeast-southwest band of igneous rock that roughly follows the same line as the CT. The Rio Grande Rift is a narrow rift valley that includes the San Luis and Arkansas valleys. Both of these features tend to push overlaying rock upward. All but one or two of the fourteeners are along these two features, and the highest and most numerous lie at the intersection of the two.

It is thought that although the entire Rocky Mountain region, including Colorado, Wyoming, and New Mexico, went through a broad uniform uplift, the fourteeners appear to be the result of an additional localized growth spurt involving these two geological features.

The results of this happy coincidence have captured the imagination of climbers ever since Carl Blaurock and Bill Ervin became the first to climb all of the fourteeners in 1923. A growing number of people have followed in their footsteps. The Colorado Mountain Club reported that by the end of 2009, well over 1,300 people had reported climbing all 54 fourteeners.

Mount Elbert and Mount Massive are the two highest peaks in the state and are tempting side trips on this stretch of the CT. No technical skills are required for either climb. Nevertheless, one must regard these as serious undertakings due to potentially adverse weather conditions and the strenuous high-altitude hiking. Be prepared—start early; carry warm clothing, rain gear, and plenty of water; and turn back if you encounter bad weather or experience symptoms of altitude sickness.

The Hayden Survey named Mount Massive (14,421) in the 1870s, and despite several subsequent attempts to rename it after various individuals, the descriptive appellation has stuck. Mount Elbert (14,433) was not so lucky. Like so many other mountains in Colorado, it was named for a politician, Samuel H. Elbert, who was appointed by President Abraham Lincoln in 1862 as secretary of the new Colorado Territory. After a succession of posts, Elbert became a Supreme Court justice when Colorado achieved statehood. Elbert the mountain is the highest peak in Colorado and second highest in the contiguous United States. Mount Whitney in California tops it by only 60 feet.

Each summit is about a 6-mile round trip hike from the CT and both can be reached from the Mount Massive Trailhead parking area on Halfmoon Creek Road (the end of Segment 10 and start of Segment 11). The Mount Massive Trail begins 3 miles from the end of Segment 10, proceeding west and then north to the summit. To scale Mount Elbert, go south on Segment 11 for 1.3 miles, then take the Mount Elbert Trail another 2.5 miles west to the top. The elevation gain from the trailhead for both summits is about 4,500 feet.

Kearney Park offers some welcome openness.
PHOTO BY BILL MANNING

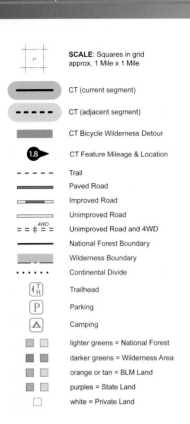

SCALE: Squares in grid approx. 1 Mile x 1 Mile

	CT (current segment)
	CT (adjacent segment)
	CT Bicycle Wilderness Detour
1.8	CT Feature Mileage & Location
- - - - -	Trail
	Paved Road
	Improved Road
	Unimproved Road
= = ‡ = = 4WD	Unimproved Road and 4WD
	National Forest Boundary
	Wilderness Boundary
· · · · · ·	Continental Divide
⊤H	Trailhead
P	Parking
△	Camping
	lighter greens = National Forest
	darker greens = Wilderness Area
	orange or tan = BLM Land
	purples = State Land
	white = Private Land

SEGMENT 10 FEATURES TABLE San Isabel National Forest

Mileage	Features & Comments	Elevation (feet)	Mileage from Denver	Mileage to Durango	UTM-E	UTM-N (NAD83)	Zone
0.0	Begin Segment 10	10,043	156.9	328.9	375,190	4,349,393	13
1.2	Cross Busk Creek	10,039	158.1	327.7	375,857	4,348,201	13
1.8	Cross Hagerman Pass Road	10,341	158.7	327.1	376,382	4,347,675	13
3.1	Reach saddle	11,094	160.0	325.8	377,283	4,346,593	13
3.3	Enter Mount Massive Wilderness Area	11,057	160.2	325.6	377,117	4,346,272	13
4.9	Reach Twin Mounds saddle	11,009	161.8	324.0	377,348	4,344,261	13
5.5	Bear right	10,644	162.4	323.4	377,345	4,343,350	13
5.7	Go left at intersection	10,660	162.6	323.2	377,205	4,343,382	13
6.4	Cross Rock Creek	10,269	163.3	322.5	377,093	4,342,766	13
6.7	Cross South Rock Creek	10,353	163.6	322.2	377,012	4,342,367	13
8.0	Cross Highline Trail	11,009	164.9	320.9	376,757	4,340,864	13
9.0	Cross North Willow Creek	11,040	165.9	319.9	376,448	4,339,375	13
9.5	Top of ridge	11,310	166.4	319.4	376,647	4,338,783	13
10.4	Intersect trail to Mount Massive	11,060	167.3	318.5	376,889	4,337,789	13
10.5	Cross Willow Creek	11,030	167.4	318.4	376,858	4,337,696	13
11.2	Cross South Willow Creek	10,804	168.1	317.7	376,992	4,336,884	13
13.6	End Segment 10	10,065	170.5	315.3	377,387	4,334,528	13

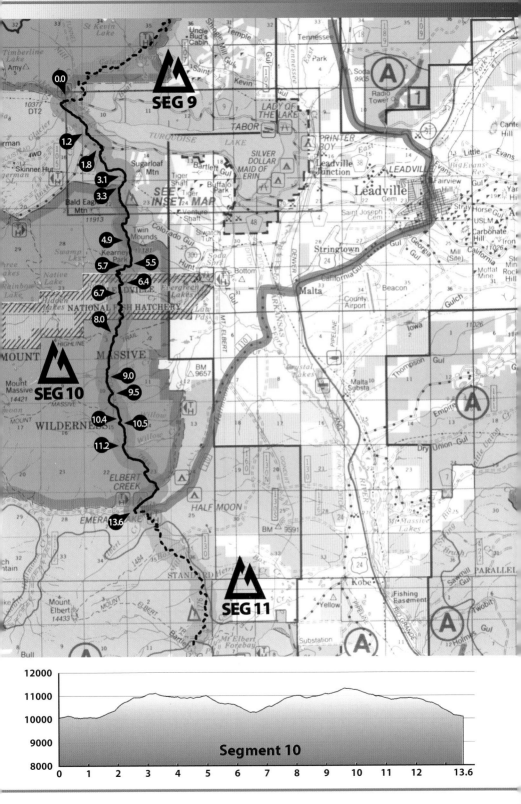

Mount Massive Trailhead to Marshall Pass (Segments 11–15)

Segment 11: Mount Massive Trailhead to Clear Creek Road

Sunset over Twin Lakes. PHOTO BY JEFF SELLENRICK

Distance: 21.5 miles

Elevation gain: Approx. 2,910 feet

Elevation loss: Approx. 4,042 feet

USFS map: San Isabel National Forest, pages 152–153

The Colorado Trail Databook 4/e: pages 28–29

The CT Map Book: pages 28–30

National Geographic Trails Illustrated maps: Nos.110, 127

Jurisdiction: Leadville Ranger District, San Isabel National Forest

Access from Denver end:

Access from Durango end:

Availability of water:

Bicycling:

"The previous route over Hope Pass has been replaced by a more direct one, eliminating 4 miles of road travel. Those still choosing to climb Hope Pass know why it is so named: 'Hope I will never have to pack over that again.'"

In 2000, access issues were finally resolved and the current lower-elevation route between the Lake Creek and Clear Creek drainages opened. The old Hope Pass route is now part of the Continental Divide National Scenic Trail.

Gudy's TIP

ABOUT THIS SEGMENT

Segment 11 starts with a steep climb up a moraine ridge that marks the edge of the Halfmoon Creek Glacier to a side trail that continues up Mount Elbert (14,433), the highest mountain in Colorado. The CT skirts the eastern flank of the peak, then descends past several creeks and beautiful displays of summer wildflowers to Twin Lakes, which lie behind another

Cyclists along the south shore of Twin Lakes.
PHOTO BY DAN MILNAR

conspicuous terminal moraine. This reservoir, which is part of the Pan-Ark Project, diverts water from the Arkansas River to Colorado's Front Range cities via tunnels.

In the fall of 2009, the CT returned to its original route over the top of Twin Lakes Dam. The trail had been diverted around the dam in 2003 due to security concerns, but thanks to the continued efforts of The Colorado Trail Foundation, authorities have deemed use of the dam trail safe. This benefits all trail users because the rerouting proved troublesome and the dam is spectacular to cross.

Along the southern edge of the lake, users may want to take a short side trip to the historic Interlaken (see sidebar on page 151). This is where the CT and CDNST diverge, having been co-located from Georgia Pass in Segment 6. After climbing away from the reservoir, the trail is well marked, but there are a lot of intersections. Be sure to keep an eye out for confidence markers in the trees and note any signs at trail junctions.

TRAILHEAD/ACCESS POINTS

Mount Massive Trailhead: 🚗 Drive south from Leadville on US Hwy 24 for about 3.5 miles. Turn right (west) onto CO Hwy 300. Drive 0.8 mile, turn left (south), and continue 1.2 miles to an intersection. Take the righthand branch (FS Rd 110). Continue 5.5 miles to the trailhead on the righthand side of the road, just after passing over a large culvert.

South Mount Elbert Trailhead: 🚗 Drive south from Leadville on US Hwy 24 for approximately 15 miles to CO Hwy 82. Turn right onto the highway and drive 4 miles. Turn right onto Lake County Rd 24, also known as Shore Pretty Drive, and proceed 1.1 miles, past the Lake View Campground, and left into the South Elbert Trailhead paved parking area.

Clear Creek Road Trailhead: 🚗 See Segment 12 on page 154.

SERVICES, SUPPLIES, AND ACCOMMODATIONS

Twin Lakes, an old mining town and perhaps Colorado's oldest resort town, is approximately 1 mile west of The Colorado Trail crossing on CO Hwy 82. The Twin Lakes Store is a delightful old general store, now a convenience and gas store, that provides the basics. It also has a small post office.

Distance from CT: 1 mile
Elevation: 9,210 feet
Zip code: 81251
Area code: 719

Twin Lakes Services

Dining
Windspirit Café & Cabins
6559 CO Hwy 82
(719) 486-8138

Gear (minimal)/ Groceries/Post Office
Twin Lakes General Store
6451 CO Hwy 82
(719) 486-2196

Laundry
Win-Mar
CO Hwy 82 and
US Hwy 24
(719) 486-0785

Lodging
Win-Mar plus Windspirit
(see above)

Twin Peaks Cabins
889 CO Hwy 82
(719) 486-2667

Twin Lakes Roadhouse
Lodge
6411 CO Hwy 82
(888) 486-4744

Medical
Nearest facilities in
Leadville

Showers
Win-Mar plus Windspirit
(see above)

TRAIL DESCRIPTION

Segment 11 starts at the south side of the Mount Massive Trailhead parking area next to Halfmoon Creek, **mile 0.0** (10,065 feet). This is the re-entry point for mountain bikers after their detour around the Holy Cross and Mount Massive wilderness areas. Cross a bridge over the creek and continue to **mile 0.3** (10,141), where the Mount Elbert Trailhead

Cache Creek in Lost Canyon, 4 miles west of the CT.
PHOTO BY DALE ZOETEWEY

access merges into the CT from the left. Keep going straight. Pass by the remains of an old log cabin and begin climbing a series of switchbacks at **mile 0.6** (10,135). At **mile 1.3** (10,590), the Mount Elbert Trail takes off to the right. The CT stays to the left at this intersection. Continue in a generally southeasterly direction, crossing another old trail. A few hundred feet beyond is a stream with a few potential campsites nearby.

Aspens in the area of North Willow Creek.
PHOTO BY ROGER FORMAN

Cross Box Creek at **mile 1.9** (10,468). Pass an old jeep trail, then cross the bridge over Mill Creek at **mile 2.1** (10,358). There are good campsites here. At **mile 2.4** (10,284), cross an old logging road. Pass over another logging road at **mile 3.2** (10,275). Cross Herrington Creek at **mile 3.3** (10,320) and continue south. Reach an intersection marked by a post at **mile 4.8** (10,513). Take a right here, joining the Mount Elbert Trail for 300 feet until that trail leaves to the right. After a descent through an aspen forest, pass by some beaver ponds, where there are a few potential campsites.

After passing the ponds, the CT comes to another intersection marked with a post and a Mount Elbert sign. Go right and cross a bridge. Just after crossing the bridge, the trail turns to the right, avoiding the road at **mile 5.2** (10,522). At **mile 5.4** (10,396), the trail crosses a small stream. At **mile 5.9** (10,012) is an intersection with a one-mile path (right) to Twin Lakes Village. Stay left on the CT and cross a bridge over a fast-moving creek below a small waterfall at **mile 6** (10,051).

Follow the CT in an easterly direction to an intersection with the trail to the Mount Elbert Trailhead parking area. Bear right and then straight ahead, and follow the trail along the southwestern edge of Lake View Campground. The trail continues just below Lake View Campground, then crosses another side trail. From this point, the trail descends along a long switchback to **mile 7.7** (9,320), where it crosses under CO Hwy 82 via a culvert. This culvert has the distinction of being the only pedestrian underpass on The Colorado Trail. This is also the beginning of a long, and potentially hot, hike along the shoreline of Twin Lakes.

The trail passes through a forest of large ponderosa pines on the south side of CO Hwy 82 and goes past the Mount Elbert Power Plant at **mile 8.3** (9,295). Cross through a log fence and over five roads in the next 3 miles. After the fifth road, the CT turns to the right and crosses Twin Lakes Dam at **mile 11.4** (9,221). This route was closed following the 2001 terrorist attacks because of security concerns. It was reopened in 2009 with the stipulation that trail users must not stop or loiter on the dam.

Follow the dam road to an intersection with a gravel road and go straight. After a few hundred feet, turn left at **mile 12.1** (9,242) and follow a small jeep trail 400 feet uphill to a gate that serves as a barricade to motorized traffic. Just past the gate at **mile 12.2** (9,257), turn right on a trail and follow it west along the south shore. Turn left at an intersection marked with a post at **mile 13.7** (9,210). The CT turns sharply to the south and ascends away from the lake. The Continental Divide National Scenic Trail (and the old CT route) splits off here (after being co-located with the CT for 99.6 miles) and follows the trail along the lake, eventually crossing Hope Pass. The old Interlaken Resort is an interesting side trip of about a mile along the lakeshore.

Follow the trail to the ridge, then descend to a jeep trail at **mile 14.6** (9,710), where the CT turns to the right. Ignore a logging trail to the left at **mile 14.7** (9,740) and continue ahead to another intersection at mile 15 (9,819).

Reflection on Twin Lakes.
PHOTO BY CARL BROWN

Turn left here. Cross a seasonal stream with potential campsites, then a small stream, where there is good camping. Intersect a road at **mile 16.6** (9,857), then enter a spectacular aspen forest. After crossing another small stream, turn left on a well-used jeep road at **mile 17.4** (9,803). For northbound hikers, it is especially important to note this junction because it is easy to overlook. At **mile 17.7** (9,787), turn right on a jeep road and then turn left 100 feet later to follow the CT.

There is an irrigation ditch to cross at **mile 18.2** (9,449), followed by another inter-section with an old logging road. Take a right and continue ahead, passing another logging trail that enters from the left shortly afterward. After crossing a seasonal stream, go right at the intersection ahead. Pass under a power line at **mile 18.8** (9,371), then turn to the right at **mile 19.2** (9,515), leaving the power line road. Turn left at an intersection marked with a post at **mile 19.7** (9,729) and continue climbing to **mile 19.8** (9,837), where the CT bears to the right on a single-track trail, gaining the top of a ridge several hundred feet later. Begin descending into the Clear Creek drainage, where the trail crosses an old canal, turns right at the jeep road, and stays below the road for the next few hundred feet. Cross Clear Creek Road to the trailhead at **mile 21.5** (8,937) and the end of Segment 11.

The Legacy of the Interlaken Resort

 Seemingly isolated and forgotten today, it's hard to imagine that one of the most popular tourist destinations in Colorado before the twentieth century was Interlaken, nestled on the shores of the present-day Twin Lakes. The complex was started in 1879 and enlarged after James V. Dexter bought the lakeside resort and grounds in 1883 and transformed it into a popular summer retreat. Visitors rode the train to a nearby stop, then took the short carriage ride to the south shore location.

The Interlaken Hotel boasted some of the best amenities of the time, with comfortable rooms and expansive views of the surrounding mountains and lakes. There was a tavern, pool hall, barns and stables, and a unique six-sided outdoor privy. An icehouse, granaries, and laundry rounded out the facility. Guests came to fish, hunt, ride horses, or just plain relax. Dexter built his own private cabin reflecting his nautical interests, including a cupola atop the second story with views in all directions.

Unfortunately, the resort fell into rapid decline after the turn of the century when the Twin Lakes were enlarged to serve irrigation interests. The entrance road was inundated and the large, but now shallow lakes, were less attractive to nature lovers. Eventually, the place was abandoned and the buildings began to deteriorate.

In 1979, as the reservoir was enlarged further, the Bureau of Reclamation stepped in and began to record and stabilize the historic district. Buildings that were to be inundated by the new dam were moved slightly uphill and extensively repaired. For CT hikers, a short side trip to the site provides a glimpse at a slice of Colorado history.

Historic Interlaken Hotel on the south shore of Twin Lakes.

PHOTO BY AARON LOCANDER

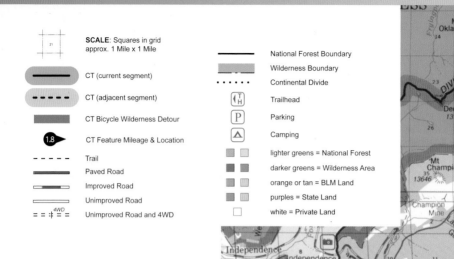

SCALE: Squares in grid approx. 1 Mile x 1 Mile

CT (current segment)

CT (adjacent segment)

CT Bicycle Wilderness Detour

CT Feature Mileage & Location

Trail

Paved Road

Improved Road

Unimproved Road

Unimproved Road and 4WD

National Forest Boundary

Wilderness Boundary

Continental Divide

Trailhead

Parking

Camping

lighter greens = National Forest

darker greens = Wilderness Area

orange or tan = BLM Land

purples = State Land

white = Private Land

SEGMENT 11 FEATURES TABLE San Isabel National Forest

Mileage	Features & Comments	Elevation (feet)	Mileage from Denver	Mileage to Durango	UTM-E	UTM-N (NAD83)	Zone
0.0	Begin Segment 11	10,065	170.5	315.3	377,387	4,334,528	13
0.3	Trail merges from left, stay right	10,141	170.8	315.0	377,835	4,334,396	13
1.3	Stay left at intersection	10,590	171.8	314.0	378,314	4,333,707	13
1.9	Cross Box Creek	10,468	172.4	313.4	378,600	4,333,054	13
2.1	Cross Mill Creek	10,358	172.6	313.2	378,859	4,332,895	13
2.4	Cross old logging road	10,284	172.9	312.9	379,251	4,332,743	13
3.3	Cross Herrington Creek	10,320	173.8	312.0	379,731	4,331,547	13
4.8	Turn right at intersection	10,513	175.3	310.5	379,535	4,329,861	13
5.2	Trail leaves road to the right	10,522	175.7	310.1	379,358	4,329,376	13
5.9	Stay left at intersection	10,012	176.4	309.4	379,922	4,328,344	13
6.0	Cross creek	10,051	176.5	309.3	379,924	4,328,451	13
7.7	Pass under road	9,320	178.2	307.6	381,986	4,328,090	13
8.3	Pass by power plant	9,295	178.8	307.0	382,842	4,328,171	13
11.4	Turn right and cross dam	9,221	181.9	303.9	387,250	4,326,731	13
11.9	Turn right onto dirt road	9,218	182.4	303.4	387,196	4,325,904	13
12.1	Turn left and go 400 feet to gate	9,242	182.6	303.2	387,085	4,325,634	13
12.2	Just past gate, turn right	9,257	182.7	303.1	387,039	4,325,596	13
13.7	Take sharp left at intersection	9,210	184.2	301.6	384,754	4,325,974	13
14.6	Turn right at intersection	9,710	185.1	300.7	385,315	4,325,204	13
15.0	Turn left at intersection	9,819	185.5	300.3	384,718	4,325,219	13
16.6	Intersect road	9,857	187.1	298.7	385,728	4,323,538	13
17.4	Turn left on jeep road	9,803	187.9	297.9	386,074	4,322,442	13
18.2	Cross irrigation ditch	9,449	188.7	298.7	385,728	4,323,538	13
19.2	Turn right	9,515	189.7	297.1	386,881	4,321,979	13
19.7	Turn left at intersection	9,729	190.2	295.6	387,022	4,320,092	13
19.8	Bear right	9,837	190.3	295.5	387,109	4,319,959	13
21.5	End Segment 11	8,937	192.0	293.8	388,946	4,319,961	13

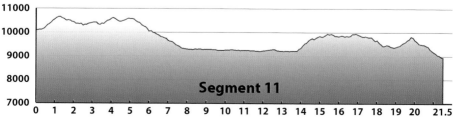

Segment 11

Segment 12: Clear Creek Road to Silver Creek Trailhead

Distance: 18.5 miles

Elevation gain: Approx. 4,866 feet

Elevation loss: Approx. 4,364 feet

USFS map: San Isabel National Forest, pages 158–159

The Colorado Trail Databook 4/e: pages 30–31

The CT Map Book: pages 30–32

National Geographic Trails Illustrated maps: Nos. 110, 129

Jurisdiction: Leadville Ranger District, San Isabel National Forest

Access from Denver end:

Access from Durango end:

Availability of water:

Bicycling:  See page 157

Sunrise over the Arkansas River Valley.
PHOTO BY KEITH EVANS

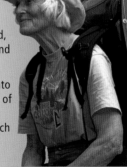

"If you have the time, a hike up Pine Creek into Missouri Basin is a rewarding side trip. In this emerald-clad basin, you are seemingly in the very heart of the sky-touching Collegiates, surrounded by four fourteeners: Harvard, Missouri, Belford, and Oxford."

This long day trip into Missouri Basin, one of the largest alpine basins in the Sawatch Range, is about 5.5 miles each way.

Gudy's TIP

ABOUT THIS SEGMENT

The beginning of Segment 12 was rerouted in 2007 to avoid the private property of Clear Creek Ranch. This required almost 3 miles of new trail construction and an 80-foot-long bridge across Clear Creek—work that was accomplished by eight crews of volunteers organized by The Colorado Trail Foundation.

Clear Creek Reservoir is cradled within the massive terminal moraine of the Clear Creek Glacier. At its maximum extent this glacier advanced far enough to dam the Arkansas River, forming a large temporary lake.

After entering the Collegiate Peaks Wilderness Area, the CT climbs into tundra, gains a ridge, then descends into another drainage. Without a doubt, this is the defining characteristic of this segment: A steep up and down, followed by another steep up and down. There are three fourteeners (Mounts Oxford, Harvard, and Columbia) within 3 miles of the trail through this segment. With a little planning, it is possible to climb all three of these peaks in a relatively short period of time. There are many great campsites throughout this segment and plenty of water sources.

TRAILHEAD/ACCESS POINTS

You can pitch a tent almost anywhere along the trail, even an undeveloped site if necessary.

PHOTO BY KEITH EVANS

Clear Creek Road Trailhead Access: 🚗 Drive north from Buena Vista for approximately 17 miles. Turn left on Chaffee County Rd 390. Drive 2.5 miles to a small, rough parking area, just west of the Colorado Division of Wildlife Campground. Three large boulders on the south side of the road mark this trailhead. There are Colorado Trail markers on both sides of the road.

Silver Creek Trailhead Access: 🚌 See Segment 13 on page 160.

SERVICES, SUPPLIES, AND ACCOMMODATIONS

These amenities are available in Buena Vista; see Segment 13 on pages 160–169.

TRAIL DESCRIPTION

Segment 12 begins by the three boulders at the Clear Creek Trailhead, **mile 0.0** (8,937 feet). The trailhead is just to the east of a pole fence marking the boundary of Clear Creek Ranch. At mile 0.3 begins a campground and possible confusion. Head east to the middle of the campground then south toward the creek. At **mile 0.5** (8,916), the trail crosses

An eighty-foot steel bridge over Clear Creek was installed by CTF volunteers in 2007. PHOTO BY KEITH EVANS

Clear Creek on a steel bridge that was built by volunteer trail crews. Begin a steady climb, passing under a power line at **mile 1.4** (9,365) and crossing an old road in Columbia Gulch at **mile 1.8** (9,655). Shortly thereafter, enter the Collegiate Peaks Wilderness Area. There are several small seasonal streams in the next few miles.

Gain the ridge off Waverly Mountain at **mile 4.8** (11,653) in a stand of bristlecone pines mixed with firs. Descend via a series of steep switchbacks. The Pine Creek Trail joins the CT from the northwest as the trail continues to the south. Cross a bridge over Pine Creek at **mile 6.4** (10,430). There are several good campsites along the creek corridor. Follow the CT as it climbs away from Pine Creek, eventually heading up several steep switchbacks before coming to a side trail that goes right to Rainbow Lake at **mile 8.1** (11,561). Continue straight ahead. Shortly after entering the tundra, gain a ridge off Mount Harvard at **mile 9** (11,845) and descend to Morrison Creek at **mile 9.8** (11,573).

At **mile 10.5** (11,520), the CT crosses the Wapaca Trail, which comes in from the east. Continue straight, heading downhill and crossing Frenchman Creek on a good bridge at **mile 11.8** (11,031). There is a good campsite on the south side of the creek. Shortly after passing this creek, cross Frenchman Creek Trail (also known as the Harvard Trail) and continue in a southeasterly direction. Gain a subsidiary ridge to Mount Columbia at **mile 12.6** (11,142), then descend to **mile 14.2** (10,646), where the CT passes a neglected mine and an old road. Cross Three Elk Creek at **mile 15.2** (10,280), pass by Harvard Lakes, and exit the Collegiate Peaks Wilderness Area at **mile 15.4** (10,246).

The CT continues to descend, crossing Powell Creek at **mile 15.9** (10,048) and passing a side trail to the A/U Ranch at **mile 16.5** (9,953). At **mile 17.8** (9,855), there is another side trail to the A/U Ranch, followed by a trail register and a right turn onto North Cottonwood Creek Road at **mile 18.3** (9,422). Head up the road for 0.2 mile, where you will come to the Silver Creek Trailhead and the end of Segment 12. There is a large parking lot with interpretive signs and a bathroom here.

Collegiate Peaks Wilderness Bicycle Detour

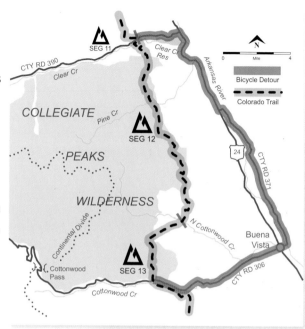

🚲 This is a mandatory bypass of the Collegiate Peaks Wilderness Area. Part of it is on busy US Hwy 24 and you'll have a hard time watching for traffic as your attention is drawn to the wonderful views of the Collegiate Peaks to the west. Although you can stay on US Hwy 24, it is more pleasant to turn onto Chaffee County Rd 371 for the 10-mile pedal into Buena Vista.

Start this detour at the end of Segment 11 (and start of Segment 12) on Chaffee County Rd 390. Ride east to **mile 3** (8,906) and turn right (south) onto US Hwy 24. Continue on the highway to **mile 8.9** (8,477), then exit left onto Chaffee County Rd 371. At this point, cross over the Arkansas River on 371 and follow the abandoned railroad bed of the Colorado Midland Railroad to Buena Vista at **mile 18.8** (7,945).

Cross the river into town and go right (west) on Main Street, past the intersection with US Hwy 24, onto Chaffee County Rd 306 (Cottonwood Pass Road). Continue to the Avalanche Trailhead parking area at mile 28.4, where you rejoin The Colorado Trail at **mile 6.6** (9,360) of Segment 13.

An unnamed, 13,000-foot peak in the Collegiate Peaks Wilderness.

PHOTO BY CARL BROWN

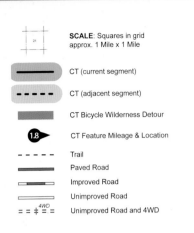

SEGMENT 12 FEATURES TABLE San Isabel National Forest

Mileage	Features & Comments	Elevation (feet)	Mileage from Denver	Mileage to Durango	UTM-E	UTM-N (NAD83)	Zone
0.0	Begin Segment 12	8,937	192.0	293.8	388,944	4,319,963	13
0.5	Cross Clear Creek	8,916	192.5	293.3	389,331	4,319,541	13
1.4	Cross under power line	9,365	193.4	294.2	388,825	4,318,814	13
1.8	Enter Collegiate Peaks Wilderness Area	9,655	193.8	292.0	388,839	4,318,542	13
4.8	Gain ridge	11,653	196.8	289.0	388,613	4,314,810	13
6.4	Cross Pine Creek	10,430	198.4	287.4	389,384	4,313,657	13
8.1	Go straight at side trail junction	11,561	200.1	285.7	389,731	4,312,397	13
9.0	Gain ridge	11,845	201.0	284.8	389,867	4,311,574	13
9.8	Cross Morrison Creek	11,573	201.8	284.0	389,916	4,310,752	13
10.5	Cross Wapaca Trail	11,520	202.5	283.3	390,901	4,310,460	13
11.8	Cross Frenchman Creek	11,031	203.8	282.0	391,074	4,308,881	13
12.6	Gain ridge	11,142	204.6	281.2	392,078	4,308,530	13
14.2	Pass neglected mine and old road	10,646	206.2	279.6	391,994	4,306,883	13
15.2	Cross Three Elk Creek	10,280	207.2	278.6	392,448	4,305,664	13
15.4	Exit Collegiate Peaks Wilderness Area	10,246	207.4	278.4	392,432	4,305,358	13
15.9	Cross Powell Creek	10,048	207.9	277.9	392,331	4,304,736	13
16.5	Cross side trail to A/U Ranch	9,953	208.5	277.3	392,844	4,304,163	13
17.8	Cross 2nd side trail to A/U Ranch	9,855	209.8	276.0	392,589	4,302,792	13
18.3	Turn right on road	9,422	210.3	275.5	392,535	4,302,469	13
18.5	End Segment 12	9,430	210.5	275.3	392,346	4,302,593	13

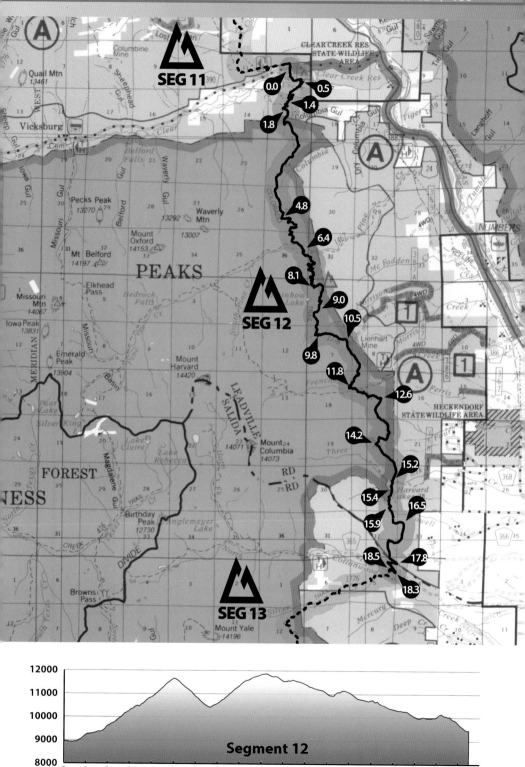

Segment 13: Silver Creek Trailhead to Chalk Creek Trailhead

Mount Princeton from Mount Yale.
PHOTO BY JEFF SELLENRICK

Distance: 22.8 miles

Elevation gain: Approx. 4,296 feet

Elevation loss: Approx. 5,343 feet

USFS map: San Isabel National Forest, pages 168–169

The Colorado Trail Databook 4/e: pages 32–33

The CT Map Book: pages 32–34

National Geographic Trails Illustrated map: No. 129

Jurisdiction: Salida Ranger District, San Isabel National Forest

Access from Denver end:

Access from Durango end:

Availability of water:

Bicycling: See page 157

"Be respectful of the long stretch of private property as the trail descends into the Chalk Creek Valley."

Although CT travel here is primarily on public corridors, there is no public camping available on the surrounding private land.

Gudy's TIP

ABOUT THIS SEGMENT

Segment 13 begins by crossing North Cottonwood Creek, then commences on a long climb that passes into the Collegiate Peaks Wilderness Area before topping out on a saddle on the east ridge of Mount Yale (14,196). The views from here are outstanding, and a short jaunt up the knoll to the east of the saddle brings the Arkansas Valley into view. It is possible to climb Mount Yale via this ridge, although there is no trail. Allow about four hours for the round trip and don't be discouraged by the false summits along the route. The descent to the Avalanche Trailhead is very steep—one trail user noted he wouldn't have minded a belay in a few spots! Trekking poles come in handy here.

! There is NO camping for the next 6.5 miles after encountering private property at the youth camp at mile 17.

The CT leaves the wilderness area just before reaching the trailhead, allowing mountain bikers to rejoin the trail. Eventually, the trail contours around the base of Mount Princeton. As it approaches Chalk Creek it descends along a moraine ridge that marks the edge of the Chalk Creek Glacier; the terminal moraine of the glacier and the broad aprons of gravel spread by its melt water are conspicuous in the valley below. Where it joins County Rd 321, the CT begins a 5.7-mile road walk to bypass private land. The Colorado Trail

West along one of the county roads near Segment 13's end with part of Mt. Princeton behind.

PHOTO BY JEFF SELLENRICK

Foundation has been searching for a way to avoid this for years, but has not had any luck yet. A soak at the Mount Princeton Hot Springs Resort can help ease the monotony of road walking, though. West of the resort the road skirts the base of the Chalk Cliffs, which are not chalk at all, but 65 million-year-old granite largely altered to white clay by water from the hot springs. The road is not well marked, so be sure to consult your *Guidebook*, *Map Book*, or *Databook* to ensure you go the right way at each road junction.

Chalk Cliffs from near Mount Princeton Hot Springs.
PHOTO BY JULIE VIDA AND MARK TABB

TRAILHEAD/ACCESS POINTS

Silver Creek Trailhead: From US Hwy 24 at the north end of Buena Vista, turn west on Crossman Street (7 blocks north of the traffic light and across the highway from the Trailhead Outdoor Gear Shop). Crossman Street is also known as Chaffee County Rd 350. Follow it for 2 miles to its end, where it intersects Chaffee County Rd 361. Turn right (north), proceed 0.9 mile, and make a sharp left turn (south) onto Chaffee County Rd 365, a gravel road. The road soon turns west and continues for 3.5 miles (some of them very rough and rutted) to the *northbound* CT trailhead. A trail register and sign identify it and there is a small informal parking area on the south side of the road. Continue 0.1 mile to the *southbound* trailhead on the south side of the road. There is a large gravel parking lot, interpretive signs, and a Forest Service toilet here. There is an even larger parking lot on the north side of the road, suitable for horse trailers. This area is the official end of Segment 12 and the beginning of Segment 13.

Avalanche Trailhead: From US Hwy 24 in Buena Vista, turn west at the traffic light onto the Cottonwood Pass Road (Main Street, which becomes Chaffee County Rd 306 at the edge of town). Drive 9.5 miles to the Avalanche Trailhead on the north side of the highway. You may spot Colorado Trail signs on both sides of the highway about 0.2 mile before the trailhead entrance sign on the righthand side. The CT crosses the parking area.

Cottonwood Lake Road Access: From the traffic light in Buena Vista, proceed west on the Cottonwood Pass Road for approximately 8 miles. Turn left onto the

Cottonwood Lake Road (Chaffee County Rd 344). After about 0.2 mile, the CT crosses the road. There is a small primitive parking area on the lefthand side.

Chalk Creek Trailhead: 🚗 See Segment 14 on page 170.

SERVICES, SUPPLIES, AND ACCOMMODATIONS

Buena Vista, as might be gathered from its Spanish name, is a beautiful place to visit because of its striking location in the Arkansas Valley between the mineralized Mosquito Range and the towering Sawatch Range. The town, approximately halfway between Denver and Durango on The Colorado Trail, is an ideal resupply point for long-distance trekkers. The most direct way to reach Buena Vista from the CT is to follow Chaffee County Rd 306. It is approximately 9.5 miles east of the Avalanche Trailhead.

Distance from CT: 9.5 miles
Elevation: 7,954 feet
Zip code: 81211
Area code: 719

Buena Vista Services

Dining
Several locations in town

Gear (including fuel canisters)
The Trailhead
707 US Hwy 24 North
(719) 395-8001

Groceries
City Market
438 US Hwy 24 North
(719) 395-2431

Info
Chamber of Commerce
343 US Hwy 24 South
(719) 395-6612

Laundry
Missing Sock Laundry
522 Antero Cir.
(719) 395-6757

Lodging
Several locations in town

Medical
Mountain Medical Center
36 Oak St.
(719) 395-8632

Post Office
Buena Vista Post Office
110 Brookdale Ave.
(719) 395-2445

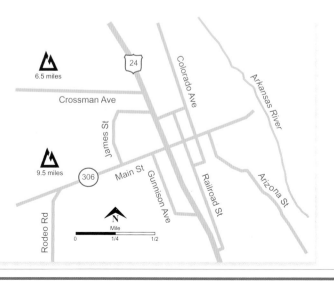

TRAIL DESCRIPTION

Segment 13 begins at the Silver Creek Trailhead on FS Rd 365, **mile 0.0** (9,430 feet). There is plenty of parking and toilets here. After crossing North Cottonwood Creek on a good bridge and passing a trail register, begin climbing through a mixed spruce and fir forest. There are many potential campsites in the first few miles of trail. Continue heading southwest, eventually following Silver Creek to **mile 2.5** (11,098), where the CT crosses the creek. Enter the Collegiate Peaks Wilderness Area at **mile 2.7** (11,269) and climb to the saddle on the east ridge of Mount Yale at **mile 3.4** (11,889). There is a potential campsite on the right. Descend from the pass into a forest of bristlecone pine and fir in Avalanche Gulch. Leave the wilderness area near a small stream at **mile 6.3** (9,502) and arrive at the Avalanche Trailhead at **mile 6.6** (9,395).

Cross Cottonwood Pass Road (Chaffee County Rd 306) and walk through a small dirt parking area. This is a good area for mountain bikers to rejoin the CT after detouring

Trekking through a grove of mature aspen.
PHOTO BY KEITH EVANS

Approach to climb Mt. Yale from the CT.
PHOTO BY JEFF SELLENRICK

around the wilderness area. Turn left on the trail and cross Cottonwood Creek on a bridge. This area is well marked. The trail bends to the southeast and follows along private property and above Rainbow Lake. Trail users are asked to stay on the trail and respect the private property. After passing a small stream, take the fork to the left when the trail splits at **mile 8.8** (9,018). From here, the trail crosses Chaffee County Rd 344 at **mile 8.9** (8,967).

The CT crosses a bridge over South Cottonwood Creek, which is the last reliable water source for the next 4.5 miles, at **mile 9** (8,921). There are a lot of good campsites in this area. The trail follows the creek for about 0.5 mile, then crosses a dirt road (FS Rd 343) at **mile 9.5** (8,862). There is another trail register here. From the register, the CT climbs a series of switchbacks to a trail junction at **mile 11** (9,641). Take a left turn here. At **mile 11.6** (9,885), gain the saddle west of Bald Mountain. After passing two creeks, cross Silver Prince Creek at **mile 13.2** (9,925) and Maxwell Creek at **mile 14** (10,003). There is a good campsite 300 feet south of Maxwell Creek. Cross Dry Creek on a bridge at **mile 15.9** (9.526), then join a dirt road (FS Rd 322) at **mile 17.1** (9,497). The CT follows roads for the next 5.7 miles in order to avoid private land. (The Colorado Trail Foundation is working with landowners to develop an alternative to this road section.)

Pass under the Mount Princeton Trail Junction sign at **mile 18.2** (8,924) and walk through the parking lot of a private camp. The paved road begins here. Follow the road to the east until **mile 18.8** (8,681), where it bends to the northeast. Turn right (south) on

Chaffee County Rd 321, another paved road. Continue following the road, bending to the east, then turning hard to the southwest. Keep an eye out for the trail markers along the side of the road. At **mile 20.3** (8,194), the CT turns right at the junction onto Chaffee County Rd 162. After another 1.4 miles, veer to the left onto Chaffee County Rd 291 at **mile 21.7** (8,303). This dirt road goes through a neighborhood to the Chalk Creek Trailhead on the left at **mile 22.8** (8,389). This is the end of Segment 13.

Mount Princeton Hot Springs

This spot was long frequented by American Indians before being taken over and developed by whites, beginning in 1860. The fortunes of the Mount Princeton Hot Springs Hotel rose and fell with the fortunes of area mines and the coming of the railroad and its subsequent departure in 1926. The elaborate hotel on the site was demolished for scrap lumber in 1950. But you can't keep a good place down, especially one that promises to "melt your cares away." Pools at the present resort are open every day of the year (admission required).

End of Segment 13 follows roads, like this Chaffee Cty Rd 162 that passes Mount Princeton Hot Springs.
PHOTO BY JEFF SELLENRICK

The Collegiate Peaks

This impressive collection of skyscraping fourteeners, with names such as Harvard, Columbia, Yale, and Princeton, are collectively known as the Collegiate Peaks, a subset of the greater Sawatch Range. These peaks were

Collegiate Wilderness boundary sign. The CT passes through six wilderness areas.

PHOTO BY AARON LOCANDER

first surveyed by a team led by Harvard Professor Josiah Dwight Whitney (for whom California's Mount Whitney is named). They started the tradition of naming the fourteeners in this area for universities after climbing Mount Harvard (14,420) in 1869. Mount Yale (14,196) was named after Whitney's alma mater. Later climbers continued the practice, adding Princeton, Oxford, and Columbia.

Despite their proximity, some of the Collegiate fourteeners don't lend themselves to a day climb from The Colorado Trail. Possibly the best opportunity comes with Mount Yale in Segment 13. At about mile 3.4 of that segment, the CT gains the long east ridge of Yale, offering a moderate, though without well-defined trail, route to the summit with a bit of rock hopping and a few false summits along the way.

Another fourteener, Mount Princeton,

also offers relatively direct access from the CT, though the round-trip hike can be 12 miles. At mile 17.1 of Segment 13, diverge from the CT and hike 3 miles uphill on a dirt road open to vehicles. (It might be feasible to trim your hiking miles by soliciting a ride from one of the many peak-baggers, especially early on a weekend morning.) Beyond where vehicles must park, hike 3 more miles to the summit.

SCALE: Squares in grid approx. 1 Mile x 1 Mile

CT (current segment)

CT (adjacent segment)

CT Bicycle Wilderness Detour

1.8 CT Feature Mileage & Location

Trail

Paved Road

Improved Road

Unimproved Road

Unimproved Road and 4WD

National Forest Boundary

Wilderness Boundary

Continental Divide

Trailhead

Parking

Camping

lighter greens = National Forest

darker greens = Wilderness Area

orange or tan = BLM Land

purples = State Land

white = Private Land

SEGMENT 13 FEATURES TABLE   San Isabel National Forest

Mileage	Features & Comments	Elevation (feet)	Mileage from Denver	Mileage to Durango	UTM-E	UTM-N (NAD83)	Zone
0.0	Begin Segment 13	9,430	210.5	275.3	392,346	4,302,593	13
2.5	Cross Silver Creek	11,098	213.0	272.8	389,394	4,301,379	13
2.7	Enter Collegiate Peaks						
	Wilderness Area	11,269	213.2	272.6	389,134	4,301,149	13
3.4	Gain saddle	11,889	213.9	271.9	388,760	4,300,634	13
6.3	Leave wilderness area	9,502	216.8	269.0	389,007	4,297,155	13
8.8	Turn left at junction	9,018	219.3	266.5	391,624	4,295,488	13
9.0	Cross South Cottonwood Creek	8,921	219.5	266.3	391,866	4,295,419	13
9.5	Cross road	8,862	220.0	265.8	392,508	4,295,787	13
11.0	Turn left at intersection	9,641	221.5	264.3	392,797	4,294,759	13
11.6	Gain saddle	9,885	222.1	263.7	393,425	4,294,630	13
13.2	Cross Silver Prince Creek	9,925	223.7	262.1	394,002	4,292,735	13
14.0	Cross Maxwell Creek	10,003	224.5	261.3	394,537	4,292,200	13
15.9	Cross Dry Creek	9,526	226.4	259.4	395,798	4,290,627	13
17.1	Join FS Rd 322	9,497	227.6	258.2	396,774	4,289,482	13
18.2	Pass under Mount Princeton						
	Trail Junction sign	8,924	228.7	257.1	397,846	4,288,577	13
19.1	Go right on Chaffee County						
	Rd 321 (blacktop)	8,615	229.6	256.2	399,035	4,288,820	13
20.3	Turn right on Chaffee						
	County Rd 162	8,194	230.8	255.0	398,830	4,287,780	13
21.7	Turn left on Chaffee						
	County Rd 291	8,303	232.2	253.6	397,328	4,286,598	13
22.8	End Segment 13	8,389	233.3	252.5	395,669	4,286,022	13

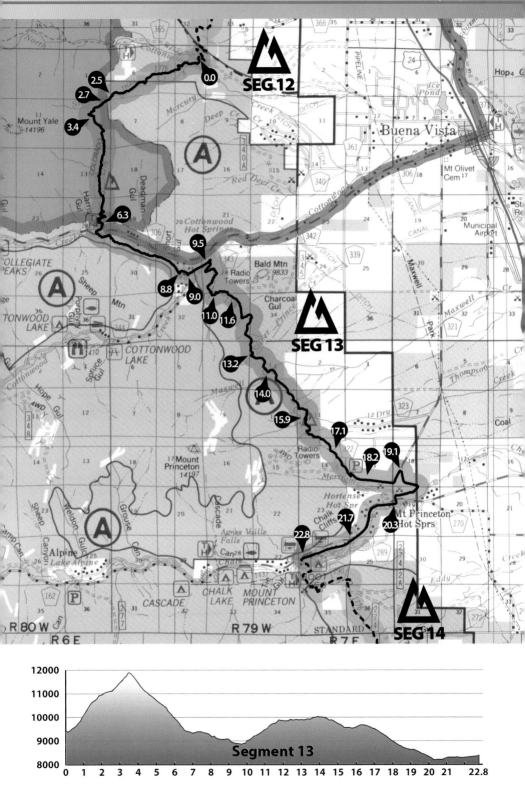

Segment 14: **Chalk Creek Trailhead to US Hwy 50**

Chalk Cliffs north of Segment 14.

Distance: 20.4 miles

Elevation gain: Approx. 4,007 feet

Elevation loss: Approx. 3,531 feet

USFS map: San Isabel National Forest, pages 176–177

The Colorado Trail Databook 4/e: pages 34–35

The CT Map Book: pages 34–37

National Geographic Trails Illustrated map: No. 130

Jurisdiction: Salida Ranger District, San Isabel National Forest

Access from Denver end:

Access from Durango end:

Availability of water:

Bicycling: 🚲

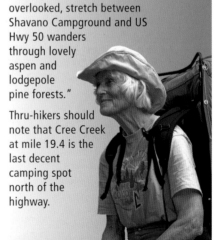

"The short (5-mile), but often overlooked, stretch between Shavano Campground and US Hwy 50 wanders through lovely aspen and lodgepole pine forests."

Thru-hikers should note that Cree Creek at mile 19.4 is the last decent camping spot north of the highway.

Gudy's TIP

ABOUT THIS SEGMENT

Segment 14 travels through the southern end of the Sawatch Range, passing Mounts Antero and Shavano and Tabeguache Peak, all fourteeners. The trail climbs steeply at the start of the section, but soon levels off and travels through forested areas before reaching the first water source since Chalk Creek, a distance of 6.6 miles. After this, there are several water sources and good camping as the northern part of the Sangre de Cristo Range comes into view ahead. The big descent at the end of the segment comes out on US Hwy 50, a good place for thru-hikers to arrange a ride to the nearby town of Salida for rest and resupply.

Waterfall on Browns Creek 1.5 miles west of the CT.
PHOTO BY DALE ZOETEWEY

TRAILHEAD/ACCESS POINTS

Chalk Creek Trailhead: Drive south from Buena Vista on US Hwy 285 to Nathrop. Turn right (west) onto Chaffee County Rd 162 for approximately 7 miles. The trailhead is on the left side of the road, slightly below road level.

Browns Creek Trailhead: Drive south from Nathrop on US Hwy 285 for about 3.2 miles. Turn right (west) on Chaffee County Rd 270 for 2 miles to where it turns north. Continue straight ahead onto Chaffee County Rd 272 for 2 miles to where it turns left (south) at an intersection. Continue south on 272 for 1.6 more miles to the Browns Creek Trailhead. Walk west on the trail for 1.4 miles to intersect the CT.

Angel of Shavano Trailhead: From the intersection of US Hwy 285 and US Hwy 50 at Poncha Springs, drive west on US Hwy 50 for about 6 miles. Turn right (north) onto Chaffee County Rd 240 (North Fork South Arkansas River Road). Proceed on 240 for 3.8 miles to the trailhead parking area opposite the Angel of Shavano Campground.

US Hwy 50 Trailhead Access: See Segment 15 on page 178.

SERVICES, SUPPLIES, AND ACCOMMODATIONS

Salida, an old railroad town and now a commercial center for the Arkansas Valley, is about 13 miles east of the CT crossing at US Hwy 50. **Poncha Springs**, 8 miles east of the crossing, has a small restaurant and a small convenience store. Monarch Spur RV Park, about a mile east of the CT on US Hwy 50, has camping and showers. Monarch Mountain Lodge, about 4.5 miles west of the CT on US Hwy 50, has lodging and a mail drop.

Distance from CT: 13 miles
Elevation: 7,036 feet
Zip code: 81201
Area code: 719

Salida Services

Bus
Chaffee Transit Center
54 Jones Ave.
(719) 530-8980

Dining
Several locations in town

Gear (including fuel canisters)
Salida Mountain Sports
110 North F St.
(719) 539-4400

Groceries
Safeway
232 G St.
(719) 539-3513

Salida Food Town
248 W. US Hwy 50
(719) 539-7500

Info
Chamber of Commerce
406 W. Rainbow Blvd.
(719) 539-2068

Laundry
Salida Laundromat
1410 E St.
(719) 530-1263

Lodging
Simple Lodge and Hostel,
224 E. First St. (719)
650-7381. Reservations
recomended.

Medical
Heart of Rockies Medical
Center
448 E. 1st St.
(719) 539-6661

Post Office
Poncha Springs Post Office
6500 US Hwy 285
(719) 539-2117

Salida Post Office
310 D St.
(719) 539-2548

Showers
Salida Hot Springs Resort
410 W. US Hwy 50
(719) 539-6738

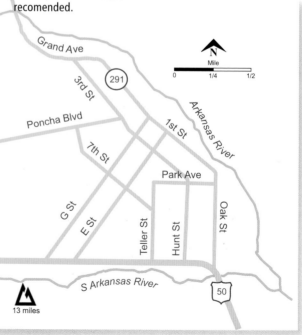

TRAIL DESCRIPTION

Segment 14 begins at the Chalk Creek Trailhead, **mile 0.0** (8,389 feet). Chalk Creek is the last reliable water until Browns Creek, 6.6 miles ahead. Go south across a bridge and begin hiking uphill. Pass the Bootleg Trail at **mile 0.1** (8,430). There is a fee campground if you take this trail left about 100 yards. At **mile 0.4** (8,506), cross FS Rd 290. The intersection is marked with a Forest Service sign for Raspberry Gulch. Ascend several switchbacks to the top of a knoll at **mile 1.4** (9,310). After heading downhill to the east, turn to the right at **mile 2.1** (9,021) and head down a steep, rocky hillside. Cross another road (FS Rd 274) at **mile 2.4** (8,901).

Contour along the northeast side of Peak 11,038, eventually crossing Raspberry Gulch Road (FS Rd 273) at **mile 3.9** (8,906). The CT crosses an eroded jeep trail at **mile 4.5** (8,963) and climbs until reaching **mile 6.1** (9,664), where the trail bears left at the junction with the Little Browns Creek Trail. At **mile 6.4** (9,546) turn right at the intersection. Cross Little Browns Creek on a bridge at **mile 6.6** (9,615) and turn left, crossing another small stream before passing over Browns Creek

Northbound hikers in Segment 14. Mount Princeton is in the background.
PHOTO BY KEITH EVANS

Bridge over Chalk Creek at the Segment 14 trailhead.
PHOTO BY KEITH EVANS

on a log bridge at **mile 6.8** (9,590). There are a few potential campsites between the two streams.

Cross the Wagon Loop Trail at **mile 7** (9,615) and head in a generally southerly direction until reaching Fourmile Creek at **mile 8.7** (9,757). Cross Sand Creek at **mile 10** (9,621) and Squaw Creek at **mile 12.2** (9,833). Both creeks offer camping possibilities. There is an intersection with the Mount Shavano Trail at **mile 12.7** (9,880). Continue straight ahead. Pass through a Forest Service gate and into an open meadow. A log fence prevents motor vehicles from accessing the trail at **mile 13** (9,812). Cross a jeep road at **mile 13.2** (9,832), continuing southwest. Descend to **mile 14.9** (9,208), where the CT reaches the Angel of Shavano Trailhead. The trail briefly re-enters some trees before crossing a road (Chaffee County Rd 240) at **mile 15**, and continuing to a bridge over the North Fork of the Arkansas River at **mile 15.2** (9,133). There are several confidence markers on trees in this area.

Begin a climb up several switchbacks, eventually reaching the top of the ridge at **mile 16.7** (9,743). From here, the CT skirts the edge of an old logging area that has been replanted. There is a spring fed pond at about **mile 17.5** (9,575). At **mile 18** (9,442), the trail crosses Lost Creek and then the Lost Creek jeep road. Follow the CT to the southwest, crossing a road next to a huge circular meadow and another road (FS Rd 248) just past the meadow. At **mile 19.5** (9,210), cross Cree Creek, the last campsite area north of US Hwy 50. Go under a double power line at **mile 19.8** (9,316), then leave the power line road at **mile 20** (9,223) on a single-track trail to the left. Cross an old railroad grade at **mile 20.2** (8,960). Segment 14 ends at US Hwy 50 at **mile 20.4** (8,861). There is a large trail marker on the north side of the highway.

Mount Shavano

Want to climb a fourteener (or two) as part of your Colorado Trail trek? The Mount Shavano Trail, which intersects the CT at mile 12.7 (9,885), is the Colorado Fourteeners Initiative's recommended route. Follow the Mount Shavano Trail west about 3.5 miles to the saddle just south of Mount Shavano. From this spot the trail is not clearly marked, but follow the ridge to the top of Mount Shavano (14,229), about 0.3 mile. From the top of Shavano, travel northwest along the connecting ridge to Tabeguache Peak's summit (14,155), less than a mile away. Return via the same route. Although technically easy and on a trail most of the way, don't underestimate the difficulties. Get an early start and be prepared for 5,000 feet of elevation gain and an arduous 10-mile round trip.

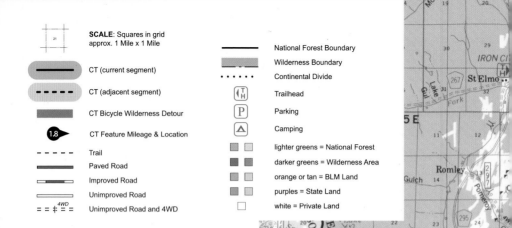

SEGMENT 14 FEATURES TABLE White River and Pike National Forests

Mileage	Features & Comments	Elevation (feet)	Mileage from Denver	Mileage to Durango	UTM-E	UTM-N (NAD83)	Zone
0.0	Begin Segment 14	8,389	233.3	252.5	395,669	4,286,022	13
0.1	Pass Bootleg Trail	8,430	233.4	252.4	395,719	4,285,900	13
0.4	Cross road	8,506	233.7	252.1	395,932	4,285,586	13
1.4	Top out on knoll	9,310	234.7	251.1	396,291	4,285,071	13
2.1	Turn right	9,021	235.4	250.4	397,268	4,285,280	13
2.4	Cross FS Rd 274	8,901	235.7	250.1	397,202	4,284,870	13
3.9	Cross Raspberry Gulch Road	8,906	237.2	248.6	398,183	4,282,952	13
4.5	Cross eroded jeep trail	8,963	237.8	248.0	398,446	4,282,224	13
6.1	Bear left at junction	9,664	239.4	246.4	397,219	4,280,808	13
6.4	Turn right at intersection	9,546	239.7	246.1	397,292	4,280,441	13
6.6	Cross Little Browns Creek	9,615	239.9	245.9	397,123	4,280,132	13
6.8	Cross Browns Creek	9,590	240.1	245.7	397,277	4,279,953	13
7.0	Cross Wagon Loop Trail	9,615	240.3	245.5	397,387	4,279,866	13
8.7	Cross Fourmile Creek	9,757	242.0	243.8	397,062	4,277,860	13
10.0	Cross Sand Creek	9,621	243.3	242.5	397,283	4,276,298	13
12.2	Cross Squaw Creek	9,833	245.5	240.3	396,242	4,273,962	13
12.7	Cross Mount Shavano Trail	9,880	246.0	239.8	395,880	4,273,299	13
13.0	Pass through Forest Service gate	9,812	246.3	239.5	395,703	4,272,954	13
13.2	Cross side trail and FS Rd 254	9,832	246.5	239.3	395,515	4,272,626	13
14.9	Reach Angel of Shavano Trailhead	9,208	248.2	237.6	393,792	4,271,443	13
15.2	Cross North Fork of Arkansas River	9,133	248.5	237.3	393,618	4,271,144	13
16.7	Reach top of ridge	9,743	250.0	235.8	393,610	4,270,555	13
17.5	Spring fed pond	9,575	250.8	235.0	393,484	4,269,554	13
18.0	Cross Lost Creek	9,442	251.3	234.5	392,870	4,269,234	13
19.5	Cross Cree Creek	9,210	252.8	233.0	391,787	4,267,794	13
19.8	Cross under double power line	9,316	253.1	232.7	391,859	4,267,336	13
20.2	Cross railroad grade	8,960	253.5	232.3	391,698	4,267,018	13
20.4	End Segment 14	8,861	253.7	232.1	391,720	4,266,827	13

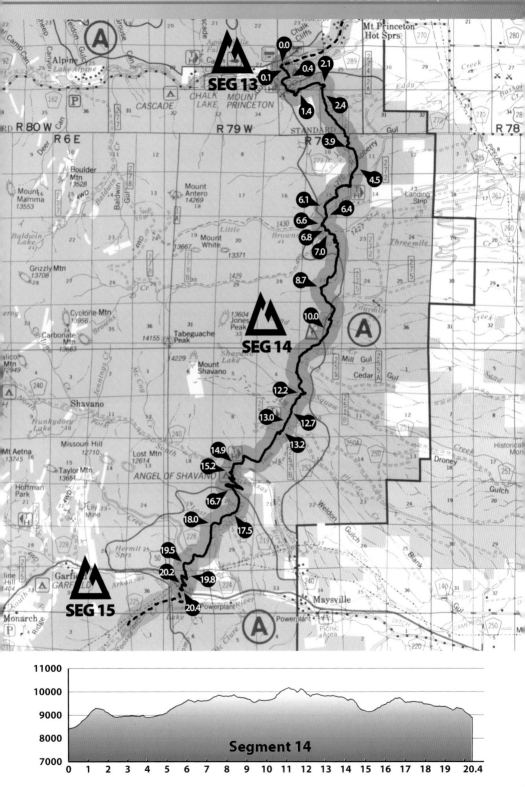

Segment 15: **US Hwy 50 to Marshall Pass**

A quiet walk in the aspens.
PHOTO BY JULIE VIDA AND MARK TABB

Distance: 14.3 miles

Elevation gain: Approx. 3,576 feet

Elevation loss: Approx. 1,608 feet

USFS maps: San Isabel and Gunnison
National Forests, pages 182–183

The Colorado Trail Databook 4/e:
pages 36–37

The CT Map Book: pages 37–39

National Geographic Trails Illustrated
maps: Nos. 130, 139

Jurisdiction: Salida and Gunnison Ranger
Districts, San Isabel and Gunnison
National Forests

Access from Denver end:

Access from Durango end:

Availability of water:

Bicycling:

"Once up on the Divide, you'll have
unobstructed views in every direction.
Three of our mightiest mountain
ranges—the Sawatch, the San Juan,
and the Sangre de Cristo—reach for
the sky."

The Divide is lofty
and remote. There
are no towns close
by for convenient
resupply, and cell
phones are unlikely to
work in an emergency.
The next 100 miles is
the least-traveled
portion of the CT.

Gudy's TIP

ABOUT THIS SEGMENT

After leaving US Hwy 50 and beginning this segment, there are no convenient resupply points for the next 100 miles until the town of Creede. *Be prepared.* The first few miles of this segment head southwest on a Forest Service dirt road, with lots of potential campsites (car and backpacking), before turning south and climbing the South Fooses Creek drainage, eventually reaching the Continental Divide and rejoining the Continental Divide National Scenic Trail (CDNST). From here, the trail follows the Divide closely until the end of the segment at Marshall Pass. Just north of Marshall Pass the trail passes out of basement rocks and into gray volcanic rocks, part of the San Juan volcanic field that covers almost 10,000 square miles and includes at least 10,000 cubic miles of volcanic rocks.

The CT intersects the CDNST when it reaches the Continental Divide and joins a well-known mountain bike route known as the Monarch Crest Trail. (See the sidebar in Segment 16 on page 187). It is a wonderful ride. If you are on foot, however, be on the lookout for mountain bikers approaching from behind. This is a very popular trail that can be very busy on the weekends during the summer.

TRAILHEAD/ACCESS POINTS

US Hwy 50 South Fooses Creek Trailhead: 🚗 From the intersection of US Hwy 285 and US Hwy 50 at Poncha Springs, drive west on US Hwy 50 for approximately 9 miles to the Fooses Creek Road (Chaffee County Rd 225). There is a wide shoulder on the south side of US Hwy 50 that provides only limited parking. This is the official beginning of Segment 15. The CT follows Fooses Creek Road for 2.8 miles to a trailhead area with limited parking. The road to the trailhead is rather primitive, but usually most cars can make it. Take the left fork at all junctions en route.

Marshall Pass Trailhead: 🚗 See Segment 16 on page 184.

SERVICES, SUPPLIES, AND ACCOMMODATIONS

These amenities are available in Salida; see Segment 14 on pages 170–177.

TRAIL DESCRIPTION

Segment 15 begins at the intersection of US Hwy 50 and Fooses Creek Road (FS Rd 225), **mile 0.0** (8,861 feet). Follow the dirt road, taking a fork to the left at **mile 0.2** (8,846) and crossing the South Fork of the Arkansas River. The road bends back to the west and eventually heads in a southwesterly direction. Pass by Fooses Lake, a small reservoir that is part of a hydroelectric project that produces power for the Salida area, at **mile 0.8** (8,960).

Mountain bikers take on the famous Monarch Crest.
PHOTO BY ANTHONY SLOAN

Stay on this main road until reaching **mile 2.7** (9,553). There is camping allowed after mile 2, with many good sites just off the main road.

At **mile 2.7**, turn left onto another small road. Reach the South Fooses Creek Trailhead at **mile 2.8** (9,551). Turn to the right and cross the creek immediately after. There are many hard-packed campsites here. From this point until mile 8.2, the trail stays near the creek, crosses multiple times, and there are many camping options available. The final crossing of South Fooses Creek comes at **mile 8.2** (11,240). This is the last water until **mile 13**. Begin a climb that ascends 668 feet in a half-mile, one of the steepest grades on the entire CT. Gain the crest of the Continental Divide at **mile 8.6** (11,908) and turn left at the well-marked intersection where the CT joins the Monarch Crest Trail and the Continental Divide National Scenic Trail. This is the beginning of a second lengthy section where the CT is co-located with the CDNST and the shared path continues 135.2 miles into Segment 24, where they again diverge.

Follow the Monarch Crest in a generally southeasterly direction, turning right at the intersection at **mile 10.3** (11,501), where the CT heads to the south. The Green Creek Shelter is just east of the trail, with water available 0.3 mile east along the Green Creek Trail. Cross the Agate Creek and Cochetopa Creek Trail at **mile 11.4** (11,814). (The summit of 13,971-foot Mount Ouray is to the east and most often climbed by following the Cochetopa Creek Trail to the Divide and traversing the ridge to the peak.) Continue ahead until joining an old jeep trail at **mile 12.8** (11,364). There is a piped spring that sometimes flows at **mile 13** (11,260). After **mile 14** (10,850) and about 200 yards before Marshall Pass Rd, cross a large ditch culvert where there is water available from Poncha Creek. Take a right turn onto Marshall Pass Road (Chaffee County Rd 200) at **mile 14.1** (10,820) and cross the road to the Marshall Pass parking area. There are USFS restrooms at the parking area. Water from Poncha Creek is available in a large swampy area 1/4 mile east of the restrooms—either follow the road to the east or just head downhill past the restrooms. If you don't mind the road traffic, Marshall Pass is good for camping given the restrooms and water. In dry years, this may be the last water available for the next 10 or 12 miles. To reach the end of Segment 15, walk up the road 0.2 mile to Marshall Pass. Turn left on a jeep trail heading south. Follow the jeep trail up the hill to where a sign marks the trail.

Continental Divide National Scenic Trail (CDNST)

The Continental Divide National Scenic Trail, commonly known as the Continental Divide Trail, passes through five Western states as it winds through the majestic Rocky Mountains from Canada to Mexico, encountering some of America's most dramatic scenery.

The Colorado Trail and the CDNST are co-located for 234.8 miles in two separate sections of the CT. The two trails join from Georgia Pass in CT Segment 6 to the south shore of Twin Lakes in Segment 11, a stretch of 99.6 miles. They are also co-located through a long section that begins in CT Segment 15 on the Divide above Fooses Creek and diverges 135.2 miles later in CT Segment 24 atop the Divide near the Elk Creek descent.

First envisioned by several far-sighted groups and individuals, including Benton Mackaye, founder of the Appalachian Trail, the 3,100-mile CDNST is about 70 percent complete today. The Colorado portion has one of the highest completion rates at 90 percent. The trail achieves its highest point in Colorado, passing over 14,270-foot Grays Peak, and includes a network of trails 759 miles long, beginning in the Mount Zirkel Wilderness Area on the Wyoming border and entering New Mexico through the spectacular San Juans.

The Continental Divide Trail Alliance (CDTA) estimates that only about a dozen people undertake the entire 6-month journey from Canada to Mexico each year. As with The Colorado Trail, few individuals finish the entire Colorado portion of the CDNST, but thousands enjoy day hikes or weeklong backpacks on segments of it.

The first complete hike of Colorado's Continental Divide National Scenic Trail was done by Carl Melzer, his son, Bob, and Julius Johnson in 1936. This was truly a pioneering trip, considering the incomplete maps and sketchy information available to them at that time. (The Melzers had a string of accomplishments. They also were the first to climb all of Colorado's fourteeners in one summer [1937] and the first to climb all of the fourteeners in the 48 states [1939]—all before Bob was 11 years old!)

For more information about the CDNST, contact the CDTA at (303) 838-3760 or visit the group's website at cdtrail.org.

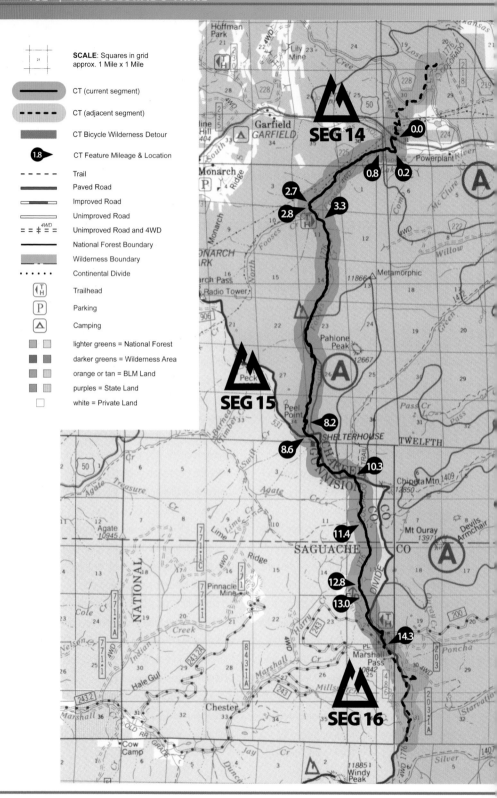

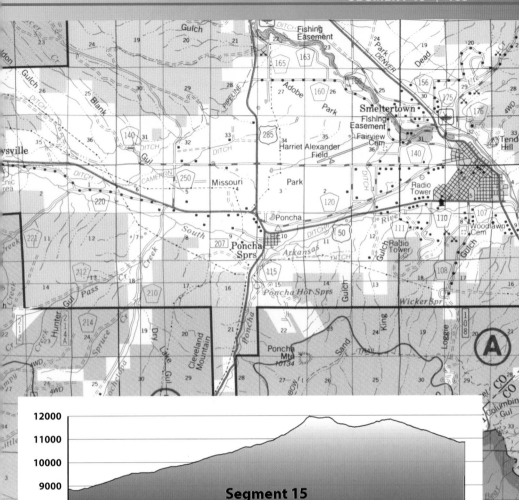

SEGMENT 15 FEATURES TABLE   San Isabel and Gunnison National Forests

Mileage	Features & Comments	Elevation (feet)	Mileage from Denver	Mileage to Durango	UTM-E	UTM-N (NAD83)	Zone
0.0	Begin Segment 15	8,861	253.7	232.1	391,720	4,266,827	13
0.2	Go left at fork	8,830	253.9	231.9	391,581	4,266,860	13
0.8	Pass by lake	8,960	254.5	231.3	391,203	4,266,465	13
2.7	Turn left	9,553	256.4	229.4	388,764	4,264,728	13
2.8	South Fooses Creek Trailhead	9,551	256.5	229.3	388,788	4,264,594	13
3.3	Creek crossing	9,699	257.2	228.6	389,112	4,264,154	13
8.2	Last water until mile 13	11,450	261.8	224.0	388,563	4,257,482	13
8.6	Go left at intersection	11,908	262.3	223.5	388,578	4,257,017	13
10.3	Go right at intersection	11,501	264.0	221.8	390,165	4,255,630	13
11.4	Go straight at intersection	11,814	265.1	220.7	390,458	4,254,050	13
12.8	Join jeep trail	11,364	266.5	219.3	390,299	4,252,010	13
13.0	Piped spring	11,260	266.7	219.1			
14.3	End Segment 15	10,864	268.0	217.8	391,128	4,250,001	13

Marshall Pass to San Luis Pass (Segments 16–20)
Segment 16: **Marshall Pass to Sargents Mesa**

Jerry Brown in camp warming up for
another long day of surveying the CT.

PHOTO BY CARL BROWN

Distance: 15.2 miles

Elevation gain: Approx. 3,184 feet

Elevation loss: Approx. 2,405 feet

USFS maps: San Isabel, Gunnison, and Rio
Grande National Forests, pages 188–189

The Colorado Trail Databook 4/e: pages
38–39

The CT Map Book: pages 39–41

National Geographic Trails Illustrated map:
No. 139

Jurisdiction: Salida, Gunnison, and
Saguache Ranger Districts; San Isabel,
Gunnison, and Rio Grande National Forests

Access from Denver end: 🚗

Access from Durango end: 🚙

Availability of water: ☕

Bicycling: 🚲

"Sargents Mesa teems with hundreds
of grazing elk and numerous trout-
filled beaver ponds."

The high mesas and rolling uplands
along the Continental
Divide, extending
from Marshall Pass
to the La Garita
Wilderness Area and
known as the Cochetopa
Hills, are excellent elk and
mule deer habitat.
Bighorn sheep also are
found around the pass
and points north. Early
morning or dusk are
prime viewing times.

Gudy's TIP

ABOUT THIS SEGMENT

This segment of The Colorado Trail and the next two segments are mostly open to motorized traffic. The Colorado Trail Foundation is looking for alternative routes through this area to avoid this conflict, but until that happens trail users should stay alert for dirt bikes approaching at high speeds.

The trail through here stays very close to the Continental Divide, which means water sources are scattered. There is water at Silver Creek, just off the trail, 4.1 miles from the Marshall Pass Trailhead. As you climb the flank of Windy Peak, you can spot a green area about a quarter-mile south at the foot of the slope. There has been a reliable spring there. About 11 miles in, you will cross Tank Seven Creek, which is also a good source of water. While walking up the meadow and approaching Sargents Mesa, there have been a couple of stock tanks with water (if you are not fussy and have a good filter). From Sargents Mesa, it is about 7 miles to water at Baldy Lake in Segment 17.

TRAILHEAD/ACCESS POINTS

Marshall Pass Trailhead: Drive about 5 miles south of Poncha Springs on US Hwy 285 and turn right (west) at the Marshall Pass and O'Haver Lake Campground turnoff. The road starts out as Chaffee County Rd 200 and toward the top of the pass morphs into FS Rd 200. It is about 13 miles from the highway to the summit of Marshall Pass. About 0.2 mile short of the pass is a parking area for about a dozen cars with a Forest Service toilet nearby. There is also limited parking at the top of the pass itself. The trailhead for Segment 16 is at the top of the hill just above the road, where a sign marks the CT trailhead.

Sargents Mesa Trailhead Access: See Segment 17 on page 190.

SERVICES, SUPPLIES, AND ACCOMMODATIONS

There is no convenient resupply point for this segment.

TRAIL DESCRIPTION

Begin Segment 16 at the smaller parking area atop Marshall Pass, **mile 0.0** (10, 864), where a sign marks the trail. The trail quickly becomes single track and the jeep roads are left behind for the moment. Follow the trail south to **mile 2.4** (11,137), where the CT merges with a jeep trail. Go left at the intersection. Motorized vehicles are allowed on this portion of the CT, so be alert to approaching motorcycles and ATVs.

At **mile 4.1** (11,238), cross the Rainbow/Silver Creek Trail and follow the CT as it bends to the west. There is a campsite and water about a quarter-mile down Silver Creek. The jeep track morphs into single-track at **mile 4.5** (11,408), cross a seasonal stream, and pass through a Forest Service gate on the Continental Divide at **mile 5.2** (11,560). The trail continues in a westerly direction, reaching a high point of 11,570 feet and then steeply

Hikers use trekking poles to keep balance and momentum on trail.
PHOTO BY BILL MANNING

descending after passing to the south of Windy Peak. Cross a jeep trail at **mile 7.1** (10,903) and continue downhill until reaching **mile 8.9** (10,629), where the trail follows a pipeline cut for 200 feet then exits to the right.

At **mile 11.0** (10,569) start a descent. Cross Tank Seven Creek at **mile 11.6** (10,351). Take a left on an old abandoned road after crossing the creek. Tank Seven Creek is the last reliable water source until reaching Baldy Lake 11.5 miles ahead in Segment 17. There are several places to camp in this area. Cross a dirt road at **mile 12.9** (10,796), where there are the remains of some crumbled buildings. Continue climbing to **mile 13.8** (11,101), where the trail crosses a gravel road. At **mile 14.7** (11,394), cross the Big Bend Creek Trail. Segment 16 ends at FS Rd 855 on Sargents Mesa, **mile 15.2** This is likely the least used and most (11,616). This is likely the least used and most poorly marked trailhead on the entire Colorado Trail.

Elk keep an eye on trail users. PHOTO BY PETE TURNER

Monarch Crest Trail

🚲 🚶 The Monarch Crest Trail has been rated by *Bicycling Magazine* as one of the top-five mountain bike rides in the country. It descends an epic 3,500 feet from tundra to sagebrush desert, covering roughly 40 miles of mostly single-track trail.

Riders begin atop Monarch Pass (a shuttle service out of Poncha Springs is available) and follow the Continental Divide National Scenic Trail south, intersecting with The Colorado Trail at Fooses Creek in Segment 15. The trail continues to Marshall Pass and on into Segment 16. Riders drop off the Divide on the Silver Creek Trail/Rainbow Trail system to reach US Hwy 285 in the valley

Mountain bikers take on the famous Monarch Crest. PHOTO BY GEORGE NESERKE

below. A swift ride down the highway returns riders to Poncha Springs.

The Legacy of Marshall Pass

📷 In 1873, troubled by a toothache and in a big hurry to get to a dentist in Denver, Army Lieutenant William Marshall "discovered" this shortcut. For centuries, of course, bands of Ute Indians had been using the several gaps in this relatively low section of the Continental Divide to travel between the intermountain parks on the east side of the Divide and their lands to the west. Famed road and rail builder Otto Mears constructed the first wagon road over the pass, following existing paths, then sold it to the Denver & Rio Grande Western railroad, which laid rails over it in 1881.

General William Palmer's D&RGW was in a battle with John Evans' Denver, South Park & Pacific Railroad to be the first to reach Gunnison and tap the mineral-rich San Juans. While the DSP&P took the shorter route on paper by tunneling under the Sawatch Range, Palmer chose the relatively low pass with modest grades for his route. The D&RGW won the race, pulling into Gunnison to an exuberant crowd on August 8, 1881. The DSP&P, meanwhile, labored for another year on its ill-fated Alpine Tunnel.

The rails are long gone today, but Chaffee County Rd 200 follows the old trackbed.

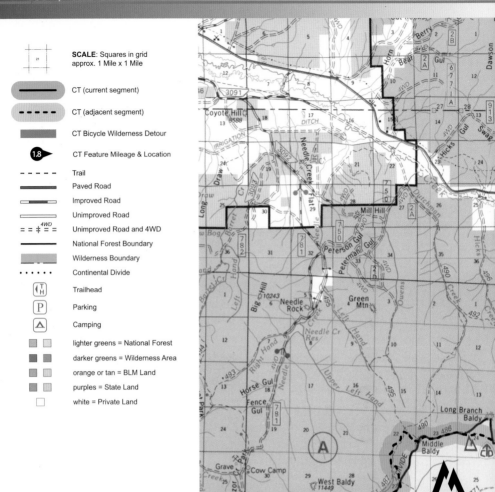

SCALE: Squares in grid approx. 1 Mile x 1 Mile

CT (current segment)

CT (adjacent segment)

CT Bicycle Wilderness Detour

1.8 CT Feature Mileage & Location

Trail

Paved Road

Improved Road

Unimproved Road

Unimproved Road and 4WD

National Forest Boundary

Wilderness Boundary

Continental Divide

Trailhead

Parking

Camping

lighter greens = National Forest

darker greens = Wilderness Area

orange or tan = BLM Land

purples = State Land

white = Private Land

SEGMENT 16 FEATURES TABLE   Gunnison National Forest

Mileage	Features & Comments	Elevation (feet)	Mileage from Denver	Mileage to Durango	UTM-E	UTM-N (NAD83)	Zone
0.0	Begin Segment 16	10,864	268.0	217.9	391,128	4,250,001	13
2.4	Go left at intersection	11,137	270.4	215.4	391,887	4,247,360	13
4.1	Cross Rainbow/Silver Creek Trail	11,238	272.1	213.7	391,513	4,245,781	13
5.2	Pass through gate	11,560	273.2	212.6	390,112	4,245,353	13
7.1	Cross jeep trail	10,903	275.1	210.7	387,754	4,245,241	13
8.9	Go right at intersection	10,629	276.9	208.9	385,322	4,244,687	13
11.6	Cross Tank Seven Creek	10,351	279.6	206.2	383,452	4,241,460	13
12.9	Cross road	10,796	280.9	204.9	382,059	4,240,605	13
13.8	Cross gravel road	11,101	281.8	204.0	380,883	4,240,101	13
14.7	Cross Big Bend Creek Trail	11,394	282.7	203.1	379,958	4,239,637	13
15.2	End Segment 16	11,616	283.2	202.6	379,441	4,238,979	13

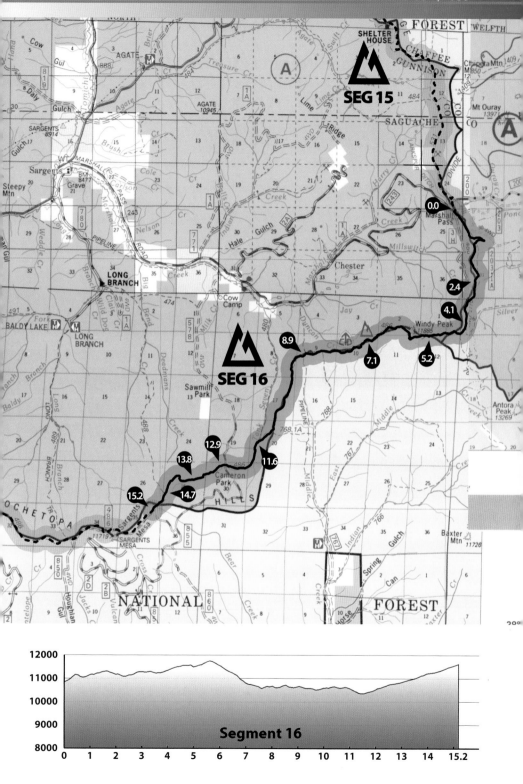

Segment 17: Sargents Mesa to CO Hwy 114

Baldy Lake. PHOTO BY JULIE VIDA AND MARK TABB

Distance: 20.4 miles

Elevation gain: Approx. 2,810 feet

Elevation loss: Approx. 4,810 feet

USFS maps: Rio Grande and Gunnison National Forests, pages 194–195

The Colorado Trail Databook 4/e: pages 40–41

The CT Map Book: pages 41–43

National Geographic Trails Illustrated map: No. 139

Jurisdiction: Saguache and Gunnison Ranger Districts; Rio Grande and Gunnison National Forests

Access from Denver end:

Access from Durango end:

Availability of water:

Bicycling:

"Baldy Lake after Sargents Mesa is worth the half-mile detour; it's a haven along a dry segment of the trail."

You'll need to plan your camps and water needs carefully on this segment. The only reliable water sources are at Baldy Lake at mile 7.5 and Lujan Creek at mile 18. All water sources should be treated as suspect because of livestock use.

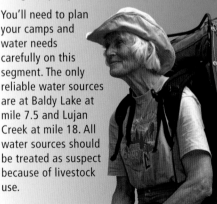

Gudy's TIP

ABOUT THIS SEGMENT

In Segment 17 the CT continues to travel along the crest of the Continental Divide. As with the previous section, water sources can be scarce. Baldy Lake, some 7.5 miles from the trailhead, is the first reliable water source. There may be water in Razor Creek early in the year or during particularly wet years, but the only reliable water source after Baldy Lake is Lujan Creek, near the end of the segment.

The CO Hwy 114 Trailhead can be difficult to locate. It is on the south side of the road at what looks more like a large turnout than a parking area. There is a confidence marker near the trailhead, but it is not visible until you are at the gate leading into the segment. If you are a thru-hiker walking on the right side of the highway, you will have to cross over the road after about a half-mile walk to find this trailhead.

Backpackers admire the broad expanse of Sargents Mesa.
PHOTO BY PETE TURNER

TRAILHEAD/ACCESS POINTS

Sargents Mesa Trailhead Access (FS Rd 855): From the small town of Saguache on US Hwy 285 in the San Luis Valley, proceed northwest on CO Hwy 114 for 10.5 miles. Take the righthand branch of the Y intersection here onto Saguache County Rd EE-38. Proceed 0.8 mile to the next Y and take the left branch, continuing on EE-38. Continue up Jacks Creek Valley for 5 miles and turn right on County Road 32JJ which morphs into FS Rd 855. From the right turn, proceed 9.5 miles to an intersection and bear left at a sign for Sargents Mesa. Continue another 0.5 miles to an informal parking area at a "Y" as you enter a large meadow. Unless you and your vehicle are well suited for extremely rough road, park here and walk the 0.4 miles further to the CT.

Lujan Creek Road Trail Access: From Saguache drive west on CO Hwy 114 for approximately 30 miles to North Pass. Continue 1.1 miles down from the pass to Lujan Creek Road (Saguache County Rd CC-31/FS Rd 785) on your right. Follow this narrow, slick-when-wet shelf road for 2 miles up Lujan Creek Valley, where it makes an abrupt right turn up a switchback. Avoid the jeep road that departs to the left. Continue 0.1 mile and cross a cattle guard. Branch left here for 0.1 mile to where the CT comes down from the mountain.

CO Hwy 114 Trailhead
Access: 🚗 See Segment 18 on page 196.

SERVICES, SUPPLIES, AND ACCOMMODATIONS

There is no convenient resupply point for this segment.

TRAIL DESCRIPTION

Trekkers enjoy easy hiking and big views on Sargents Mesa.
PHOTO COURTESY OF COLORADOTRAILHIKING.COM

Segment 17 begins at the obscure Sargents Mesa Trailhead on FS Rd 855, **mile 0.0** (11,616 feet). The trail follows an old jeep trail south and west to **mile 2.3** (11,176), where The Colorado Trail abruptly leaves the jeep trail to the right at a well-marked intersection. Cross Long Branch Trail at **mile 2.4** (11,168) and continue climbing and descending along the Continental Divide. Reach the Baldy Lake Trail intersection at **mile 6.9** (11,517). The lake is 0.5 mile to the north of the CT and is a good place to camp. It is the last reliable water source until reaching Lujan Creek, more than 11 miles ahead.

After more ups and downs along the Divide, reach the summit of Middle Baldy Peak at **mile 9.2** (11,685). Bear to the left at the intersection with Dutchman Creek Trail at **mile 9.8** (11,378), then cross Razor Creek at **mile 10.5** (10,943). This creek is seasonal, usually gone by early August, and may not run in dry years. After following the creek for 0.3 mile, turn left at the intersection with Razor Creek Trail at **mile 10.8** (10,848).

Cattle graze in the Cochetopa Hills.
PHOTO BY JULIE VIDA AND MARK TABB

Regain the Continental Divide at **mile 11.5** (10,819), then bear left at the intersection with the Razor Creek Spur Trail at **mile 12.4** (11,073). The CT continues along the Divide, heading left onto an old jeep road at **mile 16.5** (11,019). Go to the right on Lujan Creek Road at **mile 17.8** (10,343), leaving the Divide.

After passing through a gate with a cattle guard, take a left to stay on Lujan Creek Road at an intersection with an old logging road at **mile 18** (10,333). Turn right at **mile 20** (9,729) to join CO Hwy 114. Head downhill to a wide parking area on the south side of the road at **mile 20.4** (9,606) and the end of this segment. This is a poorly marked trailhead. There is a gate where the trail continues into Segment 18.

Pocket Gophers

The long, sinuous casts packed with dirt that you see scattered over the grasslands and meadows of this and other segments of The Colorado Trail are evidence of pocket gophers at work.

This small, thickset, and mostly nocturnal animal is a regular biological excavation service, with burrow systems that may be more than 500 feet long, requiring the removal of nearly three tons of soil. Excess soil is thrown out in characteristic loose mounds. But it is the conspicuous winter casts that attract the attention of curious hikers. These are actually tunnels made during the winter through the snow and along the surface of the ground and packed with dirt brought up from below. Sometimes the endless burrowing activities of pocket gophers can undermine an area to such an extent that a passing hiker can be surprised when the ground suddenly gives way under foot.

In Colorado, pocket gophers are found well up into the meager soils of the alpine zone and are a major factor in the soil-building process in mountain areas.

Pocket gopher at work.
PHOTO COURTESY OF JIM HERD

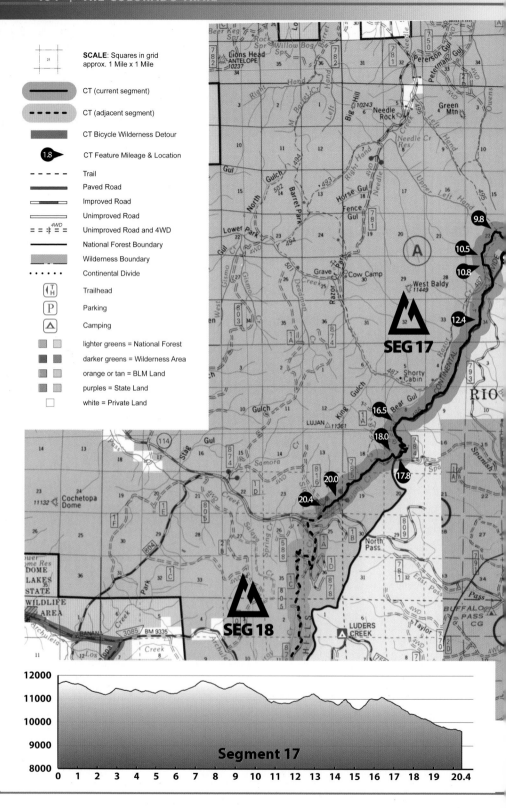

SCALE: Squares in grid approx. 1 Mile x 1 Mile

CT (current segment)

CT (adjacent segment)

CT Bicycle Wilderness Detour

1.8 CT Feature Mileage & Location

Trail

Paved Road

Improved Road

Unimproved Road

Unimproved Road and 4WD

National Forest Boundary

Wilderness Boundary

Continental Divide

Trailhead

Parking

Camping

lighter greens = National Forest

darker greens = Wilderness Area

orange or tan = BLM Land

purples = State Land

white = Private Land

SEG 17

SEG 18

SEGMENT 17 FEATURES TABLE Gunnison National Forest

Mileage	Features & Comments	Elevation (feet)	Mileage from Denver	Mileage to Durango	UTM-E	UTM-N (NAD83)	Zone
0.0	Begin Segment 17	11,616	283.2	202.6	379,441	4,238,979	13
2.3	Go right at intersection	11,176	285.5	200.3	376,575	4,238,035	13
2.4	Cross Long Branch Trail	11,168	285.6	200.2	376,345	4,237,950	13
6.9	Baldy Lake Trail intersection	11,517	290.1	195.7	371,858	4,241,633	13
9.2	Middle Baldy Peak Summit	11,685	292.4	193.4	368,575	4,241,881	13
9.8	Bear left at intersection	11,378	293.0	192.8	367,802	4,242,074	13
10.5	Cross Razor Creek	10,943	293.7	192.1	367,273	4,241,134	13
10.8	Go left at intersection	10,848	294.0	191.8	367,292	4,240,849	13
12.4	Go left at intersection	11,073	295.6	190.2	367,087	4,238,717	13
16.5	Bear left onto jeep road	11,019	299.7	186.1	363,625	4,234,859	13
17.8	Turn right onto road	10,343	301.0	184.8	363,682	4,233,580	13
18.0	Go left at intersection	10,333	301.2	184.6	363,421	4,233,706	13
20.0	Go right at CO Hwy 114 intersection	9,729	303.2	182.6	361,204	4,232,024	13
20.4	End Segment 17	9,606	303.6	182.2	360,700	4,231,743	13

Segment 18: CO Hwy 114 to Saguache Park Road

Vast pastureland characterizes this part of the CT.
PHOTO BY CARL BROWN

Distance: 13.8 miles

Elevation gain: Approx. 1,447 feet

Elevation loss: Approx. 1,534 feet

USFS map: Gunnison National Forest, pages 202–203

The Colorado Trail Databook 4/e: pages 42–43

The CT Map Book: pages 43–45

National Geographic Trails Illustrated map: No. 139

Jurisdiction: Gunnison Ranger District, Gunnison National Forest

Access from Denver end: 🚗

Access from Durango end: 🚗

Availability of water: ☕

Bicycling: ❌ See page 200

"Water sources on the ranch roads in this segment are few and far between, and what can be found is often besmirched by cow pies. However, spring water is available at Luders Creek Campground two miles east of the CT."

Lujan, Pine Archuleta, and Los creeks may have small flows at times, but are unreliable in dry years and later in the summer.

Gudy's TIP

ABOUT THIS SEGMENT

While previous editions of this guidebook have not spoken highly of this segment, the summer wildflowers and relatively easy walking can make it very enjoyable nonetheless. Thru-hikers who have just dropped down from the Continental Divide will appreciate the change in terrain and scenery. This is cattle country; the views are expansive and have an entirely different feel from the forested ridges above. Reliable water sources are nonexistent once you've passed Pine Creek at the beginning of the segment. The next reliable water source is Cochetopa Creek, approximately 21 miles ahead. Be prepared for this, especially when temperatures are high. Much of the terrain in this segment is directly exposed to the sun.

Hiking through the Cochetopa Hills.
PHOTO BY ANDREW SKURKA

TRAILHEAD/ACCESS POINTS

CO Hwy 114 Trailhead Access: From Saguache on US Hwy 285 in the San Luis Valley, drive west on CO Hwy 114 for approximately 30 miles to North Pass. Continue 1.1 miles down the pass to Lujan Creek Road (Saguache County Rd CC-31/FS

Rd 785) on your right. Continue down CO Hwy 114 for 0.4 mile to a wide shoulder on the south side of the highway. Overnight parking here on the highway right-of-way has generated two tips from authorities: 1) place a visible "Do Not Tow. Using The Colorado Trail" so it's evident that the car is not abandoned, and 2) if parking for an extended time, longer than 72 hours, communicate the license plate number and plan to Montrose State Patrol at (970) 249-4392. This is the beginning of Segment 18 and the end of 17.

Cochetopa Pass Road (Saguache County Rd NN-14) Trail Access: From Saguache on US Hwy 285, go west on CO Hwy 114 for approximately 21 miles and take the left branch onto Saguache County Rd NN-14. Follow NN-14 for approximately 10 miles to Luders Creek Campground, which has a continuously flowing spring in the back (north end). Continue 1.8 miles to Cochetopa Pass and another 1.2 miles to where the CT joins NN-14 from the north. From this point, the CT follows NN-14 for 0.5 mile down two switchbacks and then leaves the road, heading south on a jeep trail. This crossing point is considered the access point. There is no formal parking area here, but there's little traffic, and an old Forest Service side road at the top of the switchbacks offers room to park a few cars.

Alternate Cochetopa Pass Road (Saguache County Rd NN-14) Trail Access: From Saguache on US Hwy 285, go west on CO Hwy 114 for approximately 5 miles. Turn

In this segment, parts of the CT follow old ranching roads.
PHOTO BY CARL BROWN

left onto FS Rd 804 (BLM Rd 3089/Saguache County Rd GG-17) for approximately 5 miles until it terminates at Saguache County Rd NN-14 (Cochetopa Pass Road/BLM Rd 3083). Turn left (east) on NN-14 for 6.5 miles. The access point is where the road starts to make a steep switchback turn to the left. The CT comes down the switchbacks and crosses NN-14, proceeding south.

Saguache Park Road Trail Access: See Segment 19 on page 204.

SERVICES, SUPPLIES, AND ACCOMMODATIONS

There is no convenient resupply point for this segment.

TRAIL DESCRIPTION

Begin Segment 18 at a wide parking area on the south side of CO Hwy 114, **mile 0.0** (9,606 feet). The trailhead is poorly marked. Pass through the gate and cross to the south side of Lujan Creek at **mile 0.1** (9,553). Follow the trail to **mile 0.6** (9,533), where the trail bends to the south and follows Pine Creek. At **mile 0.9** (9,529), join a logging road. Ignore a side road at **mile 1** (9,550) and cross Pine Creek at **mile 1.7** (9,680). Go right at the fork at **mile 1.8** (9,708), heading uphill in a northwesterly direction. The CT bends back to the south at **mile 2.5** (9,930). The road turns into single-track trail at **mile 3.6** (10,000) and heads steeply uphill.

Reach a saddle at **mile 3.8** (10,259) and pass through a Forest Service gate. Turn left on FS Rd 876, an old logging road, at **mile 4** (10,198). Follow this road until coming to another gate at **mile 6.4** (9,774). Pass through a third gate at **mile 6.6** (9,750), then turn right onto the Cochetopa Pass Road at **mile 6.7** (9,744). (If you need water at this point and are willing to travel just over 3 miles—one way—for it, go east on Cochetopa Pass Road [NN-14] to Luders Creek Campground. You'll find flowing spring water that must be filtered in the back [north] end of the CG.) To continue on the CT from where it meets the road, follow the NN-14 road west and downhill on two long switchbacks until coming to FS Rd 864-28 at **mile 7.2** (9,628). Turn left here, following the trail as it heads slightly uphill. Pass through yet another gate at **mile 8** (9,769) and bend to the west. At **mile 8.3** (9,756), the CT crosses an intersection. Ignore the fork to the left.

Travel alongside Los Creek (water likely) from mile 8.6 to **mile 9** (9,628), where the jeep trail is closed off by several large boulders. Turn left up the hill. At **mile 9.2** (9,666), turn right onto the faint trail and head west until reaching **mile 9.6** (9,619), where the trail turns to the right down the hill. Turn to the left at **mile 9.7** (9,566). This area, which some trail users have found confusing, was rerouted several years ago to avoid the sensitive wetland area along the valley floor. The trail begins to descend after contouring around Peak 9841 and begins to follow a fence at **mile 10.5** (9,631).

Ignore a left fork at **mile 11.0** (9,424), pass through a gate at **mile 11.9** (9,366), and bear to the right at the intersection just beyond the gate. Turn left onto Saguache Park Road at **mile 12.2** (9,339). Cross a cattle guard at **mile 13.4** (9,500) and continue the gentle climb on the road to the intersection of FS Rd 787.2D and Saguache Park Road at **mile 13.8** (9,527). This is the end of Segment 18.

Late season thru-hiker and dog enjoy the expanse.

PHOTO BY LAWTON "DISCO" GRINTER

La Garita Wilderness Bicycle Detour

This long mandatory detour avoids the La Garita Wilderness Area. It is pleasant, however, and passes through a very remote part of Colorado, heavily timbered with aspen trees and spectacular in the fall. Part of the route was the planned itinerary of the infamous Alfred Packer, convicted for eating his snowbound companions in 1874. The detour passes the old Ute Indian Agency, which was Packer's destination.

The route begins where The Colorado Trail intersects the Saguache Park Road in Segment 18 at **mile 12.2** (9,339). Ride north on the road for 2.4 miles to an intersection with Saguache County Rd NN-14, where you turn left (west).

Continue west along NN-14 and pass an intersection with FS Rd 804 at **mile 5.7** (9,190), turning northwest. Pass another intersection before Dome Lakes at **mile 7** (9,132). Camping is allowed around the lakes. Follow the road in a more northerly direction past the lakes to **mile 10.8** (9,000) and an intersection with FS Rd 3084, also identified as Saguache County Rd KK-14. Turn left (southwest) and follow the road to **mile 16.4** (9,097). This is the old Ute Indian Agency location, now a Forest Service facility. Continue along the road to an intersection at **mile 20** (9,341). Take the right fork and continue on the Los Pinos-Cebolla Road to **mile 28.5** (10,183). Ignore the road leaving to the left and continue ahead to Los Pinos Pass at **mile 29.6** (10,510).

Head downhill to **mile 35.1** (8,918) and turn left on FS Rd 788 (8,920). Pass through a Forest Service cattle guard at **mile 40.2** (9,180). There are several campgrounds along Cebolla Creek, as the road follows the creek upstream. After a prolonged climb, arrive at an intersection with CO Hwy 149 at **mile 50** (11,360). It is near this point where Packer and his party became snowbound. There is a Forest Service campground before the intersection.

To continue on the CT, turn left onto CO Hwy 149 and pedal 4.6 miles south to Spring Creek Pass, the end of Segment 21 and the start of Segment 22.

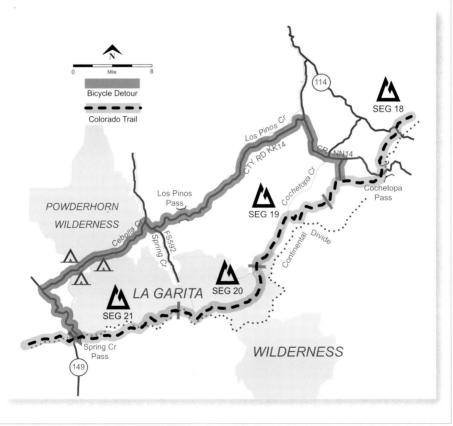

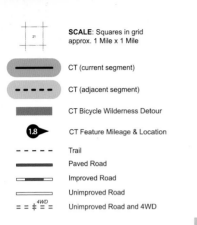

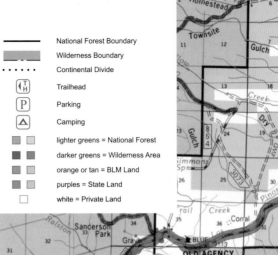

SEGMENT 18 FEATURES TABLE Gunnison National Forest

Mileage	Features & Comments	Elevation (feet)	Mileage from Denver	Mileage to Durango	UTM-E	UTM-N (NAD83)	Zone
0.0	Begin Segment 18	9,606	303.6	182.2	360,700	4,231,743	13
0.1	Cross Lujan Creek	9,553	303.7	182.1	360,600	4,231,545	13
0.6	Trail turns south	9,533	304.2	181.6	359,973	4,231,245	13
0.9	Join logging trail	9,529	304.5	181.3	360,046	4,230,889	13
1.0	Ignore side road	9,550	304.6	181.2	360,175	4,230,731	13
1.7	Cross Pine Creek	9,680	305.3	180.5	360,104	4,229,678	13
1.8	Go right at fork	9,708	305.4	180.4	360,083	4,229,501	13
3.6	Join single track	10,000	307.2	178.6	359,592	4,228,767	13
3.8	Reach saddle	10,259	307.4	178.4	359,441	4,228,335	13
4.0	Turn left	10,198	307.6	178.2	359,368	4,228,136	13
6.4	Pass through gate	9,774	310.0	175.8	358,310	4,225,269	13
6.7	Turn right	9,744	310.3	175.5	358,028	4,224,952	13
7.2	Turn left	9,628	310.8	175.0	358,003	4,224,742	13
8.0	Pass through gate	9,769	311.6	174.2	357,933	4,223,755	13
8.3	Cross intersection	9,756	311.9	173.9	357,527	4,223,661	13
9.0	Turn left & cross Los Creek	9,628	312.6	173.2	356,417	4,223,655	13
9.2	Turn right	9,666	312.8	173.0	356,464	4,223,477	13
9.6	Turn down hill	9,619	313.2	172.6	355,898	4,223,488	13
9.7	Turn left	9,566	313.3	172.5	355,763	4,223,681	13
11.0	Ignore left fork	9,425	314.6	171.2	353,785	4,223,851	13
11.9	Pass through gate	9,366	315.5	170.3	352,329	4,223,622	13
12.2	Turn left onto road	9,339	315.8	170.0	352,000	4,223,820	13
13.8	End Segment 18	9,527	317.4	168.4	351,270	4,221,765	13

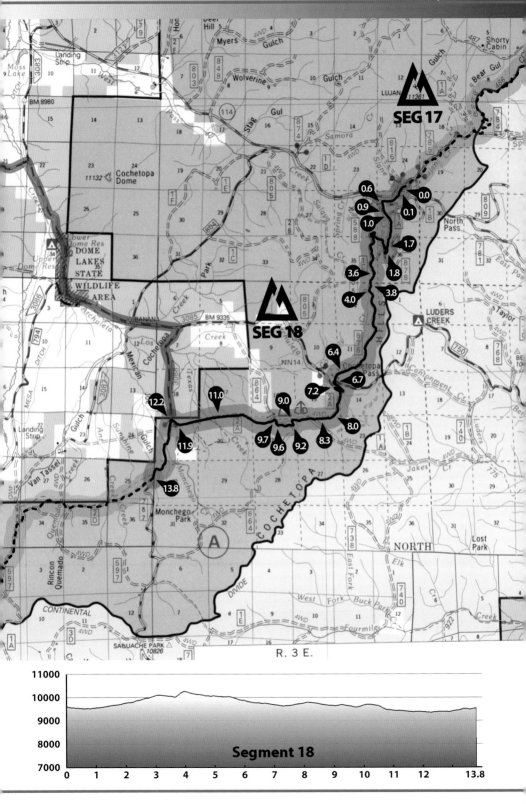

Segment 19: Saguache Park Road to Eddiesville Trailhead

Southbound on Van Tassel Gulch Road.
PHOTO BY LUCI STREMME

Distance: 13.7 miles

Elevation gain: Approx. 2,239 feet

Elevation loss: Approx. 1,442 feet

USFS map: Gunnison National Forest, pages 208–209

The Colorado Trail Databook 4/e: pages 44–45

The CT Map Book: pages 45–47

National Geographic Trails Illustrated map: No. 139

Jurisdiction: Gunnison Ranger District, Gunnison National Forest

Access from Denver end:

Access from Durango end:

Availability of water:

Bicycling: See page 200

"The La Garita Wilderness is so remote that few travel here and you are unlikely to meet other hikers. The loneliness is offset, however, by the complete solitude you find."

If you seek solitude, this is one of the least-traveled segments of the CT. The trailheads are remote and can be difficult to reach in wet weather. Don't expect your cell phone to work out here.

Gudy's TIP

ABOUT THIS SEGMENT

This segment rolls through cattle country, passing fields of summer wildflowers including paintbrush, larkspur, and various types of sunflowers. When the blooms are at peak, flatter areas around the trail appear like carpets of flowers. The segment is very dry until reaching Cochetopa Creek, where there's a log bridge over the creek that was built by volunteers. You'll find grassy meadows along the east side of the creek. The trail continues in a southwesterly direction, crossing into the La Garita Wilderness Area and one of the most remote parts of the CT before reaching the end of the segment at the Eddiesville Trailhead.

Trekkers cross Cochetopa Creek.
PHOTO BY PETE TURNER

> Many hikers have reported overlooking the intersection of the Saguache Park Road with FS Rd 787.2D. Pay close attention.

TRAILHEAD/ACCESS POINTS

Saguache Park Road Trail Access: From Saguache on US Hwy 285, go west on CO Hwy 114 for approximately 35 miles. Turn left onto FS Rd 804 (BLM Rd 3089/Saguache County Rd GG-17) for approximately 5 miles until it terminates at Saguache County Rd NN-14 (Cochetopa Park Road/BLM Rd 3083). Turn left (east) on NN-14 for 1 mile, then turn right (south) on BLM Rd 3088 (FS Rd 787) for 3.5 miles. Note the jeep road (FS Rd 787.2D) branching off to the right (southwest). This intersection is the end of Segment 18 and the beginning of Segment 19. There is no parking area at this trail access.

Eddiesville Trailhead: See Segment 20 on page 210.

SERVICES, SUPPLIES, AND ACCOMMODATIONS

There is no convenient resupply point for this segment.

TRAIL DESCRIPTION

Segment 19 begins where FS Rd 787.2D intersects Saguache Park Road from the southwest, **mile 0.0** (9,527 feet). There is no trailhead marker here. Follow FS Rd 787.2D

Old log fence.
PHOTO BY LUCI STREMME

Beaver dam on Cochetopa Creek.
PHOTO BY LUCI STREMME

Van Tassel Gulch Road.
PHOTO BY LUCI STREMME

and go left at the fork at **mile 0.1** (9,527). The trail heads in a southwesterly direction and gradually bends to the west. Pass through a gate at **mile 1.2** (9,728) and continue straight at **mile 1.5** (9,781), where a road joins the CT on the left. Turn right at **mile 2.2** (9,773) and head toward the fenced area ahead. Turn left at **mile 2.4** (9,703), cross a small wetland area that is protected by a fence, and continue on the four-wheel-drive road until passing through a Forest Service gate at **mile 3.2** (9,946). There is a fenced-in spring at mile 3.6 next to the trail where you replenish water without crossing the barbed wire.

The road ends at a T intersection at **mile 3.8** (9,835). Turn left and head uphill on the Van Tassel Gulch Road. Reach a saddle at **mile 5.4** (10,404) and bear to the right. Pass through another Forest Service gate at **mile 5.6** (10,280) and descend to **mile 6.6** (9,888), where the CT turns left at an intersection. Turn to the left again at **mile 6.8** (9,815), passing a muddy stock pond and continuing in a southwesterly direction on the road closest to the water. The trail descends a steep hill, leaves the road to the left, and becomes single track at **mile 7** (9,719). Cochetopa Creek is a reliable water source just to the west of the trail. During the next 2.5 miles, the trail gradually climbs above the creek and then descends back to it. There are a few good campsites in this area and the trail is well marked by posts with confidence markers.

Cross Cochetopa Creek on a good two-log bridge at **mile 9.7** (9,894), then climb steeply up the west bank of the creek to **mile 9.8** (9,977). Turn left here and head to the southwest. Cross Nutras Creek, pass a few good potential campsites, and enter the La Garita Wilderness Area at **mile 10.9** (10,047). Leave the wilderness at **mile 13.7** (10,310) and proceed through a camping area to the end of the segment at the Eddiesville Trailhead.

Trekking with Llamas

Llamas have been used for centuries in South America as pack animals, as well as for their fiber and meat. Increasingly on long-distance trails, such as the CT, hikers are enjoying the advantages of these unique personal porters.

Llamas may be used for short hikes or may be fully loaded for traveling through the mountains on multiday outings. An adult animal (3 years or more) can carry about 20 percent of its body weight in rough terrain, or about 70 pounds. Llamas have two-toed padded feet, which do much less damage to the terrain because they do not tear up the ground the way hooves do. Llamas are browsers, not grazers, which limits overgrazing of delicate backcountry meadows.

Highly social animals, llamas travel well in a string and are easy to train. Most importantly, they are calm and trusting with people. The common stigma, that llamas spit, is true in the sense that they use that to gain advantage in their social structure. Just don't get stuck between two angry llamas.

With their panniers fully loaded, llamas can be expected to go 5 to 9 miles per day in the mountains. Smaller and far more maneuverable than other pack animals, their pace is perfectly suited for comfortable hiking. Being herd animals, llamas like to travel with companions and become anxious when separated from them. A good pack llama will follow its human leader willingly (nearly) anywhere, including areas where it might get hurt; so, the animal's welfare should be your primary concern at all times.

Several Colorado outfitters offer trekking services on the CT using llamas. As the price of pack stock continues to drop dramatically, they also are coming into use by individuals as well as by the Forest Service. Check with land management agencies in the segments you wish to travel about any restrictions regarding pack animals. The Colorado Trail Foundation's website (ColoradoTrail.org) also has a lot of good information about using llamas for pack stock.

Using llamas to haul camping gear is a great way to go!
PHOTO COURTESY OF THE COLORADO TRAIL FOUNDATION

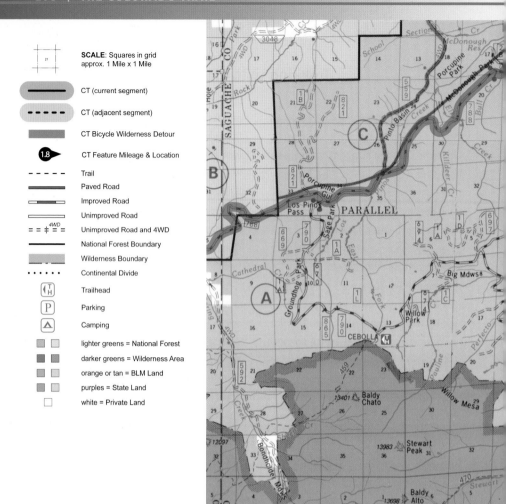

SCALE: Squares in grid approx. 1 Mile x 1 Mile

CT (current segment)

CT (adjacent segment)

CT Bicycle Wilderness Detour

1.8 CT Feature Mileage & Location

Trail

Paved Road

Improved Road

Unimproved Road

Unimproved Road and 4WD

National Forest Boundary

Wilderness Boundary

Continental Divide

Trailhead

Parking

Camping

lighter greens = National Forest

darker greens = Wilderness Area

orange or tan = BLM Land

purples = State Land

white = Private Land

SEGMENT 19 FEATURES TABLE   Gunnison National Forest

Mileage	Features & Comments	Elevation (feet)	Mileage from Denver	Mileage to Durango	UTM-E	UTM-N (NAD83)	Zone
0.0	Begin Segment 19	9,527	317.4	168.4	351,270	4,221,765	13
0.1	Go left at fork	9,527	317.5	168.3	351,057	4,221,625	13
2.2	Turn right at intersection	9,773	319.6	166.2	348,138	4,220,768	13
2.4	Turn left at intersection	9,703	319.8	166.0	347,924	4,221,028	13
3.2	Pass through gate	9,949	320.6	165.2	346,842	4,220,837	13
3.8	Turn left at intersection	9,835	321.2	164.6	346,235	4,220,294	13
5.4	Reach saddle	10,404	322.8	163.0	345,517	4,218,032	13
5.6	Pass through gate	10,280	323.0	162.8	345,139	4,217,871	13
6.8	Pass by stock pond	9,815	324.2	161.6	344,260	4,218,844	13
7.0	Turn left at intersection	9,719	324.4	161.4	344,115	4,218,569	13
9.7	Cross Cochetopa Creek	9,894	327.1	158.7	342,274	4,214,912	13
9.8	Turn left	9,977	327.2	158.6	342,142	4,214,923	13
10.9	Enter La Garita Wilderness Area	10,047	328.3	157.5	341,325	4,213,583	13
13.7	End Segment 19	10,310	331.1	154.7	339,005	4,210,354	13

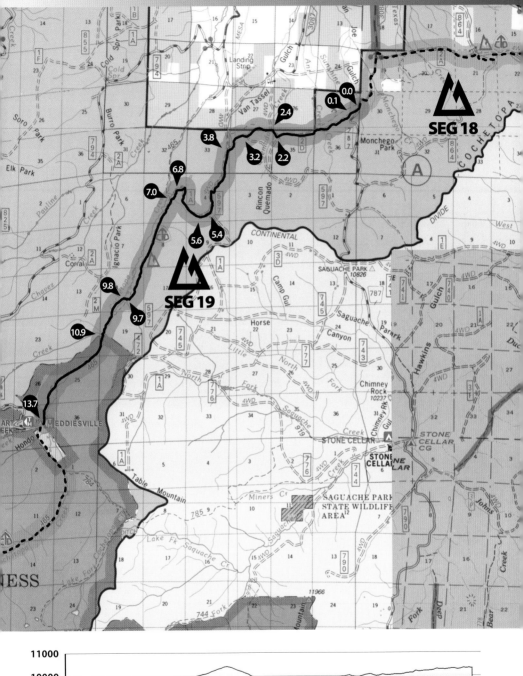

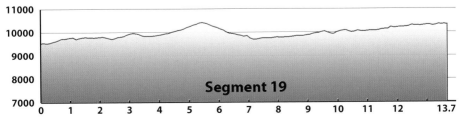

Segment 19

Segment 20: Eddiesville Trailhead to San Luis Pass

Hoodoos carved from layers of volcanic ash, remnants of volcanic activity 27 million years ago.

PHOTO BY ELLIOT FORSYTH

Distance: 12.7 miles

Elevation gain: Approx. 3,104 feet

Elevation loss: Approx. 1,478 feet

USFS maps: Gunnison and Rio Grande National Forests, pages 214–215

The Colorado Trail Databook 4/e: pages 46–47

The CT Map Book: pages 47–49

National Geographic Trails Illustrated map: No. 139

Jurisdiction: Gunnison Ranger District, Gunnison National Forest

Access from Denver end:

Access from Durango end:

Availability of water:

Bicycling: ⊗ See page 200

"It is a temptation to climb 14,014-foot San Luis Peak, but the high incidence of lightning storms in that area can make it a dicey proposition. Be sure to check the cloud patterns and weather before ascending."

It's best to depart for the pass quite early. Drop the bulk of your gear on the pass for the jaunt to the top, then resume your trek before afternoon thundershowers move in.

Gudy's TIP

ABOUT THIS SEGMENT

Segment 20 immediately re-enters the La Garita Wilderness Area, detouring around some private property. The trail slowly bends westward as it climbs up the Cochetopa Creek watershed, eventually reaching the saddle with San Luis Peak to the north. It is a relatively short side trip to the top of the peak (14,014), consisting of a 1,400-foot climb in 1.25 miles. San Luis Peak and the surrounding ridges are made up of volcanic tuff (consolidated volcanic ash). The ash was

A hiker takes a break along the saddle beneath San Luis Peak.
PHOTO BY PETE TURNER

erupted about 27 million years ago from a huge volcanic depression known as the Nelson Mountain caldera. Much of the ash from the eruption spread out to form tuff layers that cap the surrounding ridges, but much of it fell back to fill the caldera and form the tuff that now forms San Luis Peak and its neighbors. It is only one of more than a dozen similar calderas in the San Juan volcanic field. There are great views of the surrounding region from the top of San Luis Peak.

From the saddle, the CT descends and ascends two more saddles before reaching the end of the segment at San Luis Pass. The trail is relatively steep throughout, but the views and summer wildflowers are terrific. After leaving tree line just above Cochetopa Creek, the trail crosses tundra until reaching the end of the segment.

TRAILHEAD/ACCESS POINTS

Eddiesville Trailhead Access: From Saguache on US Hwy 285, go west on CO Hwy 114 for approximately 35 miles. Turn left onto FS Rd 804 (BLM Rd 3089/Saguache County Rd GG-17) for approximately 5 miles, until it terminates at Saguache County Rd NN-14 (Cochetopa Pass Rd/BLM-3083). Turn right (west) and follow NN-14 for 1.5 miles to Upper Dome Reservoir. Turn left (west) onto Saguache County Rd GG-15 (BLM Rd 3086/FS Rd 974). Follow it around the west side of the reservoir, where it curves and heads south. Proceed south for 3 miles to an intersection with Saguache County Rd DD-14 (FS Rd 794). This road may also be labeled as Stewart Creek. Follow it for about 21 miles to the Eddiesville Trailhead. This road can be very challenging when wet.

Climbing out of Cochetopa Creek toward the saddle beneath San Luis Peak.
PHOTO BY LEN GLASSNER

San Luis Pass Trail Access: 🚙 See Segment 21 on page 216.

SERVICES, SUPPLIES, AND ACCOMMODATIONS

These amenities are available in Creede; see Segment 21 on pages 216–223.

TRAIL DESCRIPTION

Segment 20 begins at the well-marked trailhead in Eddiesville, **mile 0.0** (10,310 feet), an old ranch inholding that is essentially a private island within the La Garita Wilderness Area. The trailhead is near the junction of Stewart and Cochetopa creeks. There are many good campsites in the area. From the trailhead sign, walk south along the dirt road (FS Rd 794) for a few hundred feet and then turn left onto a dirt road. Cross Stewart Creek on a bridge and turn right onto a single-track trail at **mile 0.2** (10,358). Enter the La Garita Wilderness Area shortly afterward and pass through a Forest Service gate at **mile 0.3** (10,412), where the trail turns sharply to the west and begins heading southeast along the edge of the private landholdings. There are small streams at **mile 0.4** (10,417) and **mile 0.7** (10,351). The trail is marked by wooden posts in the area and is easy to follow.

Pass through a gate at **mile 1.3** (10,348) and by another wilderness boundary sign. Intersect the Machin Basin Trail, which comes in from the east side of the valley at **mile 1.6** (10,362). The trail heads south, then bends to the southwest before passing through another Forest Service gate at **mile 3.7** (10,642). There are many small stream crossings between mile 3.7 and mile 7.6. Follow along the north side of Cochetopa Creek as the trail climbs and heads to the west, crossing the Stewart Creek Trail at **mile 7.5** (11,749). There are several good campsites in the area. Cross Cochetopa Creek at **mile 7.6** (11,755) and climb to the saddle with San Luis Peak at **mile 8.8** (12,612). From here, many people climb to the top of 14,014-foot San Luis Peak to the north. There is excellent camping in the alpine meadows below the saddle.

Descend steeply from the saddle, then climb to another saddle just off the Continental Divide at **mile 10.1** (12,366). Cross the Spring Creek Trail at **mile 10.5** (12,146) and continue heading in a generally westward direction. Cross a stream at **mile 10.9** (12,029), ascend to another saddle on the Divide, and head downhill to San Luis Pass at **mile 12.7** (11,944). There is an old sign marking the pass. This is the end of Segment 20.

Climbing San Luis Peak

The Colorado Trail's closest encounter with a fourteener comes when it passes gentle-giant San Luis Peak (14,014 feet) at mile 8.8 of Segment 20.

Despite the popularity of fourteener bagging, if you elect to climb San Luis Peak while passing by on your trek, you may be lucky enough to have it all to yourself. According to the Colorado Mountain Club, San Luis Peak is one of the least climbed of the fourteeners. The ascent is not a difficult one, with its Class 1 rating and 1,400 feet of elevation gain in about 1.25 miles. Proceed north from the saddle, following the gentle ridge to the top. Plan on an early start, though, to avoid afternoon storms. Allow about 4 to 5 hours round trip.

A climber ascends a talus-covered slope.
PHOTO COURTESY OF COLORADO MOUNTAIN EXPEDITIONS

Camping below the saddle.
PHOTO BY AARON LOCANDER

SCALE: Squares in grid approx. 1 Mile x 1 Mile

CT (current segment)

CT (adjacent segment)

CT Bicycle Wilderness Detour

CT Feature Mileage & Location

Trail

Paved Road

Improved Road

Unimproved Road

Unimproved Road and 4WD

National Forest Boundary

Wilderness Boundary

Continental Divide

Trailhead

Parking

Camping

lighter greens = National Forest

darker greens = Wilderness Area

orange or tan = BLM Land

purples = State Land

white = Private Land

SEGMENT 20 FEATURES TABLE Gunnison National Forest

Mileage	Features & Comments	Elevation (feet)	Mileage from Denver	Mileage to Durango	UTM-E	UTM-N (NAD83)	Zone
0.0	Begin Segment 20	10,310	331.1	154.7	339,005	4,210,354	13
1.3	Pass through gate	10,348	332.4	153.4	339,553	4,208,767	13
1.6	Cross Machin Basin Trail	10,362	332.7	153.1	339,756	4,208,363	13
3.7	Pass through gate	10,642	334.8	151.0	337,996	4,205,956	13
7.5	Cross Stewart Creek Trail	11,749	338.6	147.2	332,659	4,204,819	13
8.8	Gain saddle	12,612	339.9	145.9	330,987	4,204,410	13
10.1	Gain saddle	12,366	341.2	144.6	329,719	4,203,859	13
10.5	Cross Spring Creek Trail	12,146	341.6	144.2	329,568	4,203,352	13
12.7	End Segment 20	11,944	343.8	142.0	326,771	4,204,498	13

San Luis Pass to Junction Creek Trailhead (Segments 21–28)
Segment 21: **San Luis Pass to Spring Creek Pass**

CT on Snow Mesa with 1500 sheep and a cowboy.
PHOTO BY JEFF SELLENRICK

Distance: 14.8 miles

Elevation gain: Approx. 3,116 feet

Elevation loss: Approx. 4,157 feet

USFS maps: Gunnison and Rio Grande National Forests, pages 222–223

The Colorado Trail Databook 4/e: pages 48–49

The CT Map Book: pages 49–51

National Geographic Trails Illustrated maps: Nos. 139, 141

Latitude 40° map: Southwest Colorado Trails

Jurisdiction: Gunnison and Divide Ranger Districts, Gunnison and Rio Grande National Forests

Access from Denver end:

Access from Durango end:

Availability of water:

Bicycling: See page 200

"Take in the views from Snow Mesa above Spring Creek. You can see the Rio Grande Pyramid and the Uncompahgre Mountains, where Ute Indians once hunted."

Ahead is a great U-shaped bend of the Continental Divide that holds the headwaters of the mighty Rio Grande River.

Gudy's TIP

ABOUT THIS SEGMENT

Sheep herder on Snow Mesa.
PHOTO BY DON WALLACE

This segment is quite the roller coaster. The Colorado Trail climbs in and out of the East, Middle, and West Mineral Creek drainages and traverses the Continental Divide to a maximum elevation of 12,785 feet. The views of the surrounding mountains are equally spectacular from the ridges and saddles as they are from the headwaters of the creeks below. There are many great potential campsites in the forests as the trail rolls in and out of the trees.

Segment 21 is well marked throughout and ends after crossing Snow Mesa. There is no shelter on Snow Mesa, so be cautious about crossing this 3.3-mile stretch if thunderstorms threaten. Even though the mesa looks relatively flat on the map, it does dip into several small creek drainages, oftentimes quite steeply. This is one of the most

A lamb checks out passing hikers.
PHOTO BY DON WALLACE

remote segments of The Colorado Trail and Snow Mesa can feel completely cut off from civilization. This can be a good thing on clear, windless days, but a scary prospect if there are lightning bolts flashing around you. The last 2 miles of the segment descend more than 1,200 feet to Spring Creek Pass and CO Hwy 149.

TRAILHEAD/ACCESS POINTS

San Luis Pass Trail Access: From the north end of Creede, proceed north into a steep and narrow canyon on FS Rd 503. The San Luis Pass access point is 9.5 miles up this canyon. Non-four-wheel-drive vehicles can drive 6.5 miles to the closed Equity Mine and a small parking area. From here it's a 3-mile hike to the pass. Four-wheel-drive vehicles can continue an additional 1.5 miles. No formal parking is available here. From this point, it's a 1.5-mile hike to San Luis Pass and the CT on a trail that prohibits motorized vehicles.

Spring Creek Pass Trailhead: See Segment 22 on page 224.

SERVICES, SUPPLIES, AND ACCOMMODATIONS

It is about a 10-mile side trip into **Creede** from San Luis Pass. Descend on a side trail south along the headwaters of West Willow Creek until you meet up with FS Rd 503. Continue on it into town. About two miles down this road is a wide area at the Equity Mine. This area is often used by people climbing nearby San Luis Peak, hunters during hunting season, and people on a self-guided mine tour. On a busy weekend, a backpacker may find an easy hitch into town. Note that Creede can also be reached, if with difficulty due to the 33-mile distance and low traffic, from the Spring Creek Pass Trailhead that is described at the start of Segment 22 (page 224). Creede is an old mining town with various watering holes that recall the town's rip-roaring past.

Distance from CT: 10 miles
Elevation: 8,852 feet
Zip code: 81130
Area code: 719

Creede Services

Dining
Several locations in town

Gear (including fuel canisters)
San Juan Sports
102 S. Main St.
(719) 658-2359

Groceries
Kentucky Bell Market
2nd and Main streets
(719) 658-2526

Info
Chamber of Commerce
904 S. Main St.
(719) 658-2374

Laundry
Creede Laundromat
101 E. 5th St.
No phone

Lodging
Several locations in town

Medical
Mineral City Public Health/Creede Family Practice
802 Rio Grande Ave.
(719) 658-2416
(719) 658-0929

Post Office
Creede Post Office
10 S. Main St.
(719) 658-2615

Showers
Snowshoe Motel
202 E. 8th St.
(719) 658-2315

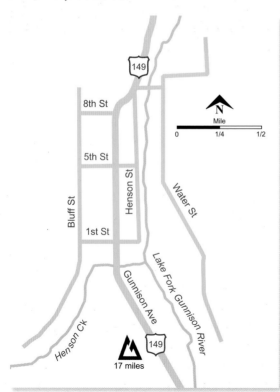

Trail users are treated to astounding views of fourteeners in the distance.
PHOTO BY ANDREW SKURKA

TRAIL DESCRIPTION

This segment begins at San Luis Pass, an obscure trailhead that also provides access to the town of Creede. Thru-hikers planning a stopover in Creede may want to consider continuing to Spring Creek Pass on CO Hwy 149, where rides are easier to obtain.

From the trail sign at **mile 0.0** (11,944 feet), head west briefly, then follow the trail as it bends to the south. Turn to the west again and pass a marker on a wooden post before climbing steeply to a saddle just north of Peak 13111 at **mile 1.3** (12,887). The trail then descends to the headwaters of East Mineral Creek at **mile 2.** Pass the East Mineral Creek Trail at **mile 2.6** (11,799) and ascend to another saddle along the ridge that divides the East and Middle Mineral Creek drainages at **mile 3.3** (12,173).

From the saddle, head downhill and cross Middle Mineral Creek at **mile 4** (11,617). The CT passes the Middle Mineral Creek Trail at **mile 4.3** (11,463), continuing to the northwest. There are potential campsites in this area. After a series of switchbacks, climb over the ridge that separates the Middle and West Mineral Creek drainages at **mile 4.8** (11,852). There is a dry campsite on the ridge. Descend again and cross a small stream at mile 5.2 (11,977), where a small camp is possible below the trail. This is the last sheltered campsite along this segment until reaching the Spring Creek Trailhead.

Climb to yet another saddle at **mile 5.8** (12,239) and pass by the West Mineral Creek Trail at **mile 6.2** (12,323). The CT continues to the west. The trail climbs gently as it passes to the south of Peak 12813 and reaches the high point of the segment at **mile 7.6** (12,785). Snow Mesa is visible to the southwest from here.

There is a well-marked intersection at **mile 8.3** (12,558). The CT stays to the left (south) here and descends toward a pond on Snow Mesa at **mile 9.5** (12,319). Head west across Snow Mesa, climbing in and out of several small drainages and passing six small streams before reaching the edge of the mesa at **mile 12.8** (12,260). There are potential campsites on top of Snow Mesa, but no shelter of any kind. After dropping off Snow Mesa, head downhill and reach tree line at **mile 13.2** (11,880). Continue west. The segment ends at **mile 14.8** (10,908), when the CT reaches Spring Creek Pass on CO Hwy 149. *The CT Map Book* shows a campground on the west side of CO Hwy 149, but this area is now marked as day-use only.

! The trail section is largely above tree line. Hikers should consider weather as a major factor when choosing campsites and determining hiking schedules. Snow Mesa can be a very unsettling experience during an electrical storm.

Wildflowers blanket a slope above Miners Creek.
PHOTO BY AARON LOCANDER

Viewing Ptarmigan

The white-tailed ptarmigan is a small alpine grouse that inhabits open tundra in summer, resorting to willows and other sheltered areas in winter. It is the only bird species in Colorado to spend the entire year above tree line. The extensive alpine terrain along the old Skyline Trail is perfect habitat for this hardy ground bird.

The ptarmigan's near-perfect seasonal camouflage helps it escape detection from predators (and even sharp-eyed trail users). Its mottled-brown summer plumage makes it almost invisible amid the scattered rocks and alpine plants. In winter, only the bird's black eyes and bill stand out against its pure white coloration.

Ptarmigan are weak flyers and are as likely to scurry away when disturbed as to burst into a short, low sail over the tundra. Despite that, they still manage to travel surprising distances in early winter to congregate in areas that harbor their favorite winter sustenance: dormant willow buds. In summer they add insects, seeds, and berries to their diet.

Nesting occurs in June with four to eight buff, spotted eggs laid in a lined depression in open ground. During breeding, males are sometimes aggressive toward interlopers passing through their territory, flying around erratically and making hooting noises, or approaching to peck comically at the boot of a resting hiker.

A recent study by ecologist James Larison of Cornell University raised a warning flag about the future of these fascinating birds. In areas of Colorado where metals from mining operations have leached into the soil, ptarmigan have accumulated high levels of cadmium in their bodies. Ultimately, this causes calcium loss and the birds can suffer broken bones in their brittle wings and legs.

Ptarmigan can be tricky to spot.
PHOTO BY TERRY ROOT

Photographers can sometimes get close.
PHOTO BY JULIE VIDA AND MARK TABB

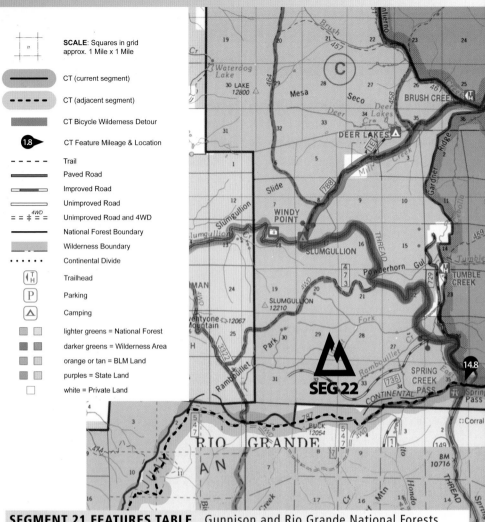

SCALE: Squares in grid approx. 1 Mile x 1 Mile

CT (current segment)

CT (adjacent segment)

CT Bicycle Wilderness Detour

1.8 CT Feature Mileage & Location

Trail

Paved Road

Improved Road

Unimproved Road

Unimproved Road and 4WD

National Forest Boundary

Wilderness Boundary

Continental Divide

Trailhead

Parking

Camping

lighter greens = National Forest

darker greens = Wilderness Area

orange or tan = BLM Land

purples = State Land

white = Private Land

SEGMENT 21 FEATURES TABLE   Gunnison and Rio Grande National Forests

Mileage	Features & Comments	Elevation (feet)	Mileage from Denver	Mileage to Durango	UTM-E	UTM-N (NAD83)	Zone
0.0	Begin Segment 21	11,944	343.8	142.0	326,771	4,204,498	13
2.6	Pass East Mineral Creek Trail	11,799	346.4	139.4	324,070	4,203,579	13
3.3	Gain saddle	12,173	347.1	138.7	323,431	4,203,260	13
4.0	Cross Middle Mineral Creek	11,617	347.8	138.0	322,627	4,203,077	13
4.3	Pass Middle Mineral Creek Trail	11,463	348.1	137.7	322,363	4,203,494	13
4.8	Gain ridge	11,852	348.6	137.2	321,838	4,203,572	13
5.2	Cross stream	11,977	349.0	136.8	321,604	4,203,060	13
5.8	Gain saddle	12,239	349.6	136.2	321,113	4,202,654	13
6.2	Pass West Mineral Creek Trail	12,323	350.0	135.8	320,568	4,202,190	13
7.6	High point of segment	12,785	351.4	134.4	319,013	4,202,624	13
8.3	Go left at intersection	12,558	352.1	133.7	317,963	4,202,880	13
9.5	Pass by pond	12,319	353.3	132.5	317,755	4,201,168	13
12.8	Drop off Snow Mesa	12,260	356.6	129.2	312,771	4,200,710	13
14.8	End Segment 21	10,908	358.6	127.2	310,289	4,201,367	13

Segment 22: **Spring Creek Pass to Carson Saddle**

The majestic San Juan Mountains.
PHOTO BY ROGER FORMAN

Distance: 17.2 miles

Elevation gain: Approx. 3,829 feet

Elevation loss: Approx. 2,385 feet

USFS maps: Gunnison and Rio Grande National Forests, pages 228–229

The Colorado Trail Databook 4/e: pages 50–51

The CT Map Book: pages 51–53

National Geographic Trails Illustrated maps: Nos. 139, 141

Latitude 40° map: Southwest Colorado Trails

Jurisdiction: Gunnison and Divide Ranger Districts, Gunnison and Rio Grande National Forests

Access from Denver end:

Access from Durango end:

Availability of water:

Bicycling:

"Don't miss the panoramas from Antenna Summit, just after Jarosa Mesa. The view overlooking the Uncompahgre Mountains is worth the climb. From Coney Summit to Carson Saddle there is a steep descent on the trail, but much better than on the jeep road. If your boot tread is worn, you'll probably slip and slide here."

Gudy's TIP

ABOUT THIS SEGMENT

After crossing Spring Creek Pass, The Colorado Trail climbs again and crosses Jarosa Mesa. The trail across the mesa is fairly nonexistent, but there are posts with CT confidence markers within view of each other that make this part of the segment easy to follow. After crossing Jarosa Mesa and passing through a forested area, the trail again climbs into the tundra as it heads toward Coney Summit and the high point on The Colorado Trail (13,271). There are two prominent bumps to pass over before coming to the side trail leading to Coney Summit at mile 14.8. The views from this ridge are fantastic. The trail descends a steep hillside on a series of long switchbacks to Carson Saddle.

As the CT descends toward Carson Saddle it affords spectacular views of Lake San Cristobal, Red Mountain, and Redcloud and Sunshine peaks. The arched course of the Lake Fork Valley marks the edge of the Lake City caldera, which erupted about 23 million years ago. High peaks beyond it are carved in volcanic tuff that fills the caldera. Lake San Cristobal first formed when a huge landslide (the Slumgullion Slide) dammed the river about 760 years ago. Parts of the slide are still moving.

TRAILHEAD/ACCESS POINTS

Spring Creek Pass Trailhead: This trailhead is located where CO Hwy 149 tops the Continental Divide at Spring Creek Pass. The pass is approximately 17 miles southeast of Lake City and 33 miles northwest of Creede. There is a Forest Service picnic area here with tables and fire rings, a toilet and an informative kiosk, as well as parking for another half-dozen or so cars. It is not unusual to see a camper or two in the picnic area. Water is usually available during the summer in a small irrigation ditch on the east side of the highway.

Above the clouds.
PHOTO BY PETE KARTSOUNES

Carson Saddle/Wager Gulch Road Trail Access: See Segment 23 on page 230.

SERVICES, SUPPLIES, AND ACCOMMODATIONS

It is approximately 17 miles north and west from Spring Creek Pass to the old mining town of **Lake City** on CO Hwy 149. That's probably too far for most backpackers to travel for resupply; nor is hitchhiking especially good on this remote byway.

Distance from CT: 17 miles
Elevation: 8,671 feet
Zip code: 81235
Area code: 970

Info
Chamber of Commerce
3rd and Silver streets
(970) 944-2527

Laundry
The Lost Sock
808 N. Gunnison Ave.
(970) 944-5009

Lodging (several)
Backcountry Basecamp
720 Gunnison Ave.
(970) 944-0181

Medical
Lake City Medical Center
700 Henson St.
(970) 944-2331

Post Office
Lake City Post Office
803 Gunnison Ave.
(970) 944-2560

Showers
Elkhorn RV Resort
713 N. Bluff St.
(970) 944-2920

Lake City Services

Dining
Several locations in town

Gear (including fuel canisters and shuttle)
The Sportsman
238 S. Gunnison Ave.
(970) 944-2526

Groceries
The Country Store
916 Hwy 149 North
(970) 944-2387

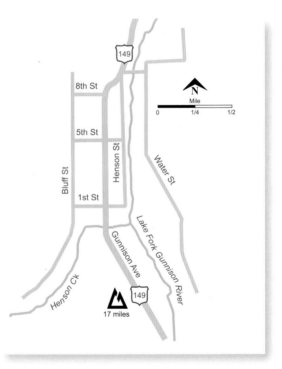

TRAIL DESCRIPTION

Segment 22 begins atop Spring Creek Pass on the Continental Divide, where there is a trailhead parking area, **mile 0.0** (10,908 feet). *The CT Map Book* and past editions of the

Guidebook have noted that this is a campground, but currently it is day-use only. Leave the parking area on a Forest Service jeep trail (FS Rd 547). CT confidence markers help guide the way. Immediately head uphill and to the west. Cross a creek at **mile 2.5** (11,327). There are potential campsites in the area. Bear right off the jeep road at **mile 2.6** (11,297) onto the old La Garita Stock Driveway. This pathway is marked with rock cairns that support tall posts with CT confidence markers. The trail is very

Backpackers refill their bottles at a high mountain lake.
PHOTO BY ROGER FORMAN

faint or nonexistent in places, but the rock cairns and posts are easy to follow. Use these trail markers as your guide for the next 3 miles.

At **mile 4.5** (12,027), reach the high point on Jarosa Mesa. Continue west, reaching a well-marked three-way junction at **mile 5.6** (11,735). Stay left (west) here. Head uphill, passing south of a mountain with a large antenna array on its summit. Reach a saddle at **mile 7** (12,074) and follow the CT along a jeep road as it bends to the southwest. Take the right fork onto a single-track trail at an intersection at **mile 7.9** (12,018) and continue to **mile 8.7** (11,713), where the CT crosses a jeep trail in a grassy valley. Follow the trail across a marshy area. In wet years, there may be water just above the trail in this meadow.

Proceed to the right on a jeep trail through the willows at **mile 9.2** (11,924), then bear left and exit the willows to the west at **mile 9.5** (12,040). Climb a series of short switchbacks and follow the CT to the southwest. Leave the trees and follow the Continental Divide, crossing the first high point after several steep switchbacks and another high point along the Divide at **mile 13.8** (13,055). There are ponds about a half-mile downhill to the south from here if a water source is needed. Top a saddle at **mile 14.4** (12,880) and head in a southerly direction until reaching **mile 14.8** (13,063), where a trail leaves the CT to the right to Coney Summit.

The Colorado Trail reaches its highest point at **mile 15.6** (13,271), then turns to the west and crosses a jeep road twice in the next few hundred feet. The trail runs parallel to the jeep road, then joins the steep jeep road heading downhill. At the bottom of the hill, turn right on an intersecting jeep road at **mile 17.1** (12,297). Head uphill on the road to a small parking area at the intersection of three jeep trails at **mile 17.2** (12,366). This is Carson Saddle and the end of Segment 22.

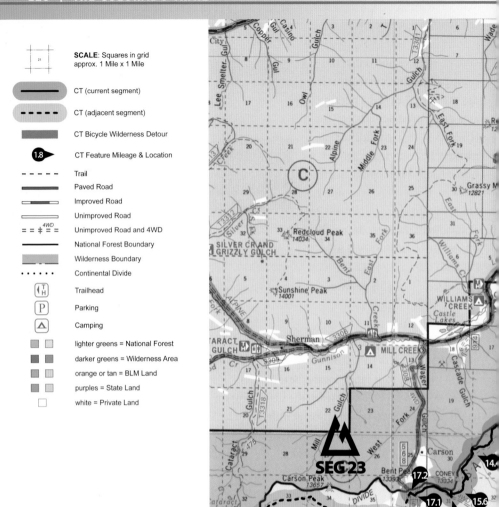

Map Legend

SCALE: Squares in grid approx. 1 Mile x 1 Mile

	CT (current segment)
	CT (adjacent segment)
	CT Bicycle Wilderness Detour
1.8	CT Feature Mileage & Location
	Trail
	Paved Road
	Improved Road
	Unimproved Road
4WD	Unimproved Road and 4WD
	National Forest Boundary
	Wilderness Boundary
	Continental Divide
TH	Trailhead
P	Parking
A	Camping
	lighter greens = National Forest
	darker greens = Wilderness Area
	orange or tan = BLM Land
	purples = State Land
	white = Private Land

SEGMENT 22 FEATURES TABLE   Gunnison and Rio Grande National Forests

Mileage	Features & Comments	Elevation (feet)	Mileage from Denver	Mileage to Durango	UTM-E	UTM-N (NAD83)	Zone
0.0	Begin Segment 22	10,908	358.6	127.2	310,289	4,201,367	13
2.6	Bear right off jeep road	11,297	361.2	124.6	306,839	4,200,325	13
4.5	Reach high point	12,027	363.1	122.7	303,954	4,200,150	13
5.6	Go left at intersection	11,735	364.2	121.6	302,268	4,200,258	13
7.9	Go right at intersection	12,018	366.5	119.3	299,464	4,199,593	13
9.2	Proceed right	11,924	367.8	118.0	299,194	4,197,912	13
9.5	Stay to left	12,040	368.1	117.7	298,901	4,197,793	13
14.4	Reach another saddle	12,880	373.0	112.8	294,095	4,193,852	13
15.6	CT highest point	13,271	374.2	111.6	293,620	4,192,498	13
16.0	Steep descent	13,153	374.6	111.2	293,263	4,192,307	13
17.1	Turn right at intersection	12,297	375.7	110.1	291,865	4,192,390	13
17.2	End Segment 22	12,366	375.8	110.0	291,701	4,192,491	13

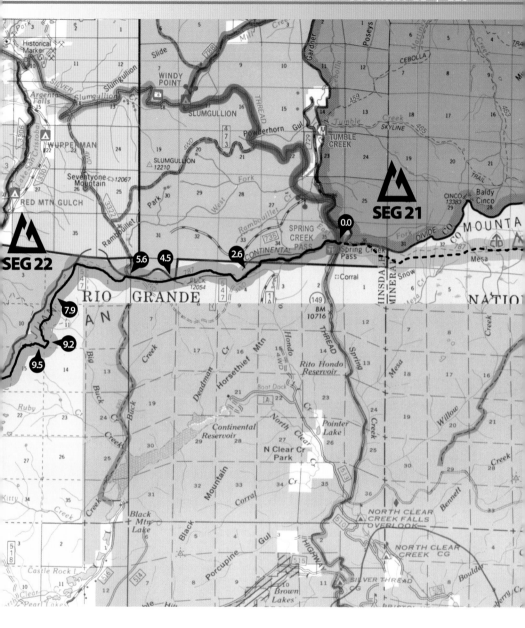

Segment 23: **Carson Saddle to Stony Pass**

Segment 23 is nearly all above 12,000 feet.

PHOTO BY JULIE VIDA AND MARK TABB

Distance: 15.9 miles

Elevation gain: Approx. 3,515 feet

Elevation loss: Approx. 3,339 feet

USFS maps: Gunnison, Rio Grande, and San Juan National Forests, pages 236–237

The Colorado Trail Databook 4/e: pages 52–53

The CT Map Book: pages 53–55

National Geographic Trails Illustrated map: No. 141

Latitude 40° map: Southwest Colorado Trails

Jurisdiction: Gunnison and Divide Ranger Districts, Gunnison and Rio Grande National Forests

Access from Denver end:

Access from Durango end:

Availability of water:

Bicycling:

"Carson Saddle draws a surprising number of people in four-wheel-drive vehicles, which can be a shock after the previous isolation of the trail."

Enjoy the spectacular above- tree-line views from the Continental Divide on this segment, but be cautious in conditions of poor visibility. A GPS receiver can be invaluable in locating the features noted in the Features Table.

Gudy's TIP

ABOUT THIS SEGMENT

The Colorado Trail leaves Carson Saddle and heads west up the Lost Trail Creek watershed, passing fields of summer wildflowers and eventually reaching an unnamed pass that is often snowy until late June. While heading down the backside of the pass, Cataract Lake eventually comes into view below and the trail reaches a clearly marked junction that is the beginning of a major rerouting of the CT. The trail originally dropped into the Pole Creek drainage on a multiuse motorized trail, but now stays closer to the Continental Divide with its spectacular views. Full-bench trail tread has not been completed in this section, but volunteers have built huge rock cairns to mark the trail, and the cairns make the route easy to follow. Mountain bikers may want to consider following the old CT route to Pole Creek to avoid difficult and sometimes unrideable sections along the new route. This is one of the most remote segments of the CT and vehicle access to Carson Saddle and Stony Pass can be quite challenging.

Sunset on Lost Trail Creek.
PHOTO BY AARON LOCANDER

TRAILHEAD/ACCESS POINTS

Carson Saddle/Wager Gulch Trail Access: ᵒ⁻ᵒ From Lake City, drive south on CO Hwy 149 about 1.5 miles to a Y in the road. The right branch leads to Lake San Cristobal. Follow this road for 9.3 miles to a turnoff on the left with a small parking area. This is the beginning of Wager Gulch Road (BLM Rd 3308/FS Rd 568). This is not a road for the squeamish. It is very steep, rocky, and narrow, with many tight switchbacks and some significant exposure. In mid-summer, expect to encounter four-wheel-drives, ATVs, and motorcycles. Follow this road for about 5 miles to Carson Saddle, a low point on the Continental Divide about a mile above the abandoned mining town of Carson. Segment 23 begins at an intersection with a jeep trail here.

Stony Pass Road: 🚜 See Segment 24 on page 238.

SERVICES, SUPPLIES, AND ACCOMMODATIONS

These amenities are available in Lake City; see Segment 22 on page 224.

TRAIL DESCRIPTION

Segment 23 begins at the jeep road intersection on Carson Saddle, **mile 0.0** (12,366 feet). Go south on the jeep trail and turn right on the single-track trail at **mile 0.5** (12,175). After a short climb, the trail bends to the west and crosses a small stream at **mile 1.2** (11,975). There is a good campsite about 50 feet below the trail. Begin a long climb up the Lost Trail Creek drainage, crossing a seasonal stream at **mile 1.7** (11,975) and a larger

A small pond offers a good spot to camp.
PHOTO BY ROGER FORMAN

Bighorn sheep look down from a ridgeline.
PHOTO BY PETE TURNER

stream at **mile 2.4** (12,220). Reach a small, unnamed pass at **mile 3.7** (12,919) and drop into the Pole Creek drainage to the west.

The Colorado Trail turns to the right at a well-marked intersection at **mile 5** (12,389). This is the beginning of the Cataract Ridge reroute of the CT, which stays near the ridgelines and avoids the Pole Creek Trail, where motorized vehicles are allowed. Cyclists should be aware that this new route is a "hike-a-bike" section, with some unrideable sections. An alternate route for cyclists is to follow the Pole Creek Trail to the bottom, then take Stony Pass Road to Silverton.

The trail heads west from here, then descends steeply to the north where it passes a small lake with several good campsites. There are also excellent campsites at Cataract Lake, about a quarter-mile off the CT to the northeast. Follow the CT as it heads back west, passing several more potential campsites before crossing a stream. After gaining the saddle at **mile 6.8** (12,673), the trail bears to the right and continues upward, crossing a wide field where elk are commonly seen. Contour along the north side of Peak 13164 and begin to follow a long string of cairns at **mile 7.8** (12,732), where the trail bends to the southwest. The cairns are tall and easy to follow.

After reaching the edge of the ridge at **mile 8.2** (12,659), drop into the valley below at **mile 8.5** (12,356). Cross the valley bottom and head up the other side in a westerly direction. Drop into a steep gully and cross to the other side at **mile 8.9** (12,591). Bear right and continue to follow the cairns, crossing the Continental Divide at a small pass above Cuba Gulch at **mile**

Volunteer-built cairns mark the trail to Stony Pass.
PHOTO BY MICK GIGONE

9.3 (12,722). From here, the trail contours into Cuba Gulch and intersects a cross trail at **mile 9.9** (12,538). A small grassy meadow, 300 feet below, makes a good campsite. Water may be found in the headwaters of Cuba Creek, a short distance ahead.

The cairns continue to mark the trail as it climbs to another saddle at **mile 10.6** (12,909). Bear to the left at the pass. Note the distinctive Cuba Peak to the northeast. Cross the top of Minnie Gulch at **mile 11.4** (12,722) and go straight through the intersection with the Minnie Gulch Trail. Climb steeply to a high point on the ridge at **mile 11.6** (12,982) and continue to **mile 12.6** (12,541), where the CT continues straight ahead at the intersection with the Maggie Gulch Trail. The CT heads to the southwest, passing a small pond at **mile 13.5** (12,819), and then continues to a high point at **mile 13.7** (12,815). Descend to another well-marked trail intersection at **mile 13.9** (12,659) and go to the left (west). Drop down to a creek at **mile 14.2** (12,412) and bear right at an intersection at **mile 14.6** (12,315), staying high on the hillside. Contour around Canby Mountain, eventually dropping down to the Stony Pass Road at **mile 15.5** (12,367). Take a right up the road to **mile 15.9** (12,524), where the trail leaves the road to the west at a trailhead sign near the top of Stony Pass. This marks the end of Segment 23.

The Stony Pass Road

The historic Stony Pass Road was constructed in 1879 as a means to transport supplies in and ore out of the booming Silverton mining district. For a few short years, it was a busy and important route for miners and others attracted by news of new-found wealth in the San Juans. After a couple years, however, the difficult route was eclipsed by the Denver and Rio Grande Western's rail route through Animas Canyon. The road quickly fell into a sorry state and gained a reputation as a "pretty rough ride."

Robert M. Ormes, of early guidebook fame, recalls struggling up it in his car, after being assured that the first car into Silverton came in this way. Finding it a lot more than his auto could handle, he encountered a man on the road who told him, "Sure it came in this way … but, it was in some wagons."

Stony Pass Road (left) beneath Canby Mountain divides Segments 23 and 24.
PHOTO BY JEFF SELLENRICK

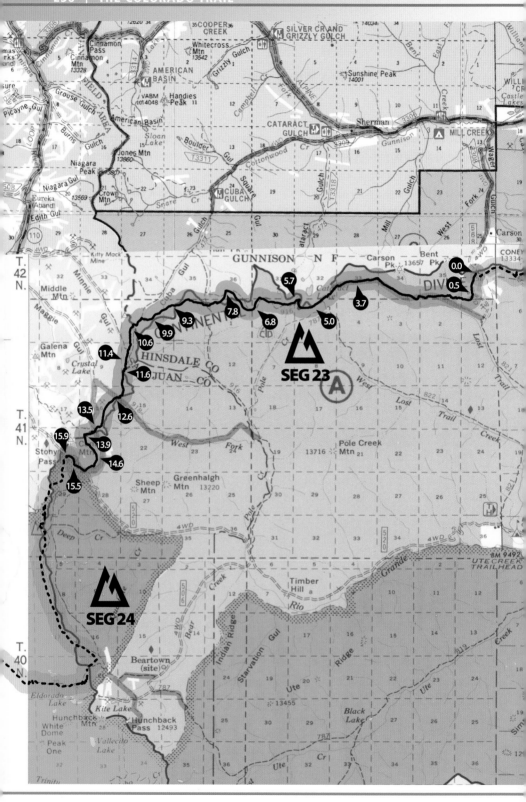

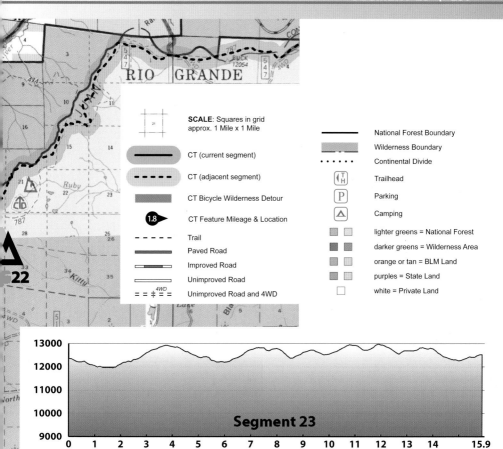

SCALE: Squares in grid approx. 1 Mile x 1 Mile

CT (current segment)

CT (adjacent segment)

1.8 ▶ CT Feature Mileage & Location

- - - - - Trail

Paved Road

Improved Road

Unimproved Road

= = ‡ = = Unimproved Road and 4WD

National Forest Boundary

Wilderness Boundary

· · · · · · Continental Divide

(TH) Trailhead

P Parking

▲ Camping

lighter greens = National Forest

darker greens = Wilderness Area

orange or tan = BLM Land

purples = State Land

white = Private Land

SEGMENT 23 FEATURES TABLE
Gunnison, Rio Grande, and San Juan National Forests

Mileage	Features & Comments	Elevation (feet)	Mileage from Denver	Mileage to Durango	UTM-E	UTM-N (NAD83)	Zone
0.0	Begin Segment 23	12,366	375.8	110.0	291,701	4,192,491	13
0.5	Go right at intersection	12,175	376.3	109.5	291,567	4,191,739	13
3.7	Gain pass	12,919	379.5	106.3	287,126	4,192,297	13
5.0	Go right at intersection	12,389	380.8	105.0	285,439	4,191,420	13
5.7	Reach unnamed lake	12,246	381.5	104.3	284,782	4,191,633	13
6.8	Gain saddle	12,673	382.6	103.2	283,195	4,191,411	13
7.8	Begin to follow cairns	12,732	383.6	102.2	282,113	4,192,071	13
9.3	Gain pass	12,722	385.1	100.7	280,050	4,191,571	13
9.9	Go straight at trail junction	12,538	385.7	100.1	279,268	4,191,105	13
10.6	Gain saddle	12,909	386.4	99.4	278,422	4,190,763	13
11.4	Go straight at junction	12,722	387.2	98.6	278,203	4,189,553	13
11.6	High point on ridge	12,982	387.4	98.4	278,100	4,189,155	13
12.6	Go straight at junction	12,541	388.4	97.4	277,777	4,188,191	13
13.5	Pass pond	12,819	389.3	96.5	277,038	4,187,096	13
13.9	Go left at intersection	12,659	389.7	96.1	276,514	4,186,805	13
14.6	Go right at intersection	12,315	390.4	95.4	276,984	4,185,969	13
15.5	Go right (uphill) at road	12,367	391.3	94.5	276,114	4,185,742	13
15.9	End Segment 23	12,524	391.7	94.1	275,826	4,186,057	13

Segment 24: **Stony Pass to Molas Pass**

Wetlands at 12,620 feet.
PHOTO BY ROGER FORMAN

Distance: 20.2 miles

Elevation gain: Approx. 3,475 feet

Elevation loss: Approx. 5,119 feet

USFS maps: Rio Grande and San Juan National Forests, pages 246–247

The Colorado Trail Databook 4/e: pages 54–55

The CT Map Book: pages 55–58

National Geographic Trails Illustrated map: No. 140

Latitude 40° map: Southwest Colorado Trails

Jurisdiction: Columbine and Divide Ranger Districts, San Juan and Rio Grande National Forests

Access from Denver end:

Access from Durango end:

Availability of water:

Bicycling: See page 244

"Once over the Divide and into the Weminuche Wilderness Area, the Elk Creek drainage and its dramatic geologic walls are topped off with views of Arrow and Vestal peaks."

This short, impressive range of peaks is known as the Grenadiers. If you have time, the short (but steep) trail that begins at the beaver ponds (mile 11.6) is an interesting side trip. See if you can spot rock climbers on the famous Wham Ridge.

Gudy's TIP

ABOUT THIS SEGMENT

Segment 24 enters the Weminuche Wilderness Area just south of Stony Pass Road and follows the trail toward Arrow and Vestal peaks, the two most prominent mountains ahead. The route is along the Continental Divide and is co-located with the CDNST. About 2 miles south of Stony Pass it passes out of the San Juan volcanic rocks and into 1.7 billion-year-old basement rocks and light- and dark-colored layered gneiss. After passing several small lakes, the trail follows a relatively flat plateau switching between double-track and single-track trail. Eventually the drop into the Elk Creek drainage will come into view, where the CT diverges from the CDNST. As it begins the descent into Elk Creek, it suddenly enters completely different rocks, quartzite interleaved with thin layers of maroon to blue-gray slate, rocks that are part of the Uncompahgre Formation. Rocks like these are found nowhere else along the CT. They are metamorphic rocks, but they have never been subjected to the high temperatures like those that produced the other meta-morphic basement rocks. They were clearly deposited as sandstone and shale after the 1.7 billion-year-old basement rocks were formed, but were lightly metamorphosed and

Alpine avens beneath the 13,627-foot White Dome.
PHOTO BY ELLIOT FORSYTH

Dramatic view from the Continental Divide before descending west into Elk Creek.
PHOTO BY JEFF SELLENRICK

squeezed into a series of tight accordionlike folds before nearby bodies of 1.4 billion-year-old granite were injected into them. The towering peaks of the Grenadier Needles that loom south of the trail are all carved from a thick north-sloping layer of the quartzite. Because the quartzite is particularly resistant to weathering, it preserves the smooth polished and striated rock outcrops shaped by the glacier that occupied this valley until about 12,000 years ago.

This is one of the most impressive sections of trail, descending a series of long switchbacks until reaching the headwaters of Elk Creek and the remnants of old mining operations below. The CT follows the creek down steeply at first, eventually reaching tree line and continuing generally westward until leaving the Weminuche Wilderness Area, crossing the train tracks for the Durango & Silverton Narrow Gauge Railroad, and passing over the Animas River on a good bridge.

As the CT climbs out of the canyon and approaches Molas Lake it passes out of quartzite and into nearly horizontal beds of early Paleozoic sandstone, shale, and limestone. From Molas Lake, access to Molas Pass, US Hwy 550, and Silverton is easy.

TRAILHEAD/ACCESS POINTS

Stony Pass Road (FS Rds 589 and 737): ☎☎ From the east end of Silverton, take the righthand branch of CO Hwy 110 toward Howardsville, which is 4 miles ahead (the lefthand branch goes to the ski area). At Howardsville, turn right on Stony Pass Road (FS Rd 589) for about 2 miles to a T intersection with FS Rd 737. Turn left on FS Rd 737, which starts a steep climb, leaving the Animas River Valley. After a little over a mile and several switch-backs, there is a Y intersection. Take the right branch. After 2 miles you'll come to Stony Pass. There is parking on the right.

US Hwy 550–Molas Pass Trailhead: 🚗 See Segment 25 on page 248.

SERVICES, SUPPLIES, AND ACCOMMODATIONS

These amenities are available in Silverton; see Segment 25 on pages 248–255.

TRAIL DESCRIPTION

Begin Segment 24 at the trail marker on the south side of Stony Pass Road, **mile 0.0** (12,524 feet). Follow the trail to the south, passing an old mine site and dropping into the valley bottom, where there is a small stream crossing. Follow the trail back to

> ❗ Don't miss the turnoff point for the CT where it drops off the Continental Divide into Elk Creek Valley. Pay close attention.

Looking south to distant Vestal Peak in the Grenadier Range.
PHOTO BY BILL BLOOMQUIST

the ridge and contour around Peak 12721. Descend to a small valley and cross the Highland Mary Lake Trail at **mile 1.8** (12,210). Climb past a small knob to the west of the trail and stay left at an intersection at **mile 2.1** (12,137). Cross a small stream at **mile 2.6** (12,322) and a small lake and side trail at **mile 3** (12,547). Stay high as the trail closely follows the Divide for the next 2.3 miles. Stay to the left at an unmarked trail intersection at **mile 3.3** (12,589).

The trail follows a faint two-track trail, with several cairns marking the way, until reaching an intersection near several small lakes at **mile 5.3** (12,522). At the intersection, head to the left and stay along the Continental Divide. At **mile 5.8** (12,456) is a signed intersection. (This is where the CT and Continental Divide National Scenic Trail go their separate ways for good, after having been co-located for 135.2 miles from Twin Lakes in Segment 11.) Turn right (uphill) at this signed intersection. Stay to the left at the intersection at **mile 6.1** (12,657) and continue south. At **mile 6.4** (12,690), the CT turns to the right and drops down a steep hillside on a series of switchbacks into the Elk Creek drainage. Pass by an old mining shed, then cross a small creek at **mile 7.4** (11,795).

Continue in a westerly direction as the canyon narrows. The trail is quite steep as it passes through a notch because of heavy spring runoff. Be mindful of your footing through this spectacular area. Cross the creek again and follow the trail as it contours

Immense rock walls line Elk Creek.
PHOTO BY PETE AND LISA TURNER

Trekkers descend the many well-built switchbacks into Elk Creek.
PHOTO BY ELLIOT FORSYTH

above the creek. After entering the trees, drop back down to the creek and cross a side trail at **mile 9** (10,720) that is used by climbers to access the saddle between Peak Two and Peak Three. There are good campsites here. Cross a side stream and then a second side stream with a trail to a hidden waterfall at **mile 9.6** (10,360). The canyon begins to widen out from here, with more campsites in the area.

Reach a pond at **mile 11.6** (9,994) with great views of Arrow and Vestal peaks. There are many good campsites on the east side of the pond. These are the last good campsites until reaching the Animas River. The trail then passes through a thick forest high above Elk Creek and descends steeply to the creek. At **mile 14.4** (9,122), the CT leaves the gorge, passing a trail register, interpretive sign, and wilderness boundary marker. Intersect a side trail at **mile 14.5** (9,117) that goes to a loading and unloading point for passengers on the Durango & Silverton Narrow Gauge Railroad.

After descending a switchback, reach the railroad tracks next to the Animas River Gorge. Follow the tracks for several hundred feet to the northwest and cross the tracks at **mile 15.1** (8,930). After passing several potential campsites, cross the Animas River on a good bridge at **mile 15.2** (8,918). Cross Molas Creek, then climb to the top of the switchbacks and bear right at an intersection with a horse trail at **mile 17.6** (10,280). Cross another horse trail at **mile 18.1** (10,246) and continue straight ahead. At **mile 18.4** (10,437), bear right at a third horse trail and go straight through the intersection with yet another horse trail at **mile 18.6** (10,504). These junctions are all clearly marked.

Take a left at the junction at **mile 18.7** (10,577) to stay on the CT. The right fork leads to Big Molas Lake. Cross Molas Creek again at **mile 19.1** (10,520) and continue to climb until reaching US Hwy 550 near the top of Molas Pass at **mile 20.2** (10,886). This is the end of Segment 24. There is a large parking area with toilets 300 feet to the south of the intersection with US Hwy 550.

Weminuche Wilderness Bicycle Detour

🚲 This detour crosses the Continental Divide at historic Stony Pass before dropping the Engineer/Cinnamon Pass Road into Silverton.

Begin at the start of Segment 24 by riding west 0.2 mile to the summit of the Stony Pass Road (12,588). Descend northwest to Howardsville and join the Cunningham Gulch Road at **mile 4** (10,071). Follow the road to an intersection with San Juan County Rd 2 (the Engineer/Cinnamon Pass Road) at **mile 6.5** (9,675). Turn left (southwest) and arrive at Silverton at **mile 10.3** (9,300). Pass through town to meet US Hwy 550 at **mile 11.1** (9,255). Silverton is the best resupply point for the ride on into Durango. Turn left onto busy US Hwy 550 and pedal up the hill to where the CT crosses the highway, just before Molas Pass at **mile 17.2** (10,520). This is the start of Segment 25.

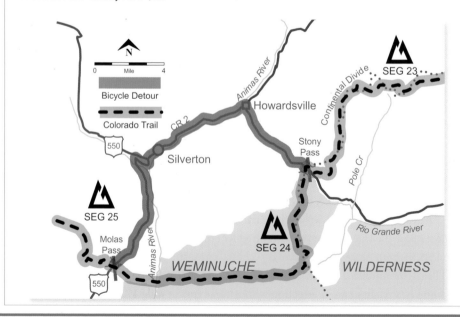

The Grenadiers

PHOTO BY JULIE MANCHESTER

Soaring faces of hard quartzite, tumbling brooks, and remote campsites characterize the beautiful Grenadier Range in the western portion of the Weminuche Wilderness Area. When the CT plunges off the Continental Divide into the Elk Creek Basin, it enters a world that is legendary with generations of Colorado mountaineers.

The Grenadiers were among the last high peaks in Colorado to be conquered; most were not climbed until the 1930s, on Colorado Mountain Club excursions and by members of the legendary San Juan Mountaineers group. They are unusual in that they are made up of quartzite, which is relatively rare in the Southern Rockies. Quartzite is a hard and resistant rock that weathers into clean, steep north faces that often require technical climbing with ropes. From the beaver ponds at mile 12.3 of Segment 24, there are excellent views of Arrow (13,803) and Vestal (13,864) peaks, the most famous of the Grenadiers and members of Colorado's Highest Hundred (or hundred highest peaks). The climbers' trail begins here, ascending steeply into the basin beneath Wham Ridge, one of the most prized climbs in the state.

The western endpoint of the short but dramatic Grenadier Range is Mount Garfield (13,074). It looms 4,000 feet over the Animas River and Durango & Silverton Narrow Gauge Railroad tracks, and is a constant companion as you labor up the switchbacks to Molas Pass.

The Durango & Silverton Narrow Gauge train approaches the Elk Creek hiker stop.

PHOTO BY ERNIE NORRIS

SCALE: Squares in grid approx. 1 Mile x 1 Mile

CT (current segment)

CT (adjacent segment)

CT Bicycle Wilderness Detour

1.8 CT Feature Mileage & Location

Trail

Paved Road

Improved Road

Unimproved Road

Unimproved Road and 4WD

National Forest Boundary

Wilderness Boundary

Continental Divide

Trailhead

Parking

Camping

lighter greens = National Forest

darker greens = Wilderness Area

orange or tan = BLM Land

purples = State Land

white = Private Land

SEG 25

SEGMENT 24 FEATURES TABLE San Juan National Forest

Mileage	Features & Comments	Elevation (feet)	Mileage from Denver	Mileage to Durango	UTM-E	UTM-N (NAD83)	Zone
0.0	Begin Segment 24	12,524	391.7	94.1	275,826	4,186,057	13
1.8	Cross Highland Mary Lake Trail	12,210	393.5	92.3	274,915	4,183,818	13
5.3	Bear left at intersection	12,522	397.0	88.8	275,888	4,179,087	13
5.8	Turn right at intersection	12,458	397.5	88.3	276,801	4,178,625	13
6.4	Turn right at intersection	12,690	398.1	87.7	276,472	4,177,596	13
7.4	Cross Elk Creek	11,795	399.1	86.7	275,535	4,177,423	13
9.0	Ignore side trail	10,720	400.7	85.1	273,836	4,177,766	13
11.6	Pass pond	9,994	403.3	82.5	270,110	4,178,016	13
14.4	Leave Weminuche Wilderness Area	9,122	406.1	79.7	266,337	4,178,801	13
15.2	Cross Animas River	8,918	406.9	78.9	265,505	4,179,581	13
17.6	Go right at intersection	10,280	409.3	76.5	264,687	4,180,604	13
18.4	Bear right at intersection	10,437	410.1	75.7	263,345	4,180,415	13
18.7	Bear left at intersection	10,577	410.4	75.4	263,152	4,180,893	13
19.1	Cross Molas Creek	10,520	410.8	75.0	262,839	4,180,625	13
20.2	End Segment 24	10,886	411.9	73.9	262,245	4,180,344	13

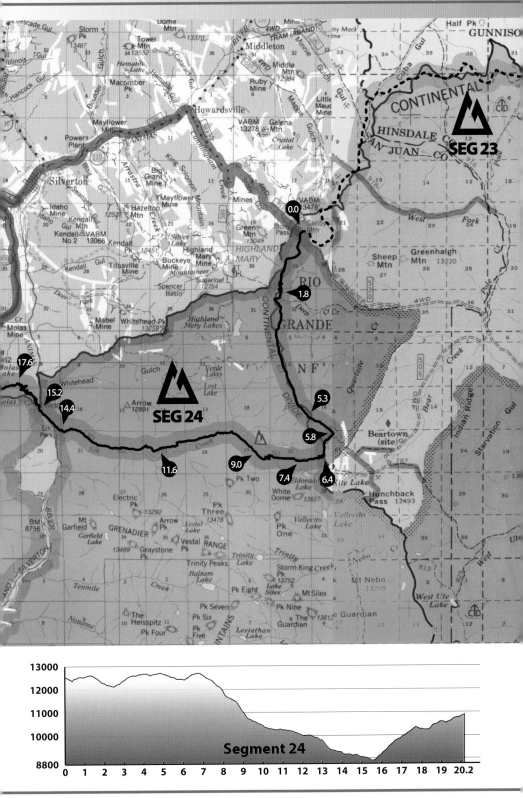

Segment 25: Molas Pass to Bolam Pass Road

Lizard Head Peak, at right, can be spotted near Bolam Pass. PHOTO BY MORGAN WILKINSON

Distance: 20.9 miles

Elevation gain: Approx. 3,799 feet

Elevation loss: Approx. 3,578 feet

USFS map: San Juan National Forest, pages 254–255

The Colorado Trail Databook 4/e: pages 56–57

The CT Map Book: pages 58–60

National Geographic Trails Illustrated maps: Nos. 140, 141

Latitude 40° maps: Southwest Colorado Trails, Durango Trails

Jurisdiction: Columbine and Mancos/Dolores Ranger Districts, San Juan National Forest

Access from Denver end:

Access from Durango end: 🚙

Availability of water:

Bicycling: 🚲

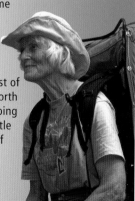

"There is a campground at Molas Pass (by Big Molas Lake) that offers showers. Don't miss it. Between Little Molas Lake and Lime Creek, wildflowers grow knee high in a kaleidoscope of colors."

Big Molas Lake, east of the highway and north of the CT, has camping on private land. Little Molas Lake, west of the highway, has public camping.

Gudy's TIP

ABOUT THIS SEGMENT

The segment starts at US Hwy 550, just north of Molas Pass, and passes through a campground near Little Molas Lake. In this area the trail passes over gently inclined beds of gray shale, sandstone, and limestone of the Hermosa Formation, which was deposited in a shallow sea that flanked the rising Ancestral Rockies between 312 and 305 million years ago. The limestone layers contain abundant fossils.

After leaving the campground, the trail climbs to the Upper Lime Creek drainage, which was heavily forested until a fire roared through in 1879. The forest has not returned to this high-elevation area since then. In the summer months, when the wildflowers along the next few miles of trail are in full bloom, the CT is ablaze in various shades of yellows and purples. The views are second to none.

A cyclist enjoys a near perfect day.

PHOTO BY NATE HEBENSTREIT

At about mile 9 the trail crosses into redbeds of the Cutler Formation, deposited in lowlands flanking the Ancestral Rockies between 300 and 285 million years ago. The spectacular cliffs on the slopes above this part of the trail are conglomerate deposited on the post-Laramide land surface before the San Juan volcanic rocks, which cap the peaks and ridges, were erupted. Large blocks that have tumbled from the conglomerate layer are conspicuous in several places along this part of the trail. As the trail descends toward Cascade Creek it encounters an irregular body of light-colored granite and

! Hikers have reported two places in this segment—at mileage points 10.2 and 12.9—where they have gotten off on the wrong trail. In both cases, they took off to the left because it appeared to be the more heavily traveled trail. At both spots the CT makes a sharp right turn!

porphyry that makes up most of Grizzly Peak. A ledge of this rock forms a nice waterfall worth visiting uphill from the CT at mile 14.3, just before crossing Cascade Creek on a good bridge built by CT volunteers. After another climb, the distinctive Lizard Head Peak comes into view. The segment is largely above tree line, so travel during safe weather periods, trying to avoid the inevitable summer afternoon thunderstorms.

TRAILHEAD/ACCESS POINTS

US Hwy 550–Molas Trail Trailhead:  This segment begins near the summit of Molas Pass, where there is a scenic pullout. Overnight parking is not permitted here, but long-term parking is allowed at the nearby Molas Trail and Little Molas Lake trailheads. The Molas Trail Trailhead is about a mile north on US Hwy 550 from the Molas Pass parking area. It is a fairly

Cascade Creek.
PHOTO BY MORGAN AND ROBYN WILKINSON

large parking area and usually has several cars in it at all times during the summer. It is approximately 5.5 miles south of Silverton on US Hwy 550. From the parking area, a jeep track, the beginning of the Molas Trail, leads south about 0.2 mile to the CT.

Little Molas Lake Trailhead: From Molas Pass on US Hwy 550, drive north 0.4 mile, turn left (west) on a dirt road, and continue 1 mile to the improved Little Molas Lake parking area. There are bathrooms and camping spots here. The CT passes on the south and west sides of the lake.

Bolam Pass Trail Access: See Segment 26 on page 256.

SERVICES, SUPPLIES, AND ACCOMMODATIONS

Silverton is approximately 7 miles north of Molas Pass on US Hwy 550. Molas Lake Campground, near Molas Lake Trailhead, offers hot showers but no longer carries grocery items nor does it have postal delivery. CT travelers have arranged for delivery of their resupply box to the campground by contacting the Chamber of Commerce.

Distance from CT: 7 miles
Elevation: 9,318 feet
Zip code: 81433
Area code: 970

Silverton Services

Dining
Several locations in town

Gear (including fuel canisters)
Outdoor World
1234 Greene St.
(970) 387-5628

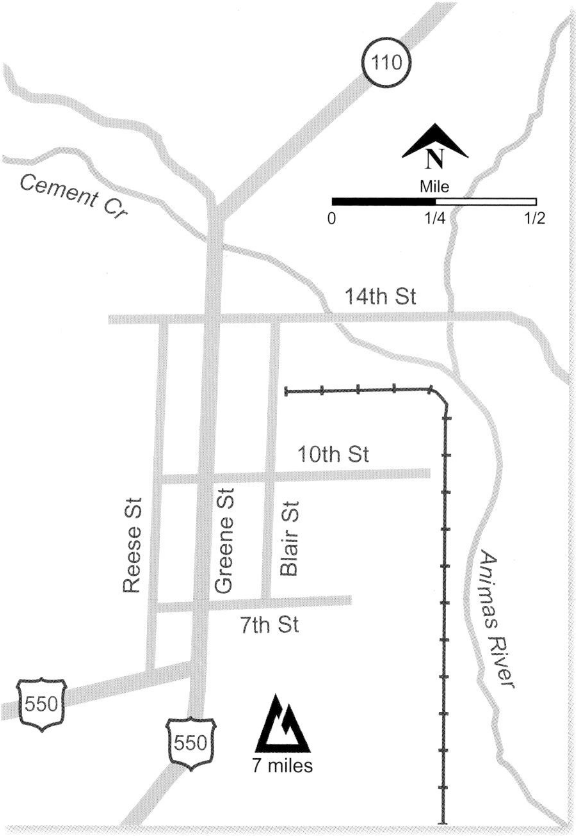

Groceries
Silverton Grocery
717 Greene St.
(970) 387-5652

Info
Chamber of Commerce
414 Greene St.
(970) 387-5654

Laundry
A & B RV Park
1445 Mineral St.
(970) 387-5347

Lodging
Several locations in town

Medical
Silverton Clinic
1450 Greene St.
(970) 387-5354

Post Office
Silverton Post Office
138 W. 12th St.
(970) 387-5402

Train Depot
Durango & Silverton Narrow Gauge Railroad
Blair and W. 12th streets
(970) 387-5416
(888) 872-4607

TRAIL DESCRIPTION

Segment 25 begins on the west side of US Hwy 550 at a large Colorado Trail interpretive sign just north of Molas Pass. There is an interpretive area with toilets on top of Molas Pass, but long-term parking is not permitted there. Long-term parking is available at a large area just off US Hwy 550, 1 mile north (toward Silverton) near mile 20.4 of Segment 24. There is another good, but smaller, parking area at Little Molas Lake Campground, west of US Hwy 550 at mile 0.9 of Segment 25. For convenience sake, most hikers take off from one of these locations, rather than from the official trailhead on Molas Pass.

After crossing US Hwy 550, **mile 0.0** (10,886 feet), pass under a power line and then around the west shore of Little Molas Lake. The trail heads to the northwest, passes through the campground, then bends to the southwest. Stay to the right on an intersecting old road at **mile 1.5** (11,097). At **mile 2** (11,205), turn right and go to the northeast at an intersection of two old roads. Continue to climb, joining a single-track trail at **mile 3** (11,626) that heads to the northwest.

Reach a saddle between Peak 12764 to the west and Peak 12849 to the east at **mile 3.9** (11,525). The trail turns to the west here and eventually crosses a tributary stream to Lime Creek on a wet ledge at **mile 5.3** (11,573). Cross Lime Creek at **mile 6.1** (11,392). There is a small potential campsite here. Continue generally westward, following confidence markers until the trail comes to a T intersection with the Engineer Mountain Trail

Saddling up after a day of trail work.
PHOTO BY PETE TURNER

In July much of the CT is an alpine garden.
PHOTO BY ROGER FORMAN

near several small lakes at **mile 10.2** (12,125). Go to the right at this marked intersection and pass a lake to the west of the trail and a smaller lake to the east of the CT. Climb up the rocky (and sometimes snowy) trail and join the Rico-Silverton Trail at **mile 11** (12,344). Bear left here, eventually reaching a series of switchbacks that gains the saddle between a 13,050-foot subpeak of Rolling Mountain to the northwest and Peak 12766 to the southeast at **mile 11.2** (12,500).

Descend from the saddle. At **mile 12.3** (11,640), bear to the left at an intersection with a side trail that goes to a campsite near a small lake. Intersect the White Creek Trail at **mile 12.9** (11,452) and go to the right. Continue downhill, passing a waterfall just uphill from the trail. Cross Cascade Creek on a bridge at **mile 14.8** (10,852). There is a good campsite 200 feet from the bridge on the east side of the creek. From here, head south to **mile 15.5** (10,948), where the CT intersects the Cascade Creek Trail. Bear to the right. The trail continues to climb, bending to the west and then crossing a creek at **mile 17** (11,162). The trail turns south again and crosses a side trail that joins with FS Rd 579 at **mile 17.3** (11,252). There are good campsites near seasonal streams in the next two miles.

At **mile 19.1** (11,761), the CT crosses a saddle in a large meadow with views of Lizard Head Peak ahead and Engineer Mountain behind. Go left on an old jeep road (FS Rd 578B) at **mile 20.1** (11,293) and turn left at the dirt road at **mile 20.7** (11,135). Pass through a forested area and reach Bolam Pass Road (FS Rd 578) near Celebration Lake at **mile 20.9** (11,094). This is the end of Segment 25.

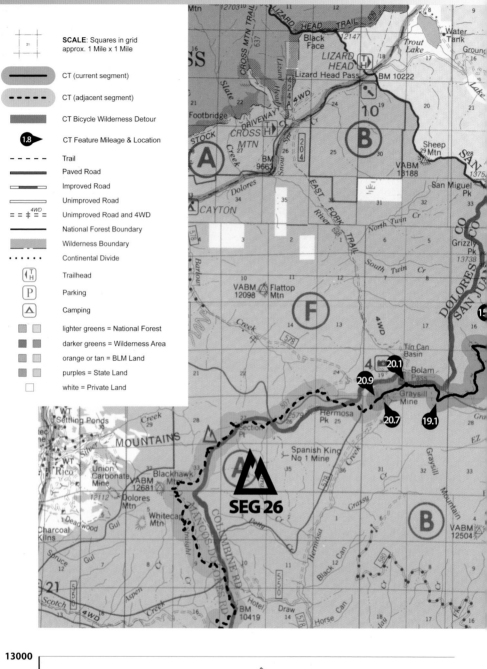

SCALE: Squares in grid approx. 1 Mile x 1 Mile

CT (current segment)

CT (adjacent segment)

CT Bicycle Wilderness Detour

1.8 CT Feature Mileage & Location

Trail

Paved Road

Improved Road

Unimproved Road

4WD Unimproved Road and 4WD

National Forest Boundary

Wilderness Boundary

Continental Divide

Trailhead

Parking

Camping

lighter greens = National Forest

darker greens = Wilderness Area

orange or tan = BLM Land

purples = State Land

white = Private Land

SEG 26

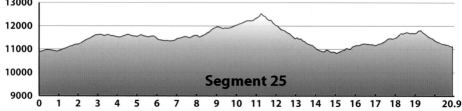

Segment 25

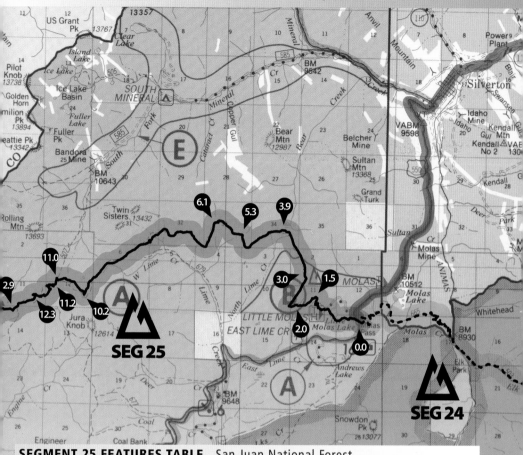

SEGMENT 25 FEATURES TABLE   San Juan National Forest

Mileage	Features & Comments	Elevation (feet)	Mileage from Denver	Mileage to Durango	UTM-E	UTM-N (NAD83)	Zone
0.0	Begin Segment 25	10,886	411.9	73.9	262,245	4,180,344	13
1.5	Go right at intersection	11,097	413.4	72.4	260,785	4,181,175	13
2.0	Go right at intersection	11,205	413.9	71.9	260,128	4,180,933	13
3.0	Join single-track trail to left	11,626	414.9	70.9	260,414	4,181,971	13
3.9	Reach saddle	11,525	415.8	70.0	259,693	4,183,401	13
5.3	Cross creek	11,573	417.2	68.6	258,281	4,183,308	13
6.1	Cross Lime Creek	11,392	418.0	67.8	257,366	4,183,709	13
10.2	Go right at intersection	12,125	422.1	63.7	252,838	4,181,383	13
11.0	Join Rico-Silverton Trail	12,344	422.9	62.9	251,950	4,181,899	13
11.2	Reach saddle	12,500	423.1	62.7	251,843	4,181,740	13
12.3	Go left at intersection	11,640	424.2	61.6	yy	yy	13
12.9	Go right at intersection	11,452	424.8	61.0	250,381	4,180,897	13
14.8	Cross Cascade Creek	10,852	426.7	59.1	249,046	4,181,555	13
15.5	Bear right at intersection	10,948	427.4	58.4	248,665	4,180,488	13
17.3	Go straight at junction	11,252	429.2	56.6	247,641	4,179,279	13
19.1	Reach saddle	11,761	431.0	54.8	246,169	4,177,932	13
20.1	Take left on road	11,293	432.0	53.8	245,102	4,178,509	13
20.7	Go left at intersection	11,135	432.6	53.2	244,274	4,178,139	13
20.9	End Segment 25	11,094	432.8	53.0	244,068	4,177,965	13

Segment 26: Bolam Pass Road to Hotel Draw Road

Distance: 10.9 miles

Elevation gain: Approx. 1,827 feet

Elevation loss: Approx. 2,551 feet

USFS map: San Juan National Forest, pages 262–263

The Colorado Trail Databook 4/e: pages 58–59

The CT Map Book: pages 60–61

National Geographic Trails Illustrated maps: Nos. 141, 144

Latitude 40° maps: Southwest Colorado Trails, Durango Trails

Jurisdiction: Mancos/Dolores Ranger District, San Juan National Forest

Access from Denver end:

Access from Durango end:

Availability of water:

Bicycling:

Ascending to Blackhawk Pass.

PHOTO BY NATE HEBENSTREIT

"The north side of Blackhawk Pass is a valley of enchantment with vast herds of elk."

Verdant alpine meadows near the pass, filled with lush mid-summer growth, attract wildlife—elk and mule deer, marmots and pika —and hikers drawn by the wildflowers and lovely vistas. Have your camera ready. Famous Lizard Head Peak is in view near the pass.

Gudy's TIP

ABOUT THIS SEGMENT

This segment follows the high ground between the Hermosa Creek drainage to the south and east and the Dolores River drainage to the north and west. The trail here is largely in flat lying beds of the Cutler Formation, cut by dikes and sills of light-colored porphyry. This segment feels very remote, descending and ascending forested ridges until climbing to Blackhawk Pass just east of Blackhawk Mountain. The views from here are outstanding. The CT then drops into the Straight Creek watershed below. There are several potential campsites after entering the forest with good access to the creek. The second crossing of Straight Creek is the last reliable water for the next 22 miles. Be sure to fill your water bottles here!

TRAILHEAD/ACCESS POINTS

Bolam Pass Road (FS Rd 578) Trail Access: 🚙 There are two ways to drive to this access point, both requiring a four-wheel-drive vehicle: from US Hwy 550 through Durango Mountain Resort (formally Purgatory Ski Area) and from CO Hwy 145, south of Lizard Head Pass and just north of Rico. For the US Hwy 550 approach, drive approximately 28 miles north of Durango to the main entrance to Durango Mountain Resort on

Cornhusk lily.
PHOTO BY NATE HEBENSTREIT

the west side of the road. At the upper parking area, bear right onto FS Rd 578. Drive approximately 15 miles to Bolam Pass. FS Rd 578 follows the East Fork of Hermosa Creek west past Sig Creek Campground, onto the main channel of Hermosa Creek, then north to Bolam Pass. The CT access point is at Celebration Lake. For the approach from CO Hwy 145, drive 6 miles north of Rico and turn right onto FS Rd 578 and drive about 7 miles along Barlow Creek. At a Y intersection, take the left branch to Celebration Lake and the CT access point.

> **!** Test the depth of the Hermosa Creek ford before driving into it.

Hotel Draw Trail Access: 🚙 See Segment 27 on page 264.

SERVICES, SUPPLIES, AND ACCOMMODATIONS

There is no convenient resupply point for this segment.

TRAIL DESCRIPTION

Segment 26 begins at the southwest edge of Celebration Lake on Bolam Pass Road (FS Rd 578), where The Colorado Trail crosses the road from the northeast, **mile 0.0** (11,094 feet). There is a small parking lot and hard-packed camping area here. Cross a

The CT is well signed in most places, but using this guide will help ensure you keep on track.
PHOTO BY NATE HEBENSTREIT

A marmot at full alert.
PHOTO BY ERNIE NORRIS

small stream flowing out of the south end of the lake and climb to **mile 0.9** (11,532), where the trail gains a saddle on the east side of Hermosa Peak. The trail contours beneath the peak to the north and passes a spring with a good campsite at **mile 1.3** (11,452). Turn left at a T intersection with a jeep road at **mile 1.6** (11,565) and head southwest. Cross a small stream at **mile 1.8** (11,486), where there is potential camping, and continue to **mile 3** (11,561), where the trail leaves the road to the right.

After reaching the top of a small saddle at **mile 3.9** (11,814), turn left when the trail intersects the old Circle Trail coming up from Silver Creek at **mile 4.1** (11,761). Pass over a small knob and down several switchbacks to **mile 5**. The trail contours around the valley ahead and begins to climb at **mile 6** (11,511). From here, pass a small stream at **mile 6.3** (11,590) and a larger stream at **mile 6.4** (11,611). Gain Blackhawk Pass at **mile 6.9** (11,985) and descend to the headwaters of Straight Creek at **mile 7.5** (11,468). There is a good campsite 0.1 mile to the south. Continue heading downhill through the forest, crossing to the east side of Straight Creek at **mile 8.4** (11,032). This is the last reliable water source for the next 22 miles. Continue in a generally southeasterly direction, passing several potential camping areas before reaching the end of Segment 26, 50 feet before Hotel Draw Road at **mile 10.9** (10,385).

> **!** Thru-hikers should be aware that the Straight Creek crossing at mile 8.4 is the last reliable water source before reaching Taylor Lake, some 22 miles away over Indian Trail Ridge.

Biking

🚲 A popular local mountain bike ride utilizes CT Segment 26, often as part of a loop using Hermosa Creek Road (FS Rd 578) and Hotel Draw Road (FS Rd 550). Riders enjoy the high elevation, views, flowers, and the challenge of Blackhawk Pass.

Maintaining the Trail: Volunteers

Maintaining all 486 miles of The Colorado Trail is an immense undertaking, requiring the efforts of hundreds of dedicated CTF trail crew and Adopt-A-Trail volunteers each year.

Every summer, The Colorado Trail Foundation organizes around 15 volunteer week-long and weekend trail crews. Each consists of 20 to 25 volunteers and takes place in June, July, and August. CT crews work on large-scale projects including bridge installation, retaining walls, trail reroutes, and rebuilding the tread. Volunteers receive training on trail work, tool use, and safety. They value spending time in the outdoors and giving back to The Colorado Trail. Volunteers enjoy the Colorado mountains, group meals, building friendships, and learning. Trail crews are hard work but a lot of fun.

Adopters and their helpers are the trail's frontline volunteers, keeping the CT passable and reporting trail conditions to the foundation. Approximately 60 adopters care for their 5- to 15-mile section by removing fallen trees, improving water diversions, and replacing CT signage. Adopters are responsible individuals, some representing a family group, Scout troop, hiking club, mountain bike group, horse club, or simply a group of friends. Adopters often stick with the task for many years, even decades, finding outdoor fun and a sense of accomplishment in keeping their adopted section in good shape for trail users.

CT volunteers are proud of their stewardship.
PHOTO BY ERNIE NORRIS

Volunteer with a Pulaski and a smile.
PHOTO BY BILL BLOOMQUIST

Reconstructing tread.
PHOTO BY LISA TURNER

If you are interested and would like more information on CTF trail crews or Adopt-A-Trail, please visit ColoradoTrail.org.

Teamwork is key to improving the trail.
PHOTO BY BILL BLOOMQUIST

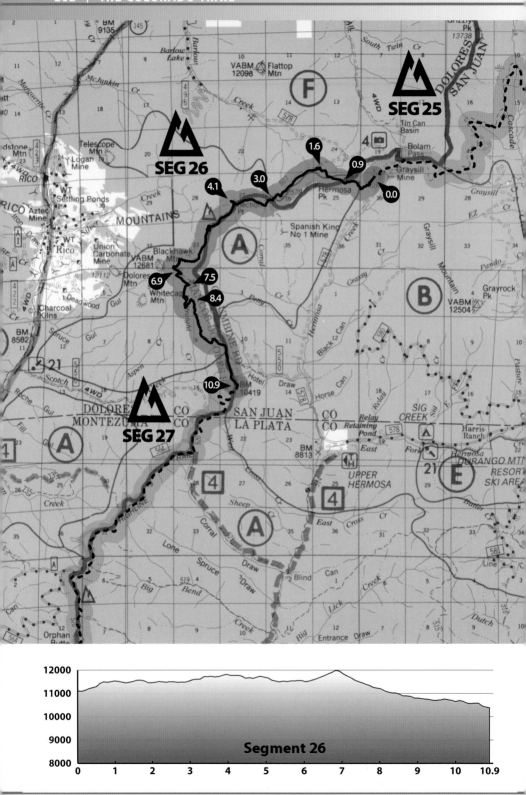

Segment 26

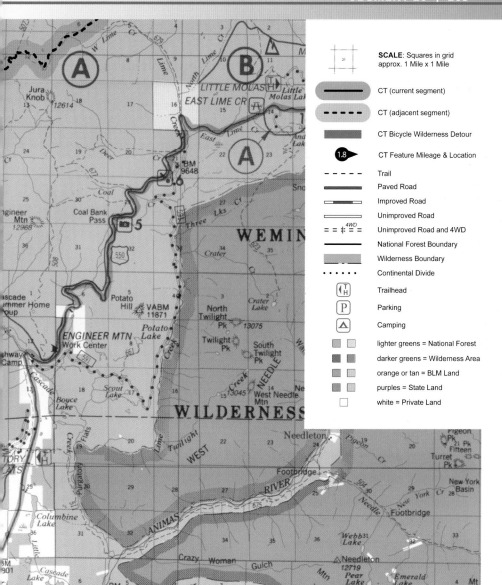

SEGMENT 26 FEATURES TABLE   San Juan National Forest

Mileage	Features & Comments	Elevation (feet)	Mileage from Denver	Mileage to Durango	UTM-E	UTM-N (NAD83)	Zone
0.0	Begin Segment 26	11,094	432.8	53.0	244,068	4,177,965	13
0.9	Gain saddle	11,532	433.7	52.1	242,958	4,177,837	13
1.6	Go left at intersection	11,565	434.4	51.4	242,181	4,178,337	13
3.0	Go right at intersection	11,561	435.8	50.0	240,516	4,177,285	13
4.1	Go left at intersection	11,761	436.9	48.9	239,089	4,177,294	13
6.9	Gain Blackhawk Pass	11,985	439.7	46.1	237,186	4,174,993	13
7.5	Cross Straight Creek	11,468	440.3	45.5	237,433	4,174,469	13
8.4	Cross Straight Creek	11,032	441.2	44.6	237,642	4,173,999	13
10.9	End Segment 26	10,385	443.7	42.1	239,125	4,171,049	13

Segment 27: Hotel Draw Road to Kennebec Trailhead

Looking south toward the La Plata Mountains.
PHOTO BY NATE HEBENSTREIT

Distance: 20.6 miles

Elevation gain: Approx. 4,186 feet

Elevation loss: Approx. 2,922 feet

USFS map: San Juan National Forest, pages 270–271

The Colorado Trail Databook 4/e: pages 60–61

The CT Map Book: pages 61–64

National Geographic Trails Illustrated map: No. 144

Latitude 40° maps: Southwest Colorado Trails, Durango Trails

Jurisdiction: Columbine Ranger District, San Juan National Forest

Access from Denver end:

Access from Durango end:

Availability of water:

Bicycling:

"From Indian Trail Ridge, a crest of cascading wildflowers and the views of Hermosa Valley and the La Plata Mountains are extraordinary."

This segment features sweeping vistas, culminating in a dramatic, 5-mile walk atop an alpine ridge at more than 12,000 feet. Wildflower enthusiasts find the incredible displays at their peak starting in mid-July.

Gudy's TIP

ABOUT THIS SEGMENT

The first 9 miles of Segment 27 encounter several infrequently used Forest Service roads and closed logging roads. For the most part the trail stays near the ridgeline, here chiefly made up of rocks of the Cutler Formation, then it climbs as it leaves the roads and logged forests behind. At mile 4 it crosses into red sandstone shale and siltstone of the Dolores Formation, deposited by streams, lakes, and winds between about 230 and 200 million years ago, after destruction of the Ancestral Rockies. As The Colorado Trail climbs toward the Cape of Good Hope it passes into still younger rocks, sandstone, shale, and limestone deposited shortly before the inundation by the Cretaceous Seaway.

Once the trail passes the junction with the Grindstone Trail, it enters the tundra and traverses Indian Trail Ridge, which is made up of a thick layer of sandstone that belongs to this group of younger rocks. From here, there are fantastic views of the surrounding mountains and drainages below. It is common to see large herds of elk below the ridge to the west. The trail stays above tree line, with no easy means of escape from sudden storms, from mile 15.5 to mile 19.4. Watch the weather patterns before committing to this section. Taylor Lake at mile 19.4 is a great sight from above for southbound hikers who have covered the last 20

Taylor Lake is a welcome sight at the south end of Indian Trail Ridge.
PHOTO BY JULIE VIDA AND MARK TABB

miles with no reliable water sources. For GPS users, note that the UTM coordinates switch from Zone 13 to Zone 12 at about mile 4.6.

TRAILHEAD/ACCESS POINTS

There are three ways to drive to the beginning of Segment 27. Two require a four-wheel-drive vehicle: from US Hwy 550 through Durango Mountain Resort (formally Purgatory Ski Area) and from CO Hwy 145, south of Lizard Head Pass and just south of Rico. The two-wheel-drive approach via FS Rds 435/654/550 is much longer but usually accessible by regular passenger cars.

US Hwy 550 Access (Hotel Draw): Drive approximately 28 miles north of Durango to the main entrance of Durango Mountain Resort on the west side of the road. At the upper parking area, bear right onto FS Rd 578. Follow this road for approximately 8 miles along the East Fork of Hermosa Creek, continuing west past Sig Creek Campground and on to the main channel of Hermosa Creek, then north along the main channel and through a ford. About a mile after the ford, make a sharp left turn onto the Hotel Draw Road (FS Rd 550). After about 3.5 miles, at the top of the ridge, the CT comes down from the north and intersects the Hotel Draw Road.

CO Hwy 145 Access: Drive 2 miles south of Rico and turn left onto Scotch Creek Road (FS Rd 550). Proceed about 5 miles to an intersection near the top of the ridge and turn left, continuing to the top of the ridge where the CT comes down the ridge on the road from the north.

FS Rds 435/654/550 Access: Drive 9 miles south of Rico and turn east onto FS Rd 435. After 6 miles, make a sharp left turn onto FS Rd 654. Continue for about 15 miles to its terminus at FS Rd 550. Follow FS Rd 550 for 1.3 miles to the beginning of the segment. FS Rd 564 intersects with the CT several times before reaching its terminus at FS Rd 550.

Kennebec Trailhead: See Segment 28 on page 272.

> **!** Test the depth of the Hermosa Creek ford before driving into it.

SERVICES, SUPPLIES, AND ACCOMMODATIONS

There is no convenient resupply point for this segment.

TRAIL DESCRIPTION

Segment 27 begins 50 feet north of a small parking area on Hotel Draw Road (FS Rd 550) at **mile 0.0** (10,385 feet). The first 10 miles or so of this segment pass through a maze of old logging trails. Much of the CT follows these old cuts. There are numerous intersections, but they are marked well by wooden posts, signs, or confidence markers, so navigating this area is not as difficult as the description may sound.

Thru-hikers will turn right and head to the southwest just before reaching the parking area. Follow a short section of new trail that parallels the road going south. In 300 feet, turn right on a closed-in logging road, then bear left at a fork a few hundred feet farther on. At **mile 0.7** (10,408), the CT continues on another logging road that turns sharply to the left (south) and uphill. A few hundred feet farther, continue straight past another logging trail. Turn right at a well-marked Y intersection at **mile 1.2** (10,444). Turn right again 500 feet farther along onto FS Rd 550, and follow FS Rd 564 to the left for another few hundred feet. Finally, turn left at a well-marked intersection at **mile 1.4** (10,408). From here, the trail climbs a forested ridge with good views to the south before reaching the top of the ridge at **mile 2.6** (10,907).

> **!** Indian Trail Ridge can be dangerous during afternoon thunderstorms.

Continue to follow The Colorado Trail in a southwesterly direction and cross the Corral Draw Trail, which drops into the Hermosa Creek drainage at **mile 2.9** (10,828). Stay high on the ridge, passing several potential campsites before meeting a dirt road (FS Rd 564) at **mile 4** (10,760). Follow it to the left. The trail leaves the road but crosses back over it several times in the next 2 miles. CT confidence markers are clearly posted throughout. Cross the Big Bend Trail at **mile 6.5** (10,617), then pass just south of the road at **mile 6.9** (10,700). The trail joins a logging road at **mile 7.1** (10,762) and turns sharply to the south. Intersect the Salt Creek Trail at **mile 7.9** (10,851). Continue heading toward Orphan Butte, the high bald knob to the south. After passing to the east of Orphan Butte and crossing two more logging roads, the trail becomes more straightforward as the logging roads are left behind.

Begin a steady climb up the ridge at **mile 11.3** (10,818) and take a series of switchbacks to **mile 12.1** (11,140). A side trail

Wildflowers galore can be found atop Indian Trail Ridge, but no water.

PHOTO BY JULIE VIDA AND MARK TABB

to good camping and a great viewpoint comes at **mile 12.3** (11,331). The trail heads northwest from here, passing a seasonal spring along the trail. The CT then bends sharply at **mile 12.5** (11,432) to regain a generally southward bearing. Encounter a wood sign identifying the Highline Trail, which is shared by the CT, at **mile 13.3** (11,617). There is another trail marker at **mile 14.7** (11,633) for the Highline Trail and the Cape of Good Hope–Hermosa Peak Road. Turn left at an intersection with the Grindstone Trail at **mile 15.2** (11,686), the last downhill exit from high ridge until **mile 18.9**.

As the trail continues to climb, it enters the tundra at **mile 15.5** (11,821) and traverses the very exposed Indian Trail Ridge. Climb to a high point on the ridge at **mile 18.3** (12,310) and reach a second, lower summit at **mile 18.7** (12,258). After a brief descent along the ridge from the second summit, turn left and head downhill toward Cumberland Basin and Taylor Lake below. After a steep, rocky descent, pass a side trail leading to Taylor Lake on the right at **mile 19.4** (11,642). Southbound hikers will appreciate this water source after 20 miles of dry trail. Continue to the southeast, eventually reaching the Kennebec Trailhead parking area and the end of Segment 27 at **mile 20.6** (11,642).

Photographing Wildflowers

Those who traverse Indian Trail Ridge in mid-summer are treated to a spectacular display of alpine flowers, including arnica, Indian paintbrush, bistort, columbine, and scores of others. Whether you still shoot film or have migrated to the latest digital technology, taking photographs good enough to enlarge and display requires the right equipment, knowledge, and patience. Here are some basic tips offered by Colorado Trail hikers whose photos appear in this guide:

Shooting columbine, Colorado's state flower.
PHOTO BY RICK TRONVIG

▲ Serious wildflower photographers enjoy the control offered by a full-featured single-lens reflex (SLR) camera, as opposed to a point-and-shoot (P&S) camera. Being able to increase depth of field by "stopping down" a camera's aperture or freezing motion on a windy day by increasing shutter speed are some of the advantages of an SLR. For P&S users, learn about the manual controls your camera might offer.

▲ While cameras and lenses often claim macro or close-focusing abilities, most do not magnify the image enough to do justice to tiny alpine flowers. SLR users can invest in a dedicated macro lens for close-focusing ability. Inexpensive di-opter lenses that screw onto a lens to boost magnification are available for SLR cameras and some point-and-shoots.

▲ Use a tripod and a cable shutter release to prevent blur from camera shake. Have a piece of cardboard handy for a wind block.

▲ If you want to shoot an expansive field of flowers, invest in a true wide-angle lens (35mm or less). Stop down the aperture for greater depth of field.

▲ Digital camera users should set a slower ISO sensitivity to avoid noise.

▲ Shoot early or late in the day to avoid intense mid-day light. Often, overcast or even rainy days are best for subtle color saturation or for the effects of raindrops on petals.

A macro shot fills the frame with vibrant colors.
PHOTO BY KEITH EVANS

Indian paintbrush, foreground, and penstemon.
PHOTO BY BILL BLOOMQUIST

Colorado blue columbine (*Aquilegia coerulea*)
PHOTO BY LORI BRUMMER

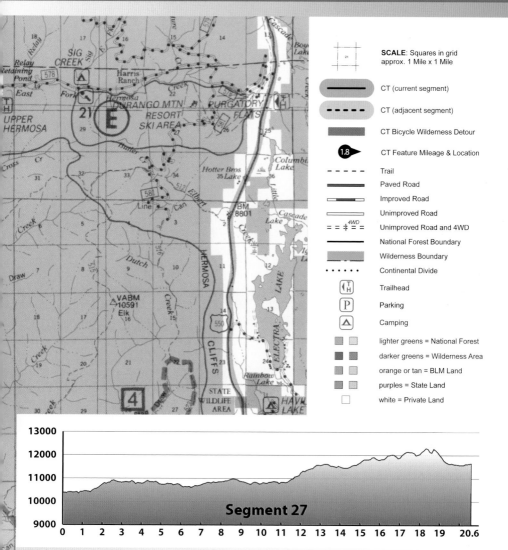

SCALE: Squares in grid approx. 1 Mile x 1 Mile

CT (current segment)

CT (adjacent segment)

CT Bicycle Wilderness Detour

1.8   CT Feature Mileage & Location

Trail

Paved Road

Improved Road

Unimproved Road

Unimproved Road and 4WD

National Forest Boundary

Wilderness Boundary

Continental Divide

Trailhead

Parking

Camping

lighter greens = National Forest

darker greens = Wilderness Area

orange or tan = BLM Land

purples = State Land

white = Private Land

SEGMENT 27 FEATURES TABLE   San Juan National Forest

Mileage	Features & Comments	Elevation (feet)	Mileage from Denver	Mileage to Durango	UTM-E	UTM-N (NAD83)	Zone
0.0	Begin Segment 27	10,385	443.7	42.1	239,125	4,171,049	13
0.7	Continue on logging road	10,408	444.4	41.4	238,476	4,170,721	13
1.2	Turn right at intersection	10,444	444.9	40.9	238,460	4,170,120	13
2.9	Cross Corral Draw Trail	10,828	446.6	39.2	237,013	4,168,800	13
4.0	Reach FS Rd 564	10,760	447.1	38.7	235,789	4,167,690	13
6.5	Cross Big Bend Trail	10,617	450.2	35.6	763,576	4,165,143	12
7.9	Intersect Salt Creek Trail	10,851	451.6	34.2	763,298	4,163,430	12
12.3	Stay left at intersection	11,331	456.0	29.8	762,217	4,158,197	12
15.2	Go left at intersection	11,686	458.9	26.9	761,759	4,154,954	12
18.3	Reach high point	12,310	462.0	23.8	762,350	4,150,637	12
19.4	Go left at intersection	11,642	463.1	22.7	762,709	4,149,685	12
20.6	End Segment 27	11,642	464.3	21.5	764,382	4,149,157	12

Segment 28: Kennebec Trailhead to Junction Creek Trailhead

Distance: 21.5 miles

Elevation gain: Approx. 1,897 feet

Elevation loss: Approx. 6,557 feet

USFS map: San Juan National Forest, pages 280–281

The Colorado Trail Databook 4/e: pages 62–63

The CT Map Book: pages 64–67

National Geographic Trails Illustrated map: No. 144

Latitude 40° maps: Southwest Colorado Trails, Durango Trails

Jurisdiction: Columbine Ranger District, San Juan National Forest

Access from Denver end:

Access from Durango end:

Availability of water:

Bicycling:

Gudy's Rest at mile 17.4 honors Gudy Gaskill.
PHOTO BY JULIE VIDA AND MARK TABB

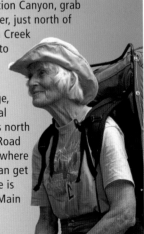

"If you didn't stop for a shower in one of the falls in Junction Canyon, grab one at the rec center, just north of where the Junction Creek Road dead-ends into Main Avenue in Durango."

Durango has a large, modern recreational center three blocks north of Junction Creek Road and Main Avenue, where hikers and riders can get a hot shower. There is bus service along Main Avenue.

Gudy's TIP

ABOUT THIS SEGMENT

The final segment of The Colorado Trail begins at the Kennebec Trailhead, climbs to Kennebec Pass, and then descends most of the rest of way to the Junction Creek Trailhead and Durango. This is an incredibly diverse segment. It starts above tree line; descends steeply; passes through stands of spruce, fir, and pine; and crosses Junction Creek at its headwaters and again where there are sturdy bridges below the bigger creek. There is dense vegetation in the Junction Creek drainage, which stands in sharp contrast to the alpine basin filled with summer wildflowers at the beginning of the segment. The views are magnificent from Kennebec Pass, but quickly disappear as the trail enters the narrow canyon carved by Junction Creek. Around Kennebec Pass and along the trail as it descends to the creek, rocks of the Dolores and Cutler formations are cut by numerous dikes, sills, and irregular bodies of white porphyry that were emplaced during the Laramide Orogeny. It passes by several mines and prospects that explored mineral deposits related to the porphyry.

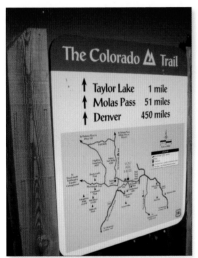

Trailhead sign below Kennebec Pass.
PHOTO BY LAWTON "DISCO" GRINTER

Camping is sporadic through the segment, compounded by a camping restriction after mile 16.9. There is plenty of water when first entering the canyon, but flat spots for camping are rare. When the CT climbs out of the canyon later in the segment, there are flat spots, but no water. Camping is not permitted after mile 16.9 because this area is heavily used and easily accessible from the south. To reduce frustration, plan your trip down this segment carefully and stop early before all the best camping sites are taken. For GPS users, note that the UTM coordinates switch back from Zone 12 to Zone 13 at about mile 1.

The beginning of this segment has previously been referred to as Cumberland Basin in earlier editions of this guidebook. Now, however, the San Juan National Forest map no longer lists Cumberland Basin. The trailhead designation is now Kennebec Trailhead. This edition has changed its designation accordingly. There is a large trailhead sign and parking area at the intersection of FS Rd 171 and The Colorado Trail. Kennebec Pass is 0.7 mile east of Kennebec Trailhead.

! Camping is NOT allowed beyond mile 16.9 of this segment (except at Junction Creek Campground, less than a half mile from CT mile 20.3).

The ridgeline ahead is one of the final climbs before reaching Durango.
PHOTO BY JULIE VIDA AND MARK TABB

This segment of the CT is spectacular in many respects. It has the most vertical travel of any segment of the trail: more than 4,700 feet of vertical gain in one direction and 1,400 feet in the other. The views are greatly reduced, though, because most of this section is in dense forest and a narrow canyon.

TRAILHEAD/ACCESS POINTS

Kennebec Trailhead: 🚜 From Durango, drive west on US Hwy 160 about 13 miles (0.5 mile beyond the village of Hesperus). Turn right on La Plata County Rd 124, which eventually becomes FS Rd 498 and then FS Rd 571, terminating in Cumberland Basin at the Kennebec Trailhead sign. The last 2 miles are rough and steep; a four-wheel-drive vehicle is strongly recommended.

Junction Creek Trailhead:
🚙 Drive north on Main Avenue in Durango to 25th Street and turn left (west). After a couple of blocks the street bears right and becomes Junction Creek Road (La Plata County Rd 204). Follow it for 3 miles and take the left branch. Continue another 0.4 mile to a cattle guard and a San Juan National Forest sign. There is a 19-car Forest Service parking lot and a toilet here. This is the southern terminus of The Colorado Trail. The road continues as FS Rd 171. In about another mile there is a switchback with seven more parking spaces. A short side trail takes you to the CT along the creek.

Sliderock Trail Access Point: 🚙 The CT can be accessed by two-wheel-drive vehicles at mile 2.4 of this segment. From the Junction Creek Trailhead previously described, continue on the gravel-improved FS Rd 171 for 17.5 miles to a side road on the left. Turn left and proceed 0.7 mile on this more rugged road to where the CT crosses. There are CT markers on both sides of the road. The trail to the right leads to Kennebec Pass, 1.7 miles away, via the Sliderock portion of this segment. The trail to the left leads to Durango, 19.1 miles away.

Julie Vida and Mark Tabb, whose photos appear in this guide, look fresh at the beginning their northbound thru-hike.

A miner's cabin sits atop redbeds of the Cutler Formation opposite a large talus slope known as Sliderock.

PHOTO BY ROGER FORMAN

SERVICES, SUPPLIES, AND ACCOMMODATIONS

Durango, an old railroad town and now the commercial center for southwestern Colorado, is approximately 3.5 miles from the Junction Creek Trailhead. The town is connected to Denver via airline and bus service, and to Silverton by the Durango & Silverton Narrow Gauge Railroad.

Distance from CT: 3.5 miles
Elevation: 6,512 feet
Zip code: 81301
Area code: 970

Durango Services

Bus
Greyhound, Durango Transit Center
250 W. 8th St.
(970) 259-2755

Dining (several)
Carver Bakery & Brewing Co.
1022 Main Ave.
(970) 259-2545

Gear (including fuel canisters)
Backcountry Experience
120 Camino del Rio
(970) 247-5830

Gardenswartz Outdoors
863 Main Ave.
(970) 259-6696

Pine Needle Mountaineering
835 Main Ave.
(970) 247-8728

Groceries (several)
City Market
South 6 Town Plaza
(970) 247-4475

Info
Chamber of Commerce
111 S. Camino del Rio
(970) 247-0312

Laundry (several)
North Main Laundry
2980 Main Ave.
(970) 247-9915

Lodging (several)
Durango Hometown Hostel
736 Goeglein Gulch Rd.
(970) 385-4115

Medical
Durango Urgent Care
2577 N. Main Ave.
(970) 247-8382

Mercy Regional Medical Center
1010 Three Springs Blvd.
(970) 247-4311

Post Office
Durango Post Office
222 W. 8th St.
(970) 247-3968

Showers
Durango Recreation Center
2700 Main Ave.
(970) 375-7300

Train Depot
Durango & Silverton Narrow Gauge Railroad
479 Main Ave.
(888) 872-4607

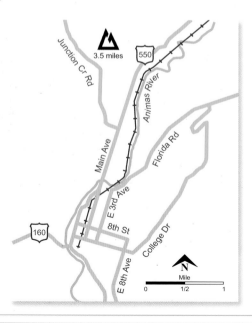

TRAIL DESCRIPTION

Segment 28 begins at the Kennebec Trailhead parking lot, **mile 0.0** (11,642 feet). The trail leaves the south side of the parking area and heads uphill to the east-southeast. Keep your eyes open for elk and other wildlife in this area. After gaining Kennebec Pass at **mile 0.4** (11,700), head downhill and take a left at the intersection at **mile 0.7** (11,713). From here the trail crosses a large talus slope that is appropriately named the Sliderock. Enter a spruce forest after crossing the talus and continue on a series of switchbacks until reaching the Champion Venture Mine Road, a spur of Junction Creek Road/FS Rd 171, at **mile 2.4** (10,351). Cross the road and continue heading downhill into Fassbinder Gulch. There are seasonal creeks at **mile 3.7** (10,003) and **mile 4.7** (9,483), but camping in this area is generally poor due to the thick vegetation.

Pass by the Gaines Gulch waterfall at a switchback at **mile 5.4** (9,250), then cross Flagler Fork of Junction Creek at **mile 5.7** (9,029). Both of these water sources are reliable year-round. The trail crosses Junction Creek three more times, then crosses it again on a bridge at **mile 7.1** (8,522). There is a great campsite just before crossing the bridge.

Begin the last notable climb on The Colorado Trail after crossing the bridge. This 4-mile climb gains more than 1,000 feet through beautiful, rugged terrain, with steep slopes dropping into the Junction Creek gorge. Water flow in the side canyons is variable, but in the canyon south of Chicago Gulch, First Trail Canyon, and Sliderock Canyon, trail users find flows all season. Where the trail reaches a ridge at **mile 8** (8,974), there is a good (but dry) campsite, with a small creek a quarter-mile farther on. At **mile 8.4** (9,001), the trail follows an old road in Road End Canyon. The trail begins following an old mining road at about **mile 11** (9,516), then continues to ascend until reaching the top of the climb at **mile 11.2** (9,557). From here the trail begins its final descent toward the Junction Creek Trailhead and Durango.

Cyclists at Champion Venture Road.
PHOTO BY BILL MANNING

At a bend in the trail at **mile 11.5** (9,415), there is an excellent small campsite on a bench above the trail and water in a small stream 200 feet below the trail. Continue heading downhill and pass through a Forest Service gate at **mile 14.4** (8,676).

Kennebec Pass is at far right beneath Cumberland Mountain.
PHOTO BY CARL BROWN

There are two more gates to pass through in the next mile and a half. Just after the first gate, take a left when the CT intersects with the Dry Fork Trail at **mile 14.6** (8,606). At **mile 16.9** (8,210), there is a year-round spring and several small campsites nearby. This is the last available camping in this segment. (Camping is available at the Junction Creek Campground, a fee area 1.5 miles east of the intersection of FS Rd 171 and the CT at mile 20.3.)

Cross the Hoffheins Trail at **mile 17.2** (7,997), then bear left and continue to Gudy's Rest at **mile 17.4** (7,970). This is a scenic overlook with a bench placed in honor of Gudy Gaskill, the remarkable woman who made The Colorado Trail a reality. After heading down a series of switchbacks, cross the bridge over Junction Creek at **mile 18.9** (7,431). Continue straight at an intersection at **mile 20.3** (7,183) and down the narrow canyon paralleling the stream. Continue ahead, eventually reaching the Junction Creek Trailhead and the terminus of The Colorado Trail at **mile 21.5** (6,983). The trailhead is about 3.5 miles from Durango via a paved road. There are several motels near the intersection of the paved road (which becomes 25th Street) and Main Avenue in Durango. The downtown area is to the right at that point.

> **!** Camping is NOT allowed beyond mile 16.9 of this segment (except at Junction Creek Campground, a mile and a half off the trail).

Viewing Dippers

A chunky, drab, wrenlike bird, the water ouzel, or dipper, would hardly attract anyone's attention if not for its unusual manner of earning a living. Dippers reside along rushing mountain streams, often perched atop a rock in the foaming center of the torrent. From this vantage point, it constantly bobs up and down, looking for aquatic insects or even small fish to eat. Spotting a tasty morsel, it then dives headlong into the water, opens its wings, and "flies" or walks submerged through the flow. Birds stake out a 75- to 200-yard length of stream for their territory, rarely venturing far from its banks.

When disturbed, dippers fly low and rapidly up and down the stream, sounding a high, ringing alarm. During winter, they move to lower levels. Their nests are a bulky ball of moss open on one side, built just above the waterline in inaccessible places such as on a rock wall or behind a waterfall.

Dippers can be found along the streams and rivers throughout western Colorado. In Segment 28, you are as likely to spot one along the lush banks of little Quinn Creek as perched on a boulder in the middle of the Animas River in downtown Durango.

American dipper.
PHOTO BY DAN GARBER

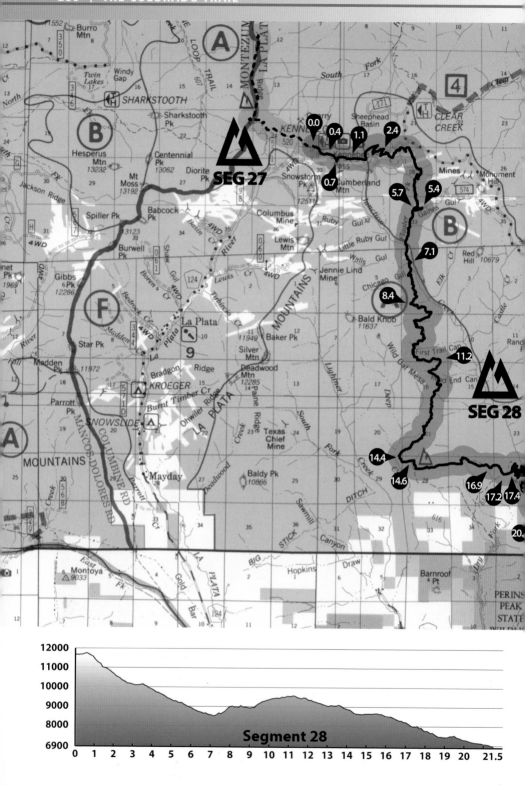

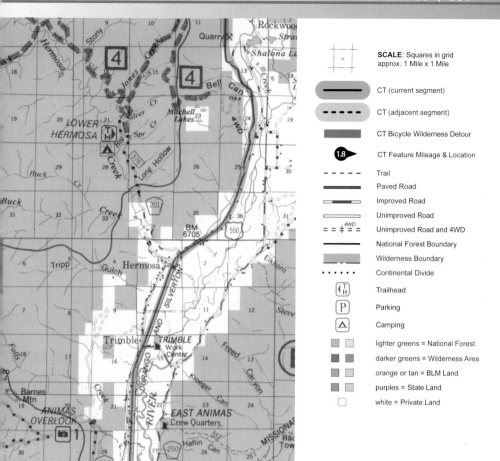

SEGMENT 28 FEATURES TABLE   San Juan National Forest

Mileage	Features & Comments	Elevation (feet)	Mileage from Denver	Mileage to Durango	UTM-E	UTM-N (NAD83)	Zone
0.0	Begin Segment 28	11,642	464.3	21.5	764,382	4,149,157	12
0.4	Cross Kennebec Pass	11,700	464.7	21.1	764,995	4,148,913	12
0.7	Go left at intersection	11,713	465.0	20.8	765,209	4,148,699	12
1.1	Cross talus slope	11,336	465.4	20.4	234,955	4,148,718	13
2.4	Reach FS Rd 171	10,351	466.7	19.1	236,016	4,149,026	13
5.4	Pass waterfall	9,250	469.7	16.1	237,369	4,147,064	13
5.7	Cross Junction Creek	9,029	470.0	15.8	237,102	4,147,083	13
7.1	Last crossing of Junction Creek	8,522	471.4	14.4	236,896	4,145,211	13
8.4	Trail follows old road	9,001	472.7	13.1	236,916	4,143,805	13
11.2	Reach top of climb	9,557	475.5	10.3	237,868	4,141,920	13
14.4	Pass through gate	8,676	478.7	7.1	236,420	4,138,600	13
14.6	Go left at intersection	8,606	478.9	6.9	236,793	4,138,500	13
16.9	No camping beyond this point	8,210	481.2	4.6	239,600	4,138,215	13
17.2	Go left at intersection	7,997	481.5	4.3	240,015	4,137,998	13
17.4	Gudy's Rest overlook	7,970	481.7	4.1	240,329	4,138,070	13
18.9	Bridge over Junction Creek	7,431	483.2	2.6	240,682	4,138,256	13
20.3	Go straight at intersection	7,183	484.6	1.2	241,314	4,136,340	13
21.5	End Segment 28	6,983	485.8	0.0	242,827	4,135,585	13

Forest Service Ranger Districts

United States Forest Service
Rocky Mountain Regional Office
740 Simms St.
Golden, CO 80401-4720
(303) 275-5350

Gunnison National Forest
Gunnison Ranger District
216 N. Colorado St.
Gunnison, CO 81230
(970) 641-0471

Pike National Forest
South Park Ranger District
320 US Hwy 285, Box 219
Fairplay, CO 80440
(719) 836-2031

South Platte Ranger District
19316 Goddard Ranch Ct.
Morrison, CO 80465
(303) 275-5610

Rio Grande National Forest
Divide Ranger District
3rd and Creede Ave., Box 270
Creede, CO 81130
(719) 658-2556

Saguache Ranger District
46525 CO Hwy 114, Box 67
Saguache, CO 81149
(719) 655-2547

San Isabel National Forest
Leadville Ranger District
810 Front St.
Leadville, CO 80461
(719) 486-0749

Salida Ranger District
325 W. Rainbow Blvd.
Salida, CO 81201
(719) 539-3591

San Juan National Forest
Columbine District
367 S. Pearl St., Box 439
Bayfield, CO 81122
(970) 884-2512

Dolores District
29211 CO Hwy 184, Box 210
Dolores, CO 81323
(970) 882-7296

White River National Forest
Dillon Ranger District
680 Blue River Parkway,
Box 620
Silverthorne, CO 80498
(970) 468-5400

Holy Cross Ranger District
24747 US Hwy 24, Box 190
Minturn, CO 81645
(970) 827-571

Useful Phone Numbers

The Colorado Trail Foundation
(303) 384-3729

Statewide road condition
(303) 639-1111

Statewide weather reports
(303) 398-3964

Colorado Division of Wildlife
(303) 297-1192

To activate a rescue group, contact the nearest county sheriff:

Seg. 1–3	Jefferson (303) 277-0211
Seg. 4–6	Park (719) 836-2494
Seg. 7–8	Summit (970) 668-8600
Seg. 8	Eagle (970) 328-8500
Seg. 9–11	Lake (719) 486-1249
Seg. 12–15	Chaffee (970) 539-2596
Seg. 16–20	Saguache (719) 655-2525
Seg. 21	Mineral (719) 655-2525
Seg. 22–23	Hinsdale (970) 944-2291
Seg. 24–25	San Juan (970) 387-5531
Seg. 26	Dolores (970) 677-2257
Seg. 27–28	La Plata (970) 385-2900

Leave No Trace

Aspen grove found in Segment 11.
PHOTO BY JULIE VIDA AND MARK TABB

The **Leave No Trace** (LNT) program is a message to promote and inspire responsible outdoor recreation through education, research, and partnerships. Managed as a nonprofit educational organization and authorized by the U.S. Forest Service, LNT is about enjoying places like The Colorado Trail, while traveling and camping with care and preserving these places for the future. The seven Leave No Trace principles of outdoor ethics are:

• PLAN AHEAD AND PREPARE

Know the regulations and special concerns for the area you'll visit.
Prepare for extreme weather, hazards, and emergencies.
Schedule your trip to avoid times of high use.
Visit in small groups when possible. Consider splitting larger groups into smaller groups.
Repackage food to minimize waste.
Use a map and compass to eliminate the use of marking paint, rock cairns, or flagging.

- ### TRAVEL AND CAMP ON DURABLE SURFACES

  Durable surfaces include established trails and campsites, rock, gravel, dry grasses, or snow.
  Protect riparian areas by camping at least 200 feet from lakes and streams.
  Good campsites are found, not made. Altering a site is not necessary.
  In popular areas:
  > Concentrate use on existing trails and campsites.

  Walk single file in the middle of the trail, even when wet or muddy.
  Keep campsites small. Focus activity in areas where vegetation is absent.
  In pristine areas:
  > Disperse use to prevent the creation of campsites and trails.
  >
  > Avoid places where impacts are just beginning.

- ### DISPOSE OF WASTE PROPERLY

  Pack it in, pack it out. Inspect your campsite and rest areas for trash or spilled foods.
  > Pack out all trash, leftover food, and litter.

  Deposit solid human waste in catholes dug 6 to 8 inches deep at least 200 feet from water,
  camp, and trails. Cover and disguise the cathole when finished.
  Pack out toilet paper and hygiene products.
  To wash yourself or your dishes, carry water 200 feet away from streams or lakes and use
  small amounts of biodegradable soap. Scatter strained dishwater.

- ### LEAVE WHAT YOU FIND

  Preserve the past: examine, but do not touch, cultural or historic structures and artifacts.
  Leave rocks, plants, and other natural objects as you find them.
  Avoid introducing or transporting non-native species.
  Do not build structures, furniture, or dig trenches.

- ### MINIMIZE CAMPFIRE IMPACTS

  Campfires can cause lasting impacts to the backcountry. Use a lightweight stove for cooking
  and enjoy a candle lantern for light.
  Where fires are permitted, use established fire rings, fire pans, or mound fires.
  > Keep fires small. Only use sticks from the ground that can be broken by hand.
  >
  > Burn all wood/coals to ash, put out campfires completely, then scatter cool ashes.

• RESPECT WILDLIFE

Observe wildlife from a distance. Do not follow or approach them.
Never feed animals. Feeding wildlife damages their health, alters natural behaviors, and
    exposes them to predators or other dangers.
Protect wildlife and your food by storing rations and trash securely.
Control pets at all times, or leave them at home.
Avoid wildlife during sensitive times: mating, nesting, raising young, or winter.

• BE CONSIDERATE OF OTHER VISITORS

Respect other visitors and protect the quality of their experience.
Be courteous. Yield to other users on the trail.
Step to the downhill side of the trail when encountering pack stock.
Take breaks and camp away from trails and other visitors.
Let nature's sounds prevail. Avoid loud voices and noises.

Aconitum columbianum monkshood.
PHOTO BY LORI BRUMMER

Leave No Trace publishes an educational booklet, *Outdoor Skills and Ethics*, that specifically covers backcountry recreation in the Rocky Mountains. To obtain a copy of this, or for more information about the LNT program, contact:

    Leave No Trace, Inc.
    P.O. Box 997
    Boulder, CO 80306
    (800) 332-4100
    LNT.org

INDEX

Snow remains in late July on Segment 8 near Searle Pass.
PHOTO BY LEN GLASSNER

Sunset over the San Juan Mountains.
BY LEN GLASSNER